ADVENTURE TREKKING

ADVENTURE
TREKKING

A Handbook for
Independent Travelers

ROBERT STRAUSS

THE
MOUNTAINEERS

Published by
The Mountaineers
1001 SW Klickitat Way
Seattle, Washington 98134

0 9 8 7 6
5 4 3 2 1

Published simultaneously in Canada by Douglas & McIntyre, Ltd., 1615 Venables Street, Vancouver, B.C. V5L 2H1

Published simultaneously in Great Britain by Compass Star Publications Ltd., Kyre Park, Tenbury Wells, Worcestershire, England WR15 8RP

Manufactured in the United States of America

Edited by Dana Lee Fos
Maps by Green Rhino Graphics
All photographs by the author except as noted
Cover design by Watson Graphics
Book design and typography by The Mountaineers Books

Cover photograph: *Hikers—Alsek Range, Tatshenshini River Valley, Yukon, Canada* © Art Wolfe/Allstock
Frontispiece: *Milford Sound, South Island, New Zealand* (Deanna Swaney photo)
Title page: *Mark of Xerxes, King of Persia (486–456 B.C.)*

Library of Congress Cataloging-in-Publication Data
Strauss, Robert.
    Adventure trekking / Robert Strauss.
        p.   cm.
    Includes bibliographical references and index.
    ISBN 0-89886-443-7
    1. Backpacking—Handbooks, manuals, etc.   2. Hiking—Handbooks, manuals, etc.
  3. Camping—Handbooks, manuals, etc.   4. Tourism—Planning—Handbooks, manuals, etc.
  I. Title.
  GV199.6.S87   1996
  796.5'2—dc20   95-25478
                                                                                          CIP

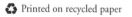

CONTENTS

◆ ACKNOWLEDGMENTS ◆

Thanks to Mark Sampson of Mobile Positioning Systems (UK) and Tony Wale of Silva (UK) for advice on the GPS and navigation; Dr. Peter Barrett of MASTA, School of Hygiene and Tropical Medicine, London, for advice on medical matters; photographer Paul Scott (London) for photographic wisdom; Joyce Strauss for enthusiastic support; computer whiz Jonny Morland of NSTA Bugfree Software; mountain guide Yossi Brain, Bolivia, for altitude advice; my old buddy Chuck Merkel, global piano-tuner and travel enthusiast, for his reappearance with new tales and reminiscences from Afghanistan, Iraq, and the Amazon; Alan Samagalski (Australia) for research; and Jonathan Kennett (New Zealand), co-author of *Classic New Zealand Adventures* (Compass Star Publications), for advice.

A special vote of thanks to the following friends and colleagues who contributed photos, wisdom, humor, and anecdotes:

Graeme Cornwallis, Scottish climber and Munro enthusiast, has trekked in many parts of the globe and is currently completing *Great Hikes & Treks in Norway* (Compass Star Publications).

Marc Dubin, author or co-author of *Trekking in Turkey*, *Trekking in Spain*, and *Trekking in Greece,* who in his old age has gone soft and opts more frequently for general-focus Rough Guides to Greece, Cyprus, Turkey, and the Pyrenees but still keeps his hiking gear in trim and can be coaxed out for long walkies. Photographer and author Mike Ford, who has trekked extensively in the Himalaya and Tibet, including a sponsored marathon walk from Ladakh to Dharamsala to raise money and awareness for Tibetan refugees. Mike recently returned to Tibet to update *The Tibet Travel Companion* (Compass Star Publications). Bradley Rowe (Stone Routes), research consultant specializing in travel, ecology, and photography in Tibet. Wendy Teasdill, who provided extracts from *Walking to the Mountain* (Hong Kong: Asia 2000, 1995), an account of her experiences en route to Mount Kailash.

A double portion of appreciation to Deanna Swaney, author of numerous travel guides to countries in Africa, Europe, South America, the South Pacific, and beyond. Deanna contributed to the climate chapter and, as partner on and off the trails, shared knowledge and encouragement, not least some devoted coaxing on the steeper gradients of this project.

Finally, to The Mountaineers Books director, Donna DeShazo; project editor, Christine Clifton-Thornton; editor, Dana Fos; and graphic arts coordinator, Alice Merrill, a megabundle of team appreciation for your guidance, patience, and equanimity during the long haul.

Pelicans awaiting handouts at the fish market, Antofagasta, Chile

◆ PREFACE ◆

Although I've been traveling since the early 1970s, during the last ten years my work has focused on writing travel guides to countries in Europe, Asia, South America, the Indian Ocean, and beyond. Much of the information in this guide is culled from traveling and trekking experiences during these years, sometimes in a professional capacity, sometimes not.

The marshalling of material, in itself an odyssey ranging from computer bytes to yellowed scraps of Indian ricepaper and dusty boxes of Chinese notebooks, triggered dormant memories: riding in dust-clogged comfort on bus roofs and hiking on high to view assembled summits of the Hindu Kush in Afghanistan; making all the wrong moves while scrambling a disintegrating slope on Lanyu Island, Taiwan; stopping on a hike in the Bolivian Amazon to marvel at the retention of desiccated shape in an armadillo skeleton, lying as it had fallen on the forest floor; walking for several days across wooded hills on a Greek island, so laden with fruit and vegetables from farmers met along the way that, staggering under the weight of the gifts, I was forced to stop and camp.

The material found in this book reflects my own experiences and research and that of many of my friends, trailmates, and colleagues, some of whose names and exploits pop up in later chapters. I am especially indebted to them for their contributions to the book, which has been enhanced with an unusually rich seam of comment derived from a combined total of many years on the move.

◆ INTRODUCTION ◆

Where I live, when autumn weather descends, some spiders feel the urge to up and disperse their species, sailing away in the air on a silken thread across gardens, counties, and even continents. Down to earth and on a human scale, what instincts provide our impetus for adventurous wanderings?

At a reflex level, trekking is a physical challenge: a simple desire to pick a path and measure up to the terrain and the elements. The adventure component adds the spice of uncertainty, raising the stakes for you to test yourself in unfamiliar territory.

On a deeper level, trekking is a bridge between ancient lifestyles: the fixed vision of a settler counterbalanced by the transient motion of a nomad. As an evolution from a simple walk into a more self-sufficient venture, trekking requires simplification, a reduction to portable basics, and implicit trust in your capability to define what you need to live.

Casting loose from civilization and living in the wilds brings you back into the guidance of clear natural rhythms. Afternoon shadows prompt the search for shelter; a healthy appetite treads hard on the heels of thirst and hunger; hard physical effort is followed by the need for the replenishment of deep slumber; birdsong and the first rays of sun raise your head in the morning; and as the day progresses you seek agreement with whichever of nature's moods comes your way, be it cloudburst, breeze, storm, or sun.

In the developing world, locals may express wonder when trekkers come from afar and spend a relative fortune—with no apparent motive for economic gain—for the opportunity to trek, as a matter of choice, the same trails often painstakingly covered by the locals as necessary toil in their daily life.

What prompts this exodus? For citizens of highly developed countries, trekking overseas can be a break from daily routine and the complexities of technology in an urban environment. At the same time, travel offers the chance to set aside secondhand representations as you seek your own perspective on the world, firsthand and at ground level.

Once you make this move outside your usual field of experience, you'll encounter differences in culture, language, dress, food, social values, and attitudes. As a result, you may note a subtle change in your own attitudes toward concepts such as needs and wants or poverty and wealth. In a reverse process, the way others view your culture will give you an outside perspective: with any luck, when you return you won't see the world quite as you did before, and you'll have a fresh pair of eyes for your former routine.

This book is aimed at both the budding adventure trekker who wants to grasp the nettle of overseas trekking, and the more experienced independent

Hiker at rest in the Kamikochi Valley, Japan

trekker and traveler who wants to browse the pages for refreshment or to kick loose the armchair muse with a romp or two down memory lane.

The general focus of this book is on the traveler with the time and tenacity to hit the trail with an independent viewpoint. While a dedicated trail guide or country guide will serve you on the trail, this book is intended as a source of reference, inspiration, and encouragement before you go.

Hikes are good for preparation, to check your fitness, to assess your compatibility with a potential trekking partner, to test new or repaired equipment before you go. At your overseas destination, they provide a break from city life and can tie in well with the first day of your trip to get rested and acclimatized or with the last day of your trip to wind down and ponder reentry into your home world.

Trekking trips cut the ties with civilization, extend the demands for self-reliance beyond that of an overnight trip, and lead longer (weeks or months) and deeper into backcountry or wilderness trails. Treks generally involve a level of independence that can only be achieved by longer periods of time spent away from civilization.

This book covers all levels of preparation for trekking overseas, from tips on choosing your destination and packing your bags to staying healthy, minimizing environmental impact, and communicating with locals in your host country.

Adventure Trekking does not cover climbing and is essentially nontechnical; in other words, it does not address treks requiring the use of crampons, ropes, and ice axes, and it does not discuss the perspectives of survival or shelter in technical terrain requiring such equipment. Once the taste for trekking has been developed, there are many excellent courses and manuals already available to lead into the technical field.

Around the world, the pursuit of trekking covers a wide spectrum beyond the basic concept of travel on foot. Bushwalking in Australia, tramping in New Zealand, hillwalking in Scotland, or fellwalking in England are just some of the variants you'll encounter. Chapter 10, "The World at Your Feet: Trekking Worldwide," is a sampler of trekking options available around the globe. Although I have emphasized treks lasting 5 days or much longer, these are supplemented with shorter or novel hiking and walking options for acclimatization or preparation. It is clearly beyond the scope of this book to catalogue each and every trek on the planet, and in my opinion such an undertaking would pull the teeth from the very notion of adventure. Between the lines of the ordered thumbnail description of trekking possibilities lies the meat of adventure: the snake on the path, the heaven of a thirst slaked at a spring, or the welcome of a stone shelter in driving rain.

Exploring the world on foot invites you to extend your interests through looking to the sky and to the earth, learning the ways of a rockhound, stargazer, botanist, wildlife enthusiast, or any of the many other facets of the jigsaw that is life on this planet.

You could follow the trails of the ancient Inca civilization in the Andes, hike the lakelands of Patagonia, walk in to the base camp of Mount Everest, or view African game on a bushwalk in Kenya or Zimbabwe. Perhaps you'll choose to observe the abundant birdlife in the tropical forests of Malaysia or Costa Rica, climb volcanoes in Japan or Indonesia, or visit the lakes and birch forests of Scandinavia.

The growth of the travel industry and the soaring popularity of trekking for recreation (in its literal sense of renewal) raise the issue of impact wherever you choose to explore. The more trekkers enjoy the trails, the more they should be mindful of the impact of their actions on the land: a plastic bottle tossed aside, human waste undisposed, or trees cleared for firewood. An individual's action multiplied over months and years by hundreds and thousands of other visitors can quickly ruin the quality of the environment. There's no better time to adopt low-impact methods for travel and trekking than now.

As you trek, remember that you share the trail with others: those who live in the surroundings; those who will follow your path; and those who have gone before you. Thoughtless fires can ruin the livelihood of hillfolk and the habitat of wildlife; piles of garbage can ruin the experience for those who follow; and disturbance of traditional or religious monuments breaks the links with the past.

I hope this book gives you the inspiration to take off and experience adventure trekking overseas, the encouragement to explore foreign cultures and environments with sensitivity, and the capacity to enjoy your discoveries both large and small.

—*Robert Strauss*

◆ A NOTE ABOUT SAFETY ◆

Safety is an important concern in all outdoor activities. No guidebook can alert you to every hazard or anticipate the limitations of every reader. Therefore, the descriptions of roads, trails, routes, and natural features in this book are not representations that a particular place or excursion will be safe for your party. When you follow any of the routes described in this book, you assume responsibility for your own safety. Under normal conditions, such excursions require the usual attention to traffic, road and trail conditions, weather, terrain, the capabilities of your party, and other factors. Keeping informed on current conditions and exercising common sense are the keys to a safe, enjoyable outing.

Political conditions may add to the risks of travel in ways that this book cannot predict. When you travel, you assume this risk, and should keep informed of political developments that may make safe travel difficult or impossible.

—*The Mountaineers*

PRIME TIME
Choice Trekking

All sorts of things and weather
Must be taken in together,
To make up a year
And a Sphere.

—Ralph Waldo Emerson,
The Mountain and the Squirrel

ONCE YOU'VE SET YOUR SIGHTS ON A TREKKING trip, an essential part of preparation is to pick the right time to take advantage of the climate and any seasonal variations. Swapping messages in electronic forums or burying your nose for a few hours in guidebooks and tourist literature can help pinpoint trekking destinations with climates to suit. Remember that summer in the Northern Hemisphere isn't always the best trekking season elsewhere in the world. Examples of variant prime trekking times would be October to November in Nepal, late November to March in New Zealand, May to September in northern Australia or December to March in the south, December to February in Kenya, and November to May in the Patagonian Andes. Don't religiously pin your hopes on exact seasons: you may get lucky with freak good weather just before or after the prime season, or you may not.

Apart from climate, keep in mind other seasonal factors, such as prices, reservations, and crowds. If you are keen to see wildlife or plant life, you'll need

---

Alchemic symbol: **Gold**; origin unknown

Which way? Kangerlussuaq, Greenland (Deanna Swaney photo)

to make arrangements so that your trip connects with such wonders as a blossoming desert in Australia or an exceptional frog hatch in Amazonia. Health risks and annoyances can occur at certain times of the year as well: insect life, for instance, is notably more abundant in the summer. Terrain and climate can combine to shape transport timetables and, hence, provide or obstruct access to trailheads. Seasonal snowfall, landslides, and swollen rivers can close passes and roads for part of the year. Similiarly, guides, porters, and pack animals may not be available during such times.

✦ CLIMATIC DETERMINANTS ✦

A basic knowledge of climatic determinants provides an introduction to the patterns and general types of climates described later in this chapter.

LATITUDE

First, a quick definition: latitude is the measurement, in degrees, of an angle formed by two lines—one drawn between the position of an object anywhere on the earth's surface and the center of the earth, and another drawn between the center of the earth and the nearest point on the equator.

Latitude is expressed in degrees north or south of the equator. Therefore, the equator lies at 0 degrees latitude, while the North Pole is at 90 degrees north latitude, the South Pole at 90 degrees south latitude, and the mainland United States between around 24 degrees north latitude (Key West, Florida) and 49 degrees north latitude (Boundary Waters, Minnesota).

In general, seasons are determined by latitude combined with the earth's 23½-degree tilt in relation to its orbit around the sun. During the northern summer—June to September—the Northern Hemisphere, which includes North America, Europe, Asia, and northern Africa, is tilted toward the sun. In the southern summer—December to March—the Southern Hemisphere, which includes Australia, New Zealand, Antarctica, the South Pacific, southern Africa, and most of South America, is tilted toward the sun. Conversely, in their respective winter months, the Northern and Southern hemispheres are tilted away from the sun.

This tilt also explains why the polar regions experience the midnight sun and the polar night. During the summer months, these regions see the midnight sun at least 1 day per year. For example, at the Arctic Circle, which lies at 66½ degrees north latitude, you can see the midnight sun on 1 day a year, the northern summer solstice (21 June). The farther north you go, the more days of continuous daylight you have. At the North Pole, that daylight lasts six months, from the northern vernal equinox (21 March) to the northern autumnal equinox (21 September).

Conversely, in the winter months, the Arctic regions experience polar night; the Arctic Circle experiences 24 hours of darkness on the northern winter solstice (21 December) and the North Pole doesn't see the sun from 21 September to 21 March.

In the Antarctic region, the same thing happens, but the seasons are reversed. The tropical and equatorial regions, however, experience roughly the same amount of daylight every day the year round, varying not more than around 2 hours from winter to summer.

The simple significance of all this is that the farther north you go in the Northern Hemisphere and the farther south you go in the Southern Hemisphere, the cooler it's going to get. On the other hand, the closer you move toward the equator, the warmer it will become.

ALTITUDE

On a local scale, altitude is also a major determinant of both temperature and weather. As you go higher in the earth's atmosphere, the molecules that make up the air become sparser and sparser. As a result, the air holds less and less heat and the temperature drops. You may take off from Miami International Airport in 90 degrees Fahrenheit (32 degrees Celsius), but once you've climbed to cruising altitude, the temperature may be -40 degrees Fahrenheit (-40 degrees Celsius) or colder.

The summit of Huashan, People's Republic of China

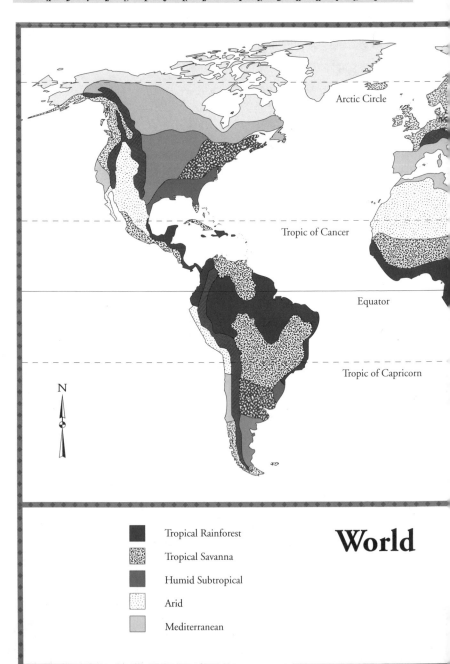

Arctic Circle

Tropic of Cancer

Equator

Tropic of Capricorn

N

Tropical Rainforest
Tropical Savanna
Humid Subtropical
Arid
Mediterranean

World

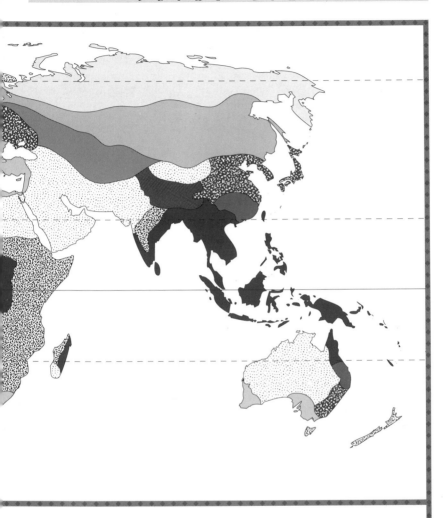

Climates

Humid East Coast

Steppe

Marine West Coast

Boreal Forest (taiga)

Polar

Major Alpine Areas

The same is true in mountain regions. As a general rule, you lose 3.5 degrees Fahrenheit for every 1,000 feet (6.5 degrees Celsius for every 1,000 meters) you ascend, although this may be affected by a number of other factors—humidity, wind direction, angle of the sun, and so on.

Altitude affects the weather in several ways. During the day, the sun warms the air enclosed in valleys, thereby reducing its density and causing it to flow up the slopes toward the cooler air above. At night, the process is reversed as the air above becomes cooler and denser and flows downward into the valleys.

In the mountains, this relationship can become typically stormy when up-drafts of warm, moisture-laden air rush toward the peaks in the morning and rapidly increase in density to build distinctive anvil-shaped cumulonimbus clouds by the afternoon. In the resulting climax, the clouds dump their moisture as rain or hail and release the electrical charge (accumulated from friction within the clouds) as lightning.

CONTINENTAL AND MARINE EFFECTS

Because water is more resistant than land to changes in temperature, large bodies of water—particularly oceans and seas—provide a stabilizing effect on the climate. This marine effect causes coastal areas to experience a much milder—and generally wetter—climate than inland areas. That is, summers are generally cooler and winters warmer than the latitude would otherwise suggest.

However, the susceptibility of large landmasses to temperature changes causes inland areas to experience the greatest temperature extremes on the planet. It isn't surprising, then, that some of the hottest summer temperatures and harshest winter climates both occur in the interior of large continents: Siberia, Central Asia, and Canada's Prairie Provinces.

For example, on Kodiak Island, off the southern coast of Alaska, the summer temperature never rises much above 55 degrees Fahrenheit (12 degrees Celsius), whereas winter temperatures rarely drop below freezing (32 degrees Fahrenheit). In Fairbanks, however, which lies 350 miles inland, summer temperatures can soar to 90 degrees Fahrenheit (32 degrees Celsius), and winter temperatures drop as low as -60 degrees Fahrenheit (-51 degrees Celsius).

This is also the mechanism that drives the monsoons around southern Asia and the Indian Ocean.

TERRAIN

Terrain can also greatly affect temperatures and weather. Air generally cools and condenses as it rises (see "Altitude," earlier). When this happens, clouds form and often result in rainfall. A range of mountains will often force air currents upward. If the air is moist enough, a bank of clouds may form along the mountain slopes, resulting in rainshowers. In most parts of the world, these showers occur in the midafternoon. A good example is along the Front Range of Colorado, where humid air moving across the Great Plains is forced upward, causing rainshowers nearly every afternoon in the summer.

On the other hand, when moist air is forced over a mountain range and descends the other side, it heats up and dries out. This is well illustrated in Washington state in the northwestern United States, where moist air from the sea dumps its moisture on the western slopes of the Cascades. As it continues moving eastward, it descends and heats up, creating dry conditions across eastern Washington.

WINDS

Although all the other factors discussed in this section will have an effect on wind direction, wind is caused quite simply by temperature differentiation. If the temperature increases, whether in a tiny localized cell or across an entire continental landmass, the heated air will rise, leaving an area of low air pressure at the surface. This semivacuum causes cooler air to pour in from surrounding areas, thus creating wind. The differential heating of land and water is a major driver of wind. In the morning, after the sun causes the land to heat up, the breeze will flow inshore. In the evening, after the land has cooled down, the sea, which is more resistant to temperature changes, remains warmer and causes an offshore wind.

OCEAN CURRENTS

Ocean currents also have a direct effect on world climate. It is beyond the scope of this discussion to go into the several driving forces behind ocean currents. Suffice to say that they generally come in two varieties: warm and cold. Warm currents originate in tropical areas, and cold currents come from more northerly or southerly ocean areas.

The effects of warm currents are most pronounced when they carry warm tropical waters into high latitudes, resulting in the meeting of warm water and cold land. When air heated by the water moves onshore, the cooler air over the land causes it to condense and form rain. It also moderates the temperature in such areas. The best example is probably the Gulf Stream, which brings wet and extremely mild climates to much of western Europe. As a result, in northern Norway trees grow well north of the Arctic Circle, while at similar latitudes in northern Canada, the coasts are icebound for most of the year.

Cold currents have their most dramatic effects when they strike warm tropical or subtropical coastlines. The cold current causes moist maritime air to condense and drop most of its moisture at sea. When the dry, cold air over the current strikes the warm air over land, it causes all moisture over the land to condense into fog. This results in extremely arid conditions. The Atacama Desert on the northern coast of Chile and the Namib Desert in southwestern Africa provide the best examples. To a lesser extent, a similar effect occurs along the coast of California.

HUMIDITY

Humidity, the moisture in the air, is responsible for putting the biting dampness in a cold day and for causing the stifling, lethargy-inspiring sultriness that characterizes hot days in moist areas. In general, regions of low humidity are more comfortable than those with high humidity.

Humidity is always relative. That is, the amount of moisture in the air is measured as a percentage of the maximum amount of moisture the air could possibly hold at its current temperature. Thanks to condensation, hot air is capable of holding considerably more water than cold air (which explains why, on hot humid days, the moisture condenses around cold drinks). Therefore, 100 percent humidity on a cold day represents much less actual moisture than 100 percent humidity on a hot day.

◆ OTHER CLIMATIC MATTERS ◆

MONSOONS

Monsoons, which occur across the southern tier of the Asian continent and around the Indian Ocean, are the result of the enormous temperature variations between the tropical Indian Ocean and the vast Asian landmass.

During the early part of the northern summer, when the land heats up and the continental air mass rises, moist sea air rushes inland and butts up against the Himalaya, which causes the air to rise, condense, and produce copious amounts of precipitation. On the Indian subcontinent, this is known as the southwest monsoon. One Indian town, Cherrapunji, receives more than 1,000 inches (2,540 centimeters) of rain annually, thanks to its unfortunate position in the foothills at the head of the precipitation funnel, the Bay of Bengal. It is these same conditions that each year cause devastating floods around the Brahmaputra Delta in Bangladesh.

In the northern winter, when the central part of the Asian continent is locked in the deep freeze, the warm tropical seas to the south cause the maritime air mass to lift, and cooler air from the continent rushes seaward. In India, this arrives around the middle of September and brings the cooler and relatively comfortable temperatures associated with the northeast monsoon.

In most of Southeast Asia—including Thailand and Indochina—the southwest monsoon brings the summer rains, whereas the northeast monsoon, which lasts from October to April, brings generally drier weather. In southeastern China, the wet monsoons occur from May to September, whereas the dry westerly monsoons from the Gobi and Takli Makan deserts arrive around October and last until March.

In the western Indian Ocean, which lies mostly in the Southern Hemisphere and includes Madagascar and the eastern coast of Africa, the monsoons are governed more by the African than the Asian continent. The wet monsoons come from the east between December and March, whereas the dry winds blow from the west and last roughly between May and October.

HURRICANES, TYPHOONS, AND CYCLONES

As we know, the earth rotates on its axis once every 24 hours, causing night and day. Because the earth is spherical, a point on the equator moves a much greater distance in one 24-hour period than a point at higher latitudes. In fact, the North and South poles don't move at all. This differentiation, which causes drag on the atmosphere and deflection away from the equator, is known as the Coriolis effect. In the Northern Hemisphere, this deflection causes counterclockwise spiraling, while in the Southern Hemisphere, it is clockwise.

In the moist tropical regions, this effect creates spiral weather patterns. These occasionally develop into enormous tropical storms, which are variously known as hurricanes (Gulf of Mexico, Caribbean Sea, and Atlantic Ocean), typhoons (western Pacific Ocean), and cyclones (South Pacific and Indian oceans). Although severe storms can occur at almost any time, the earth's tilt generally causes the cyclone belt to move north of the equator from March to September and south of the equator from September to March. The hardest hit areas normally lie between about 15 and 30 degrees of latitude, north or south.

◆ GENERAL CLIMATIC ZONES ◆

So how can you use all this climatic information? Hopefully, it will help you decide the best time to set off on a trekking trip, but before you start making any complicated calculations, have a look at this section, which should simplify things considerably. This is because the various climatic determinants coincide in various parts of the world to create general climatic tendencies. For example, you'll find similar climatic conditions in Seattle, Scotland, southern Chile, and the South Island of New Zealand; in San Francisco, Rome, Cape Town, and Adelaide; and in Manaus, Bangkok, Darwin, and Kinshasa.

These patterns should make it easier to select the best season for the sort of trek you're hoping to make. Remember, though, that seasons in the Southern Hemisphere are the reverse of those in the Northern Hemisphere.

ALPINE

The alpine climate is the most variable climatic region and is more a function of altitude than geographic location. However, because most trekking occurs in mountain areas, it is a highly relevant issue. Generally, the alpine regions of the world can occur at any latitude and are normally defined as areas above the local tree line. On the equator (Mount Kenya, for example), this limit is around 12,000 feet (3,600 meters), while at 65 degrees north or south latitude (as on Mount McKinley), it can be as low as 1,000 feet (300 meters) or lower. In alpine regions, you can expect cold, harsh conditions—including snow—at any time of year.

The world's major alpine areas include parts of the Himalaya, Pamirs, Karakorum, Altai, and Japan Alps in Asia; the Andes in South America; the Rockies, Sierra Nevada, Cascades, and various Alaskan ranges in North America; the Alps, Caucasus, Carpathians, and Pyrenees in Europe; the Atlas, Simiens, Ruwenzoris, and Drakensberg and the Mount Kenya and Mount Kilimanjaro massifs in Africa; and the Southern Alps in New Zealand.

TROPICAL RAINFOREST

The tropical rainforest climate forms a band along either side of the equator. Because the seasons are indistinct in this region, it is difficult to lay down set climatic rules but, in general, there are no summers or winters, only "wet" and "dry" seasons. The wet season, which falls in the summer months, is extremely hot, humid, and wet, whereas the dry season, which falls in the winter months, is just as humid but less hot and less wet.

The tropical rainforest climate prevails through much of coastal West Africa, central and west-central Africa, the Amazon Basin of South America, eastern Mexico and Central America, northern Australia, Southeast Asia, and most of southern and eastern India and Bangladesh.

TROPICAL SAVANNA

The tropical savanna climate, named for the open savanna grassland vegetation that characterizes most of the region, is marked mainly by hot, humid summers, punctuated by frequent rainshowers, and cooler, drier winters. These conditions occur in southern Florida, most of Mexico and Central America, northeastern South America (northeastern and west-central Brazil, southern Venezuela, and north-central Bolivia), most of the Sahel region (which forms a band from eastern Senegal eastward to southern Sudan), East Africa, most of southern Africa north of the Cape region, and central India.

The higher altitude areas in the tropical savanna regions can be extremely comfortable, however, and actually resemble a sort of reversed Mediterranean climate, with dry winters and wet summers. This occurs on the plateaus of southern Africa (Malawi, Zambia, Zimbabwe, most of Botswana, central Namibia, and northern South Africa), the highlands of Mexico and Central America, and the highlands of central South America (central Bolivia). In these areas, the summers tend to be warm and damp, whereas the winter days are warm and dry, but the nights cold.

HUMID SUBTROPICAL

The humid subtropical climate is characterized by hot and humid summers, punctuated by frequent rainstorms and mild, damp winters, with occasional steady rains.

Areas with a humid subtropical climate include most of the southeastern United States from Virginia to central Florida, eastern China, the southern coast of Queensland and northeastern coast of New South Wales in Australia, and southern Brazil.

ARID

The desert regions of the world, which are defined simply as regions of low rainfall, come in two major varieties: hot and cold. You may be surprised to learn that the polar regions, for example, are considered desert areas, although they don't exactly fit the image most people have of deserts. Polar climates are discussed later in this chapter.

Some deserts, such as the Atacama and the Namib, are extremely dry and, in some areas, no rainfall has ever been recorded. Other deserts, such as the Mojave and Sonoran, do experience occasional rainfall, most often in violent storms that occur during the summer months.

Major deserts or desert regions include the Mojave, Great Basin, Sonoran, and Chihuahuan (southwestern United States and northwestern Mexico); the Atacama (northern Chile and southern Peru); the Gobi and Takli Makan (Mongolia and northwestern China); the Thar (northwestern India and southeastern Pakistan); the Kara Kum and Kyzyl Kum (Central Asia); the Dasht-e-Kavir and Dasht-e-Lut (Iran); the Arabian (the Arabian peninsula); the Negev and Sinai (southern Israel and northeastern Egypt); the Nubian (northeastern Africa); the Sahara (northern Africa); the Kalahari (Africa); the Namib (southeastern Africa); and the Great Sandy, Great Victorian, Simpson, and Gibson (central, northern, and western Australia).

MEDITERRANEAN

The Mediterranean climate, which is generally considered the most comfortable of all climates, is characterized by warm to hot, dry summers and cool to warm, rainy winters.

The areas that experience a Mediterranean climate include (of course) the Mediterranean area, from Portugal to Greece, western Turkey and Israel, and along the North African coast; western California; central Chile; the southern tip of Africa; the coast of South Australia; and the southwest coast of Western Australia. Note, however, that conditions can vary considerably within these regions. For example, the marked variation between San Francisco and San Diego (both considered to enjoy a Mediterranean climate) is comparable to that between Porto (Portugal) and Tunis (Tunisia).

HUMID EAST COAST

The humid east coast climatic region, so-called because it most often occurs on the eastern coast of continents, experiences hot, humid summers and cold to cool, snowy winters.

It is prevalent in the northeastern and midwestern United States, southeastern Canada, eastern China, southeastern South America from Uruguay to northeastern Argentina, and southeastern Australia, and across eastern Europe from the north German plains to Belarus and western central Russia.

STEPPE

The steppe climatic zone experiences hot, dry summers and cold, harsh winters, and its generally flat landscape has relatively few features to break the typically strong, cold wind.

The continental steppe climate occurs in a band across Central Asia from eastern Poland to Mongolia, and across the Great Plains of North America from northern Texas north to Manitoba and Saskatchewan.

MARINE WEST COAST

The marine west coast climatic zone appears most often on the western coast of continents between 35 and 55 degrees of latitude. This climate is identified by cool maritime temperatures, with mild, rainy winters and cool, mostly rainy summers.

The most prominent areas with this sort of climate include the northwest coast of North America from northern California to southeastern Alaska; New Zealand; southern Chile; and most of northwestern Europe, including Britain, Ireland, northern Spain, Scandinavia, and most of France.

The Routeburn Track, South Island, New Zealand (Deanna Swaney photo)

BOREAL FOREST (TAIGA)

The boreal forest climatic zone, which covers a vast area, is characterized by hot, dry summers and extremely cold, dry winters. The name comes from the vegetation cover, which consists mainly of birch forest or coniferous trees that have been stunted by underlying permafrost (permanently frozen ground).

This region takes in the vast continental areas of north-central Eurasia, from Finland across central Russia to the eastern edge of Siberia and northeastern China. Similar conditions also occur all across central Canada, from the Yukon and northeastern British Columbia eastward to southern Labrador.

POLAR

The polar climatic zone experiences extremely cold, dry, and dark winters and cool to mild, dry summers.

The polar climatic regions generally take in those areas beyond the tree line in both the northern and southern polar regions. These include the continent of Antarctica, Greenland, northern Canada, northern and western Alaska, and the northern and northeastern areas of Russia.

◆   PERSONAL ANGLE   ◆

Your choice of timing for your trek will depend not only on climatic factors, but also on the local travel and trekking infrastructure.

If you travel during the peak holiday season, you can expect to pay peak prices for transport and accommodation. The structure of airline fares rises and falls to reflect seasonal demand. Be aware of public holidays, festivals, and religious holidays at your destination: these may lead your travel plans a merry jig.

Peak season can also produce unpleasant surprises for those who have not booked permits and huts far in advance in popular trekking regions, where the influx of visitors has prompted the introduction of fees and quotas. You may also find trails more heavily traveled, especially during school holidays.

If you have no choice but to go during peak season, then be prepared to book ahead, pay higher prices, and meet more people on the trail. You could also consider a less well-known trek or region at a popular destination or compromise further by choosing a country less visited.

If you have the experience and the equipment, you can enjoy winter or wet season treks abroad and take advantage of great price reductions. In many cases, you'll find the trails uncrowded, but you may have to be more self-reliant because facilities such as hotels and transport close down outside the main season.

FIRST STEPS
Travel Arrangements

TRAVELING INDEPENDENTLY YOU'LL HAVE TO take care of organizing the necessary documents for travel overseas, applying for visas to your destination and booking flights to get you there. You'll also need to budget for the trip, take money in the appropriate form, and know your way around foreign currency. As a safety net, the right travel insurance will provide peace of mind.

Organized tours can be booked "off-the-peg" or you can approach a specialist company to tailor a trip for your group. As a semi-independent option, popular in Europe, some companies will prebook your transport and accommodation, provide maps and instructions, and leave you to hike at your own pace. Although an organized tour handles your arrangements while overseas, you will still need to know about necessary arrangements and take an active role in organizing passports, visas, and other errands covered in this chapter. Trekking preparations for independent and organized travelers are discussed in chapter 5, "Setting the Pace: Trek Preparation and Technique."

Approach travel arrangements with patience, flexibility, and humor. If the embassy ties you up in red tape, see if there's another route to the coveted visa. Perhaps the official will respond more efficiently if you explain your interest, or you might be better off applying through the well-oiled channels of a visa agency. If flight dates are full, maybe there's space for you at the top of a waiting list for cancellations or you could fly a different route. If the bank hasn't heard of the foreign currency you need, then perhaps a smile and a few sample phrases in an exotic language will generate some action. Travel planning can provide valuable lessons applicable at home and abroad: you don't have to accept what you can change, but what you cannot change you may have to accept.

Magic scarab: **Good luck**; Assyrian

◆ OBTAINING INFORMATION ◆

Taking the seed of an idea and nurturing it through the planning and takeoff stages of your trip requires information. With knowledge at your fingertips you'll be able to hunt around for alternatives and be flexible in your choices and decisions. Ideally, you should apply yourself to research several months in advance so that you can chop and change in good time, putting shape into your plans. Focus on the personal perspective: where possible ask the people supplying information about their own trips and experiences; often this will give you a much livelier idea of what's available and perhaps encourage a considerably better deal or even friendlier service.

Where you look for your adventure trekking information depends on the time you have at hand and the type and depth of information you require. For example, a quick check through CD-ROM listings at the library may give you a selection

of general articles about the country you have in mind, while the time taken to contact the relevant tourist office might yield a stack of brochures and contact details for hiking groups and associations. You could also put your feet up in front of the fire and dip into a guidebook. At a more personal level, if you are computerized, you might join a special interest group on the Internet to chat on-line with someone who has just returned from your proposed destination and has the latest scoop on trail conditions.

Whether you seek traveling companions, visa advice, language tips, flight information, weather charts, or the latest methods to zap the bugs, there's an impressive array of

Traveling in Southwestern Bolivia

sources at your disposal. Throughout this guide, you'll find references to resources and cross-references to contacts as well as further reading in appendices A and B.

MEDIA

Regular travel programs are aired on TV and the radio. Given the competition and expense of broadcast media, you're more likely to see or hear topics covered in "taster" format and aimed at a broad audience, but keep a lookout for the occasional series on outdoor pursuits. Newspapers tend to cover travel in dedicated sections of the weekend editions where you'll find both general travel articles and useful discussions on related travel topics, such as gear, insurance, and health. Magazines for general readership usually have a travel section, and the specialist publications, aimed at trekkers or hikers, will be a rewarding read.

CLUBS AND ASSOCIATIONS

Both at home and abroad there are many clubs and associations for travelers, hostelers, hikers, trekkers, and any number of other special interests. These organizations can be a good source to seek advice on organized trips and referral, for example, if you are looking for trekking companions, used gear, maps, or publications.

GOVERNMENT SOURCES

Government sources of information include special services for the public, such as voice phone, fax, or modem access to the latest information on health or security alerts, and publications offering advice on passport applications, representation abroad, and background details for specific countries.

NATIONAL TOURIST OFFICES

Many national tourist offices can supply extensive literature, including specialist brochures on hiking, trekking, or backpacking in their country and listings of accommodation. They are also a good source for travel planning questions that you have been unable to solve elsewhere. Note, however, that there is a growing trend to cut office overheads by providing such information via premium-rate phone numbers. Obviously, given the promotional emphasis of these offices, you should also read between the lines of any glossy brochurespeak and adjust your expectations accordingly. Because these offices are usually sited in the capital or largest cities of a country, contact details can usually be obtained through the relevant phonebook or from guidebooks.

MANUFACTURERS

Don't overlook manufacturers as a handy source of information. If you've purchased something secondhand, they should be able to provide advice on the care and repair of equipment before you go or during your trek. You can also contact them for the latest product specifications, sales brochures, and details of imminent upgrades.

You can find contact names, addresses, and toll-free phone numbers for manufacturers by looking in library reference sections, outdoor shops, specialist magazines, and telephone directories. Specialist outdoor magazines review gear throughout the year, but in the spring they usually run a bumper issue devoted to equipment complete with comprehensive listings of manufacturers. There is also a growing trend for manufacturers to provide information and technical assistance on-line.

LIBRARIES

Your local library is a prime resource for books, newspapers, magazines, cassettes, and other reference materials. Pop in to browse or take out on loan all sorts of publications, such as guidebooks, language primers (often with sets of cassette tapes), collections of travelers' tales, and survival manuals. Browse through microfiche, CD-ROM, or on-line databases to find books or magazine articles on your chosen topic. You can also consult highly detailed reference works to find, for example, local or international clubs and societies. Some libraries have introduced computer terminals that are linked to the Internet and available for public use.

THE INTERNET

The advances in electronic communications are of direct value to the travel industry and to virtually any individual thinking about taking a trip abroad. As

Help is available for even the least-prepared traveler; sign in Tibet

this book goes to press, new developments continue to change this sector, but travelers are already benefiting from the speedy and comprehensive access to reference material and the ability to locate and contact people or organizations on a global scale.

The Internet is a network of thousands of computers linked around the world that transfers information and messages. As an entity, it has no overseer (although some would like to try!) and the system functions along the lines of a "pass-the-parcel" operation.

You can scour addresses on the Internet to make personal contacts, search for information, and purchase goods. For example, using e-mail (letters sent electronically from your computer) you can seek foreign friends and contacts as part of a trip you're planning. By joining forums or newsgroups and subscribing to discussions, you can seek and give advice on topics such as cheap flights, equipment, places to avoid, or hikes to savor.

If you need to check on the hotspots in the world, the U.S. State Department issues advisories and travel briefings on-line and similar services are available from the Foreign Office in the United Kingdom. Updates on health requirements, visas, and airline schedules are also provided by commercial services, although you may need to pay an additional fee for access. At the same time, more and more information from government sources, ranging from meteorological centers to the Central Intelligence Agency, is being made more widely available on the Internet.

To keep up with travel angles in the news, you can also contact hiking magazines, travel sections of newspapers, or authors and publishers of guidebooks.

Given the speed at which this whole sector moves, there's little point in providing lists of addresses here, although I have provided a few electronic addresses for some of the companies listed in appendix A. Once you join up, you'll see how fast the technology can be harnessed to search for your own favorite topics and sites.

GUIDEBOOKS

Before you set off on your travels, background reading can sharpen your knowledge of your destination and prime your senses when you are there. A selection of useful addresses and contacts for guidebook publishers is provided in appendix A.

Whatever you read, the viewpoint you receive will be that of the author. Make sure that you leave yourself some leeway to form your own opinions and set the parameters for your own trip.

Very few travel guidebook researchers get to see and do everything that goes into the book. In addition to on-site visits, information is compiled from tourist offices, local contacts, letters from readers of previous editions, and other sources. This jigsaw of perceived and received information is then massaged into the final text.

Many travelers swear by guidebooks, plan with them, eat with them, fall asleep with them, and quote them. If time is lacking, this is definitely one way to be organized. Other readers with more time on their hands may "dip and skip" or only use hard data in emergencies. When arriving at the wrong time in the wrong part of town, a guidebook can be your best bet.

Too much meticulous planning, too much reliance on guidebooks, can rob your trip of impromptu experience; on the other hand, used sparingly, they can be an excellent tool to inspire your instincts for personal adventure.

When assessing guides published as part of a series, it helps to first find a title covering a place you are familiar with. Take a look at the maps and text. Do they mesh and complement each other? Does the author's assessment of the place agree with your own experience there? And is the author's style of travel similar to your own? If the answer is yes, then you can expect that a guide in the same series that covers your destination will be informative and useful.

Bear in mind that the full production cycle for a guide may take twelve months or longer from research trip to submission of copy to final editing, printing, and delivery to store bookshelves. The imprint page at the front of the guide provides various clues. For a rough idea of when the information was gathered, subtract one year from the year printed after the copyright symbol (©).

If there's a reference to the text being a translation, check the date on the original-language version carefully—translation rights for guidebooks aren't always sold simultaneously, which means the information could be vintage stuff. Some translations read fluently, whereas others require the reader to hack through a thicket of forced grammar to reach the information in the interior.

In recent years, there has been a surge in the numbers of specialist guides dedicated to walking, hiking, and trekking in familiar and unfamiliar parts of the globe. The breadth of titles offered ranges from Alaska to Papua New Guinea, from Greenland to Tasmania.

Some titles focus on specific routes combined with precise mapping; others offer a general overview of trail networks, akin to a menu, and refer the reader to locally available maps. It's up to the user to decide the level of detail and flexibility applicable to his or her level of experience.

Some trail guides concentrate on the routes and assume the reader will turn to a separate guide for general information such as that on fauna and flora, language, and culture and customs; others spin a wider net to combine all this information in one volume. If the added weight of more comprehensive books poses a problem, you can cut out the relevant parts.

Whichever type of trail guide you pack for reference, keep your eyes open for your own interpretation and improvisation.

Traveling by **mokoro** *(dugout canoe) in the Okavango Delta, Botswana* (Deanna Swaney photo)

◆ DOCUMENTS ◆

PASSPORT

For travel overseas you'll need to pack a passport. Before you become engrossed in other aspects of planning, check that it is still valid and that there are enough spare pages for visa stamps.

Most countries require passports to be valid at least for the length of your visit, and many stipulate validity for six months or more beyond that. If you fall in love with a country, you'll appreciate having enough leeway to extend your stay.

It's amazing how fast embassies, border officials, police, and others can take up space in your passport with entry visas, exit visas, extensions, travel permits, and associated official marks. Some officials take delight in placing a microscopic stamp plumb in the middle of a clean page, whereas others will diligently search for the elusive white space on a page already pockmarked with entries.

In Portugal, a sharp-eyed hotel owner took my passport away for registration and brought it back sopping wet. It transpired later that he thought I was a look-alike for an English antiques forger reported on the run. Hoping for fame as a sleuth, he had rubbed the number of the suspicious document in water.

Passport Application and Renewal

Apply for a new passport or renew an old one well in advance of your intended departure date, especially if it falls during a peak travel season, when all the folks who forgot to apply are deluging the issuing offices with applications.

Passport photos to accompany applications should show the front view of your face, preferably as you normally look (for example, with glasses and a beard if that's your style) but without a hat or sunglasses. On your travels you'll need a handful of these photos for visas, so stock up at the same time.

If you plan to visit a number of countries, ask for a passport with more pages. In the United States and United Kingdom, for example, passports are available with twice the number of pages than in the standard version. It's worth paying the extra to avoid the hassle of running out of pages in a remote spot. If a passport is lost or stolen, report this to the police and contact your nearest embassy or consulate, which may require another document to provide proof of citizenship, sometimes two forms of identifiction, and possibly a police report before issuing a replacement.

U.S. Citizens. Applications and renewals for passports are handled by the U.S. Passport Agency and at designated post offices and federal and state courts

Pirate ship ferry, Alcântara, Maranhão, Brazil

in most cities. Apply at least six weeks before your departure, earlier if possible. As backup in case of loss, you can obtain a duplicate birth certificate from the Bureau of Vital Statistics of the state where you were born.

Canadian Citizens. Pick up an application form at a local post office or regional passport office. You can obtain a duplicate birth certificate from the Bureau of Vital Statistics in the province in which you were born. Processing time takes from one week to a month.

British Citizens. Pick up an application form at the post office, at least a month (preferably three months) in advance. A copy of your birth certificate can be obtained either from your local registration office in the district where you were born or by applying in person to the Public Search Room in London. For postal applications, apply to the General Register Office.

Australian Citizens. Apply for a passport in person at a passport office or post office. You can obtain a duplicate birth certificate from the Registry of Births, Deaths, and Marriages in the state where you were born. Processing time takes approximately 7 working days.

New Zealand Citizens. Pick up an application form from a local post office, Link centre, or travel agent and send it to the New Zealand Passport Office. Processing takes approximately 10 days or can be reduced to around 3 days if an additional urgent fee is paid. A duplicate birth certificate can be obtained from the Registrar General's Office.

Passports and Political Disputes

Some countries, the United Kingdom, for example, allow you to hold two passports. This is useful for visitors to countries that refuse to admit travelers with specific stamps in their passports. Many Arab countries will refuse entry if a passport contains an Israeli stamp. If you can avoid it, don't carry both passports at the same time. In the event of a search, you could raise suspicion.

Another option is to ask for the entry stamp of the problem country on a separate piece of paper that is inserted into your passport for the length of your stay and then retained by passport control when you exit.

Passport Care

Take good care of your passport; it provides proof of your identity at border posts and in banks, hotels, bicycle rental shops, and more. For passport security before you go and during the trip, follow the advice given in chapter 6, "Look Sharp: Security Basics."

Learning by heart (or by reciting like a mantra) the number, expiration date, and place and date of issue of your passport will save you digging in your luggage time and time again to fill out yet another form. This rote knowledge might also speed up the issue of a replacement in the event of loss.

VISAS

Permission to enter or leave a country is usually granted with a visa obtained either before you go or on arrival. Your visa status depends on your country of nationality, the nature of your trip, and your destination. Some countries have reciprocal arrangements to waive visa requirements for each other's citizens; others can tie up visitors in the proverbial red tape. In some cases, tourist visas are issued routinely, but business or work visas are hedged round with complicated requirements. Countries with political or other agendas may restrict the validity of your visa to one region and exclude another.

Where to Apply

If you apply at home, you have the certainty of a visa in hand rather than a chancy visa in the bush. This may also save you time during your trip. A visa of short duration, valid from date of issue, has the disadvantage that unpredictable transit travel could lose you time. Visas that are valid from date of entry into the country are also usually granted for use, in other words entry, within a couple of months of issue. This provides leeway if you are traveling overland for several weeks or months before reaching the country.

Those planning longer trips often prefer to apply abroad for visas, for example in adjacent countries, so that they can keep itinerary options open. On the other hand, regulations may be more involved, possibly including a demand for a letter of introduction or reference (as a pro-forma gesture to prove you are genuine) supplied by your embassy. If you know before you go that there is only a vague chance of obtaining a visa at the border, you'll have one less worry if you can obtain it at home.

Visa Types

In most cases, stating the purpose of your trip as "tourism" will be enough to obtain a tourist visa. If you are transiting one country to reach another, you may have to apply for a transit visa.

If you intend to enter and exit a country several times, you'll need to consider applying for a multiple-entry visa, which will cost considerably more but save you the complication of repeated applications for single-entry visas.

Visa Procedures

Travelers with money and little time or interest in pursuing their visa can pay specialist visa agencies to do the work. Those with time on their hands can run the errands in person or apply by mail. When applying in person, a neat appearance helps to smooth the paths of visadom. If you apply by mail, be sure to use registered post.

If you leave your application until the last minute, don't be surprised if the

Rail travelers, Santa Cruz, Bolivia
(**Deanna Swaney photo**)

price rises dramatically due to urgent telecommunications charges or just plain bureaucratic whimsy; after all, an applicant in a hurry is not in the best of bargaining positions.

Most visa applications require a fee (factor this into your budget), a couple of passport photos (always keep half a dozen of these handy), and a completed application form.

Sometimes you may also be asked to show enough money, such as traveler's checks, to cover your stay and possibly evidence, such as an outbound airline ticket, that you really are going to depart. To save expense, it's sufficient for your exit ticket to be a short hop across the border into a neighboring country rather than a long-haul flight back home.

Sometimes requirements extend to evidence of prebooked accommodation, such as vouchers or itineraries supplied by travel agents. When visas are only granted to groups, you may have to join up with an organized tour or gather together enough independent travelers to constitute a group.

Questions on a visa application cover your personal details and your profession. If you work in the field of journalism, radio, or TV, some countries may question whether or not you really are just visiting for leisure. Jotting down a run-of-the-mill profession, such as teacher or student, generally sidesteps such interest. If you are asked to supply the address of your accommodation in the country, even if you have none booked, it is usually a sufficient sign of intent to pick the name of a hotel from a guidebook. If you know you will have to fill out forms in duplicate, triplicate, or larger multiples, save time and penwork by taking along some carbon paper.

As for the length of stay, try for the maximum number of days or months applicable to your visit; if you later find yourself with fewer days than you need, you may have to waste time getting an extension.

In one instance, where I mentioned authoring of travel guides on my application form, I was granted a visa (for two weeks) on condition that I obtain a letter of introduction from my embassy and agree not to write anything about the country. On another occasion, I mentioned my work as an editor to an immigration official. Instantly I was surrounded by top brass demanding to know my assignment and newspaper. Although they were satisfied with the travel guide angle, their rapid reaction did make me wonder if there wasn't a juicy tale or two under wraps.

When you are handed your visa, check it carefully to ensure that it covers the right dates, places, and length of stay.

Visa Extensions and Exit Visas

Visa extensions are usually handled at immigration or security offices. As long as you provide a simple reason and are not using the system for other means (work, for example), your first extension is rarely a problem, but subsequent applications may require more bureaucratic investigation, perhaps even a whole new revalidation ballgame known as visa renewal.

Exit visas are sometimes required before you can leave the country. These are usually obtained from a local security or police post in a town near the border or at the border. Avoid last-minute surprises, such as being turned back at the airport prior to departure, by planning ahead.

Sources of Visa Information

One certainty about visa regulations is that they change rapidly. How do you keep informed? Embassies, consulates, and tourist offices can provide advice over the phone, although in peak season you may have trouble getting through. In some cases, callers are charged for their call on a premium-rate number.

Travel agents have on-line databases and reference works available for their day-to-day work. If they are too busy to sort out a query over the phone, politely ask to borrow the latest edition of their travel agent reference manual, or consult them in your local library. If you have access to the Internet, many of these works can be accessed on-line, although some may be restricted to subscribers only.

In return for a fee, visa agencies will take the visa worries off your hands; some also operate a premium-rate phone information service.

Feedback from recently returned travelers is another good source, as are the travel sections in weekend newspapers and special update sections in travel magazines.

INTERNATIONAL DRIVER'S LICENSE

If you intend to drive at your destination, perhaps hiring a car in a group to reach a trailhead, you may need an international driver's license. In the United States, contact the American Automobile Association (AAA), 1000 AAA Drive, Heathrow, FL 32746 (phone toll-free 1-800-222-4357, or (407) 444-7000); in the United Kingdom, call the Automobile Association (AA) (phone 01256-

201223) or the Royal Automobile Club (RAC) (phone 0181-6860088); and in Australia, call the Australian Automobile Association (AAA) (phone 06-2477311).

HOSTELING CARD (YOUTH HOSTEL CARD)

The concept of youth hostels has been expanded to cater to hostelers of all ages, hence the recent change of name to Hostelling International from the former International Youth Hostel Federation (IYHF). Most of the affiliated international organizations are in the process of making similar name changes. If you join up with your local hosteling association (the typical annual fee is around U.S.$20), you'll receive a membership card that entitles you to a discount when used at participating hostels at home and abroad. A selection of useful addresses and contacts is provided in appendix A.

INTERNATIONAL HEALTH CERTIFICATE

If you are traveling in South America, Africa, or Asia, an international health certificate is useful to record vaccinations. In addition to documenting your personal health history and all immunizations and prophylactics you've received, it can also be used for the official documentation of immunization against yellow fever, as required by many countries where the disease is prevalent. Certificates are obtainable from either a qualified immunization center or your local health authority. It's preferable to carry the certificate inside your passport rather than risk the hygienic uncertainties of a compulsory jab at the border. For an overview of immunizations that can be entered on the certificate, see chapter 4, "In Good Shape: Staying Healthy."

◆ FLIGHTS ◆

Flying is certainly a quick, if uncomfortable, method to get you to trekking destinations in far corners of the world. It's also relatively safe compared to the perils of road transport. One effect of flying is that you may need a few days on arrival at your destination to settle temporary physical and emotional upheaval after rapidly crossing several time zones into a new climate and culture.

Before you book your flight you'll need to consider your options. The price you pay will vary according to the season you travel, the route you take, and the comfort and convenience you require.

A selection of useful addresses and contacts is provided in appendix A.

RESEARCH

For library research at the source, refer to the *Official Airline Guide* (or *OAG*), an enormous listing of flights and their price data, published monthly and also available for on-line reference.

Landing at Narsarsuaq, Greenland (Deanna Swaney photo)

Another good place to start looking for flights is in the travel sections of major weekend newspapers. In the United States, try the *New York Times, Los Angeles Times,* or *San Francisco Chronicle.* In the United Kingdom, scan the pages of the weekend national press or periodicals such as *TNT, Time Out, City Limits, Loot,* and *Exchange & Mart.*

TICKET OPTIONS
If you are looking for tickets at a discount, you have several options.

Airlines Direct
When you lay out money for an airline ticket, there are various ways to sharpen your bargain. Most airlines structure fares around seasons, typically designated as peak, shoulder, and low.

When you are quoted a price, ask how the fare is structured; if you can shift your dates, you may be able to slip into a cheaper season. If you fly on a weekend or require a ticket valid for more than a few months, you may have to pay a supplement. Rather than spend extra time and money traveling to a major airport miles from your home, it may be more convenient to catch either a direct or feeder flight from a nearby airport.

Look carefully at cheap flights. In some cases very small savings may be gained by taking "milk run" flights, which will get you to your intended destination, but stop all over the place and take a lot longer or involve long transit waits.

When booking flights for travel during the peak months, such as August and September, you'll be in competition with many other buyers, so aim to book several months in advance.

Excursion. Offered at a reduced rate on scheduled flights, this ticket requires the purchaser to complete travel within specific dates, but flight changes are usually allowed.

Advance Purchase Excursion (Apex). As the name implies, this ticket must be bought in advance. The purchase must be made from a few days to a month or more before the departure date. A minimum stay is often stipulated, and stopovers are usually excluded. Once you've bought the ticket, you may have to pay extra to change flights.

Round the World. For long-haul destinations it may be cheaper (and provide an enjoyable bonus) to link together a series of destinations to form a round-the-world itinerary. Most bargain tickets of this type are not with a single airline but, rather, composed of individual sectors with different airlines. You can usually shave costs by traveling to major cities around the globe (for example, New York, London, Bombay, Bangkok, Hong Kong, Singapore, Sydney, and Los Angeles), by keeping to a circular route (east to west or vice versa), and by avoiding backtracking.

Given the complicated "stitching" involved with this type of arrangement, you should check restrictions for each sector closely. Common ones are a minimum number of stopovers, a minimum number of days' duration for the entire trip or for a specific stopover, and options to change prebooked dates. You do not have to use flights to connect every leg of your trip, so you can also include overland travel. Interestingly, jet lag is much less of a problem if you fly round the world from east to west.

Open Jaw. This type of ticketing lets you to fly to one airport and depart from another, a nifty option to explore overland routes without backtracking— for example, Miami–Manaus–La Paz surface Lima–Los Angeles or London–Colombo–Singapore surface Bangkok–Hong Kong surface Beijing–London.

Air Passes. These passes allow a number of stopovers within a country or region and can be a great way to get to know a specific area in depth. Note that some airlines stipulate that their passes may only be bought before arrival at the destination, and there may be restrictions on eligible flights during peak times of use.

Standby Fares. If you can be very flexible about the time and destination for your trip, you might want to go standby. This means you wait until the last day or hour before a flight departs to see if any seats are available. Rather than lose money by flying with an empty seat, the airline waits until the last moment before selling it at a large discount.

Consolidators

Consolidators (also known as bucket shops) make bulk purchases of tickets from airlines and then sell them at a discount. This can be a good deal as long as you make a close check on any restrictions on routings, stopovers, validity, and re-funds.

Available in various permutations, charter flights are booked in advance and may form part of a package deal or can be booked at the last minute at huge discounts—the closer you are to the departure date, the greater the risk for the agent that the seat will be left unsold, hence the willingness to drop the price. The flip side of the gamble is that you could be stranded on your anticipated departure day without a ticket. A selection of useful contacts is provided in appendix A.

When purchasing airline tickets from an agency, check if it is a member of a trade association, such as the International Air Transport Association (IATA), which offers some financial protection of the traveler's money should the agency fail to deliver the goods.

In the United Kingdom, a similar protective role is performed by the Association of British Travel Agents (ABTA), the Air Travel Organiser's Licence (ATOL), and the Association of Independent Tour Operators (AITO).

To protect yourself against failure of the airline or agent to provide travel, pay with a credit card. This should further protect your purchase, assuming that the credit card company honors its obligation to ensure provision of service. You can also purchase travel insurance offering this specific coverage.

Before paying for your ticket, run through the details in full: dates, routing, flight numbers, and flight times. Ask about additional costs, such as airport taxes, security charges, surcharges for credit card payment, and the fees payable if you cancel.

Courier Companies

Major discounts are offered if you fly as a courier, escorting documents through customs for courier companies operating out of major cities worldwide. If you have specific dates and destinations in mind, you are advised to book well in advance. However, you can also snap up very good deals if you travel at the last minute and are prepared to make an almost instant decision to simply go with what's available.

Basic requirements include a smart appearance and flexible schedule. Courier tickets are usually sold as return fares for solo travel, although it may be possible, for example, for two people to book separate flights timed so that they arrive on consecutive days. There is generally a minimum stopover requirement (for example, 3 days) and a maximum permitted stay, ranging from a few days or weeks to a year. Because the courier company uses your baggage allowance, you will usually be restricted to one or two pieces of carry-on luggage. Further contacts for courier flight information are provided in appendix A.

◆ MONEY ◆

Whichever trekking destination you choose, you're going to need money to get there, for daily expenses on the road before you get to the trailhead, to cover your running costs while you trek, and to get home again (if you can bear the thought).

BUDGET

While you can quickly gain an idea of your flight costs by scanning the travel advertisements in magazines and newspapers or calling travel agencies, the amount of money you'll need at your destination will depend on your lifestyle.

Put together an estimate for the time you expect to stay, including your anticipated expenses for accommodation, food, and transport. Put aside some money for delays and emergency use, and add some leeway for impromptu brighteners or treats to give your spirit a boost when it needs it—a tight budget is fine, but continuous worry about finances can ruin the zest of a trip.

You can make savings by teaming up with a fellow traveler for accommodation, using public transport, and generally adapting to local levels of life.

Once you hit the trail, your costs drop dramatically because, in most cases, you become self-sufficient for shelter (tent), food (supplies bought in advance or en route), and transport (your own two feet). This means that countries or regions that might initially scare the living daylights out of your wallet start to look quite viable once you reach their trekking territory (Japan and Scandinavia, for example). At times, though, you'll have to draw on the budget for specific trekking costs, such as guides, porters, and pack animals; trail permits; hut fees; and park admittance charges.

When making your budget choices, bear in mind that the way you spend your money has an environmental and cultural impact on the places you visit (see chapter 7, "Minimum Impact: Trekking and the Environment," and

*Motorbike taxi, Guayaramerin,
Bolivian Amazon*

chapter 8, "Foreign Cultures: Meeting the Locals"). Spending the lowest possible amount on your trip doesn't necessarily mean you'll have the most rewarding time; sometimes spending a little extra on local assistance can be the best move you make.

There's obviously a massive potential spread between the tightest "bread and water" budget and the most luxurious safari, so treat the following comments as general in scope. In most of Asia (with some exclusions such as Japan), South America, and Africa, you'd be looking at a rock-bottom, "on-the-trail" budget of around U.S.$8 per day, whereas a similar budget in Europe, the United States, Australia, New Zealand, and Japan might vary between U.S.$12 and U.S.$25 or more depending on compulsory entry or hut fees. Bear in mind these are on-the-trail estimates that do not include your transport costs to and from the trail or your equipment acquired prior to the trip.

HOW TO PACK MONEY

There are three major methods to carry money: cash, traveler's checks, and credit cards. All three have advantages and drawbacks, so the broadest advice for your budget is to strike a balance among the trio, say, 30 percent in cash (including an emergency reserve and a small foreign currency buffer), 50 percent in traveler's checks, and the rest available on a credit card (if not accepted or used at your destination, substitute with traveler's checks).

Predeparture research is necessary to establish what sort of banking facilities are available at your destination. In most cases you can expect to change traveler's checks or money in towns close to the trekking region and then pay cash in local currency for your expenses on the trail. Credit cards are most often used for emergencies and an occasional splurge, such as a celebratory meal and a comfortable bed in a hotel after a demanding trek. All three methods require basic precautions against theft and misuse. In addition to the tips given here, also refer to chapter 6, "Look Sharp: Security Basics."

Cash

Cash is a quick and easy way to dispose of travel funds. For the same reason, it's also the most desirable commodity for a thief. You'd be wise to carry only part of your funds in cash, preferably covered by travel insurance and secured on your person and in your baggage.

If possible, buy some of the local currency—enough for expenses for a couple of days at your destination—before you depart. This buffer stock of cash stands you in good stead, for instance, if you arrive when everything, including banks and exchange bureaus, are closed, or the only options available are sharks offering scandalous rates.

The U.S. dollar is the most widely known and accepted foreign currency. There are still a few countries where other currencies are in equal favor, such as the British pound in India and Nepal, the French franc in Francophone Africa, and the German mark in Turkey and Namibia.

Pay careful attention to the denomination of dollar bills. Carry a few singles and low denomination bills as a quick way to pay small items, such as taxi fares, and as a means to exchange a small amount of money, adjusting the level of your local funds, just before leaving a country. Take larger denomination bills, such as U.S.$50 and U.S.$100 as emergency money, to be wrapped in plastic and stashed in a secret place (such as a shoe sole, backpack frame, or zippered belt).

Take only crisp, clean bills; torn, soiled, or defaced ones are often spurned as potential forgeries. The issue of forgery is assuming enormous proportions and causing headaches across the globe, from the largest corporate banks to the solo operators cruising the back streets of tourist centers. The Bank of England reportedly has an employee whose sole task is to monitor the reprographic qualities of each new range of photocopiers.

At its simplest level, you'll see crude forgeries, such as the dayglo U.S.$20 bill I saw a lady vigorously jabbing at a clerk in an exchange booth on the Argentine border. His curt negative response to her request was accompanied by an expression of disdain at this lurid piece of green paper lighting up the counter. At the other extreme are crash-hot forgeries like those being pumped out of Lebanon and Iran. Designed by engravers from the former East German intelligence organization, these U.S.$100 bills come virtually complete with all the hi-tech counterfeit measures intended to deter forgers. Understandably concerned by the stockpiling of several billion dollars' worth of these bills, the U.S. government has reportedly considered missile strikes on the presses.

Traveler's Checks

Traveler's checks, an invention dating back to 1891, can be exchanged for foreign currency at banks, exchange bureaus, and hotels or used in the same manner (subject to agreement) as cash or a personal check when making a purchase.

They are also replaceable if lost or stolen, hence safer than cash, and convenient to use. However, they are not readily accepted in remote areas, and their purchase entails a commission (effectively the price of insurance against loss), typically between 1 and 5 percent, although some banks waive this for their regular customers.

The issuers with the widest networks are American Express, Thomas Cook, and VISA. Checks are available in most major currencies, the U.S. dollar being the most popular. If you take checks denominated in the local currency at your destination, they will not be subject to fluctuations. Take mostly large denominations with a few smaller ones for ballast. When exchanging checks, you may be charged commission on each check, in which case it's in your interest to change one or two large checks rather than a lot of small ones. Contact details for American Express, Thomas Cook, and VISA are provided in appendix A.

If you purchase traveler's checks, make copies of your receipt before you depart and leave one at home for reference in emergency. Keep another copy (together with a note of the emergency numbers to call in case of loss) in a safe place in your baggage—separate from your checks. Never carry your checks and passport together. Keeping a separate tally of your checks as you spend them gives you a quick overview if they are stolen.

If you deposit checks in a hotel safe, always seal them in an envelope and then sign across the flap and tape over it. When you reclaim them be sure to count that they are *all* there. Some crafty operators have been known to extract from the middle of a wad rather than the top, which would be more obvious.

In the event of loss or theft, apply for replacement or refund of your checks by contacting the appropriate emergency phone number. For smooth processing of your claim, you must present the purchase receipt and a list of the check serial numbers—if you are lucky you'll be back in the money within 24 hours.

Credit Cards

Another useful way to spread your options is to use credit cards from major companies. Use them for emergencies (medical bills or flights) and the occasional splurge, but don't rely on them exclusively. Remember that the temptations of easy spending soon come home to roost on your statement.

Credit cards are useful for drawing cash advances in local currency from a bank or, using your secret PIN (personal identification number), from an ATM (automated teller machine), which stays open long after the other sources of cash are shut. Glitches can happen with ATMs, so don't be totally reliant on them for your finances. Although you will pay a fee, typically 1.5 percent for each transaction, the exchange calculations are generally better because they are negotiated at special interbank rates.

Smart travelers with spare cash place it in an interest-bearing account at home and arrange to have their credit card bills paid from it automatically. You can also avoid paying charges for a cash advance by paying in money to your account in advance.

Credit cards can provide quick access to cash in emergencies. If your credit card is stolen or lost, cancel it as quickly as possible, and make sure before your departure that you know the relevant emergency phone numbers to report any loss.

New-style credit card coupons do not have carbon paper inserts and offer more protection against misuse. If you sign an old-style coupon, be sure to ask for the carbon inserts and destroy them after use. Similarly, destroy any coupons that have been filled out incorrectly. These are worthwhile precautions against unwanted duplication of your signature or credit card.

As a general rule, don't let your card out of your sight. In shops and restaurants, you might prefer to ask for the vouchers to be prepared at the counter or at your table. There have been reports, especially in Asia, of shop assistants and waiters whisking cards into back rooms or kitchens where details and signature are quickly copied for card duplication.

Always keep your credit card receipts so that you can tally them against your statements. Check carefully for discrepancies in currency exchange. It's not unknown for nefarious characters to slip a couple more zeros into any blank spaces you've skipped between figures, particularly in countries where the currency runs in units similar to telephone numbers.

WHERE TO CHANGE MONEY

Rates and commissions vary considerably depending on where you change your money. Banks and exchange bureaus in town centers generally offer better deals than those in airports, where rents may be high and the clientele short of time to make cost comparisons. Exchange rates at hotels are generally much worse.

Before you go, find out the current exchange rate for your destination, by checking with a bank or travel agent or in the business pages of newspapers.

Learn the numbers and script for the currency of your destination and watch those decimal points. To name just a few random examples, the Italian lire trades at over a thousand to the dollar; the Vietnamese dong, Russian rouble, and Romanian leu run to several thousand; and, at the time of this writing, a dollar buys hundreds of thousands of Ukrainian karbonavets. Some travelers carry a wafer thin, solar-powered calculator to keep track of the figures.

Find out if the currency has recently been changed and what is happening with obsolete currency. Locals often react well to such a request and, as happened to me during a round of Brazilian inflation, you may well receive insights into the latest foibles and jokes. If the currency change is recent, you may be able to trade old for new at the bank. As a foreigner with less knowledge of local streetlore, you may also be intentionally landed with a few duds. Because there's usually very little value at stake, it's best to spare the blood pressure and assign the duds to the souvenir bag.

Incidentally, small change from home is a good gift or discussion starter; for many it's a chance to get a close-up view of figures such as the British Queen or George Washington. Small change from foreign currencies, particularly those produced in stunning designs, makes good souvenirs. Australian bills, plastic-based to resist forgery (and washable), are a novelty.

In some countries, you'll find a chronic shortage of change. In this case, whenever you change money be sure to break large notes. Even if there is no shortage of change, be discreet about showing large-denomination bills that might draw the attention of thieves. Traders on the street, especially in remote trekking areas (where banks may be few and far between), may have genuine problems finding change. If, however, you find the lack of change story is a frequent ploy to extract more than the agreed price, then ask if the trader has change *before* you hand over the cash. In lieu of small amounts of change, you may also be offered a stick of gum, sweets, or matches.

EXCHANGE CONTROLS AND CURRENCY RESTRICTIONS

Countries with ailing currencies or teetering economies, or both, may introduce controls and regulations for fixed (as opposed to floating) exchange rates and place controls on the flow of money to and from the country. For foreign visitors, this often means paperwork, the occasional search, and acquaintance with the black market, whose denizens minister to foreign exchange wishing to float free.

Traveling in Brazil a few years ago, I watched the regulation process in action. The government decided to ride yet another wave of inflation by declaring to amazed and enraged savers that, overnight, a hefty percentage of their savings had been frozen. At the same time, the outbound flow of foreign exchange was stopped, and the resultant hiatus prompted vigorous black market trading. As a countermeasure (and incentive for tourism), the government introduced a "tourist exchange rate," which was set at a competitive level to undermine the black market rate.

I've also encountered the black market in the former Soviet Union and China, where foreign travelers entering the country were required to fill in a currency declaration, detailing all the currency carried. Whenever money was exchanged, it had to be entered on the declaration by the official bank or exchange agent, and when the foreigner left the country the figures were rigorously tallied. The discovery of discrepancies was treated as a serious misdemeanor.

Variations on this theme include the establishment of designated government shops authorized to sell goods for hard currency, restrictions or a total ban on the export or import of local currency, and the setting of a minimum daily exchange quota.

Information on controls or currency restrictions is usually available from travel agents, travel reference works, or similar on-line databases, travel news-letters, and banks. Because this type of information changes rapidly, guidebooks are rarely accurate on this topic. If possible, talk to travelers returning from your destination for the freshest picture on any restrictions or black market developments.

In countries where the economy is fragile, unbalanced, or totally down the tubes, there is usually a black market supplying the populace with money and goods. This circumvents all the legalities of the stricken official economy—which may or may not be the root of the problem.

Blackmarketeers appreciate that foreigners have access to foreign goods and currency and offer to buy both—primarily cash U.S. dollars—at a premium well above bank rates (for currency) or street rates (for goods rarely available on the street).

If you change money on the black market, your deal is by definition beyond the law, which will not protect you if the deal goes wrong and may even be used against you if you're caught.

◆ INSURANCE ◆

It makes very good sense to be insured. After all the money and effort you've spent on your trip, it's just not worth seeing it thrown out of the window as a result of mishap.

Seek advice on the type of insurance suited to your trip. If you already hold home insurance and personal health insurance, then you should find out if you are covered for some or all risks on an overseas trip. By putting together a package to cover yourself for specific risks, you may be able to reduce the premium.

How many trips do you make abroad each year? Short-term insurance taken out several times in one year can often work out to be more expensive than one annual policy. Ask the insurer about the maximum length of any one trip and whether it's possible to extend your policy while abroad.

Before you purchase insurance, ask to see a specimen policy. Look carefully at the small print of exclusion clauses, the often-minute text that tells you when and why you won't be covered. Some policies do not automatically include sports and activities considered high risk, such as bungee jumping, mountaineering, white-water rafting, or in some cases even trekking. For some sections of coverage an excess is payable on the first part of a claim.

Once you've purchased insurance, keep a copy of the policy number and telephone assistance number with you as proof and reference in case of emergency.

POLICY CONTENT OPTIONS

The following are broad policy content options you should consider for coverage.

Medical expenses coverage will pay for expenses incurred should you fall ill or meet with an accident during your trip. Because you may require air ambulances, attention by a mobile medical team, repatriation, and so on, aim for over U.S.$1 million coverage. In a medical emergency, you'll want to be insured with a company that runs an efficient 24-hour phone assistance service with multilingual backup.

For coverage against death or permanent disablement, inquire about *personal accident* insurance. If you purchase *baggage and personal effects* insurance, check carefully to see if there is a limit on the value of any one item. If you already have home insurance for your property, see if this extends to overseas trips. *Money and documents* insurance covers the loss of small amounts of personal money and documents such as airline tickets. *Personal liability* insurance applies to your legal liability for injury or damage caused to others and their property.

Delayed departure benefit covers you for reimbursement of your trip costs in the event that you have to cancel your trip due to accident, illness, jury service, bad weather, and other specified causes of delay. *Legal expenses* coverage will pay legal costs and expenses for pursuit of compensation and damages for personal injury or death.

EMERGENCIES AND CLAIMS

In the event of loss or theft, you will need to file a police report as soon as possible, at the latest within 24 hours of the occurrence, and obtain a copy for your insurance company, whom you should notify within the time limits set in your policy.

Keep a separate note of 24-hour emergency assistance numbers provided by your insurer. Retain all receipts involving any of the preceding insurance options—this applies especially to claims for medical costs and expenses, which you must support with receipts from doctors, hospitals, and pharmacies.

• 3 •

GEAR TO GO
What to Take

 ONCE YOU KNOW WHERE YOU'RE GOING, AND with an additional idea of the trekking you're going to tackle, you can take a hard look at the type of equipment you will use. What goes onto your gear list depends on your trip, but there are general categories that cover most situations.

You will need documents, such as a passport; some form of shelter, such as a tent or bivvy bag (unless you are trekking from hut to hut); sleeping gear; clothing to keep your body comfortable in the prevailing climatic conditions; toiletries and medical items to maintain hygiene and health; cooking equipment (unless catering is provided en route); an emergency kit for survival; lighting and navigation gear to find your way; miscellaneous items; and, finally, a suitable pack to carry it away.

• LESS IS MORE •

"He who would travel happily must travel light."
—Antoine de Saint-Exupéry, French novelist (1900–1944)

What you take with you depends on the climate and terrain of your trekking destination; whether you'll be sharing gear with a companion, using gear supplied by an organized trekking group, or trekking from hut to hut; and your standards of comfort and personal preferences. Some gear is essential—without it you may not survive. Other equipment enhances the trip but can be easily replaced or jettisoned if necessary. Lastly, there are items that are casually included due to tempting shape, color, or function but return from the trip having served only as clutter or deadweight.

Magic amulet: **Makes garments auspicious**; origin unknown

The best way to start your trip on the right foot is to minimize the weight you carry. With a lighter pack you will require less energy, which in turn means you will need to consume less to produce that energy. You will also put less stress on your body, both physically and mentally. In environmental terms, a heavily laden trekker (in a manner similar to that of megatrucks on a highway) also gives the trail an extra pounding, transmitting the added weight through the sole of the boot or crushing the vegetation when a pack is deposited at a trailside stop.

Trekking with one or more companions offers several advantages when it comes to gear. Up-front expenditures can be cut by sharing the expenses of community items such as a tent and cooking gear. These same items can be distributed among trekking partners, thereby cutting down on the carrying load. But beware: even the best of friends can part under the strain of a foreign culture and the demands of trekking. Be prepared for the possibility of splitting gear before the end of your trip by planning possible improvisations, such as carrying an extra tarp for use as an impromptu shelter. Even better, decide beforehand who gets what in case of a split so you'll know what you're up against should

Lighten the load on your mind; Kathmandu, Nepal (Mike Ford photo)

PLEASE MIND YOUR HEAD

Even the best hiking companions sometimes disagree! Western Samoa (**Deanna Swaney photo**)

this occur. Often, losing gear, through a difference of opinions or theft, can mean the end of a safe trip.

Ask yourself why you are taking something. Is it essential or optional? What would happen if you didn't take it—how would it prevent you from functioning? If it's an item for comfort or entertainment, would you be miserable without it? Look for ways to cut down weight and size; opt for double-use or collapsible items, or share components with a companion. Eliminate redundant paper and plastic packaging. You'll find more detailed suggestions on this theme later in this chapter.

◆ FIRST CHOICES ◆

When making your choices, beware of the gearhead syndrome, where the equipping process becomes a steeplechase of detail or bagging of technological peaks. Focus on the task at hand: the purchase of what you need, for the purpose you have in mind, at a price that fits your overall budget.

SOURCES

Find out as much as you can from relevant magazines, mail-order companies, and salespersons in specialist shops. Pick up leaflets from the shops, visit outdoor travel exhibitions, try your library for appropriate publications, or, if you are into electronic communication, send your request for advice to trekking forums or special interest groups. Hiking clubs are clearly a good place to find people who have had good and bad experiences with various types of equipment. Here, too, you might find a source of secondhand equipment. Also note that manufacturers are starting to produce items such as backpacks, boots, and jackets in fittings, sizes, and styles designed specifically for women. For a brief list of mail-order suppliers, see appendix A.

QUALITY

If you plan to do plenty of trekking and have the money for high-quality gear, you'll usually find that it outlasts cheaper versions. Compare the cost, for example, of using one pair of boots for five years or the equivalent multiple annual purchase of a pair of cheap boots. As a bonus you may also save on repairs and receive many years of comforting support on the trail. It can be quite a wrench for trekkers when the old faithful backpack, for example, has become more patch than pack and requires honorable "retirement."

On my first trip to India, I discovered a shop in New Delhi that sold rudimentary gear for porters and hikers. For around U.S.$8 I purchased a canvas backpack constructed with a bamboo frame, lashed together with strips of cane and nails, and thick canvas webbing for back support. This excellent contraption lasted several decades and numerous mishaps, including falling off the top of an Afghan bus (the flexible bamboo frame bounced out of this almost unscathed!), before succumbing to European woodworm.

RELIABILITY AND AVAILABILITY

Reliability and availability of equipment are important factors when traveling abroad. In general, you'll be best prepared if you buy your gear at home before departure, thereby giving yourself a chance to give equipment a trial run and to benefit from manufacturer guarantees.

If you buy essential gear abroad, you may have to pay a premium for imported goods. The close proximity of your trekking destination may be tempting, but don't rush into your trek without first giving the equipment a good testing.

As a compromise between these two options, there's the opportunity in some countries, such as Nepal, New Zealand, and Kenya, to rent equipment. This can be cost-effective, especially if you are only going to be in the area for a short time or you are not sure if you'll be doing enough trekking at home or abroad to merit outright purchase of specialist equipment. If your trek is part of a longer general trip around the world, renting equipment will also mean you can continue your trip after the trek without loading your pack with redundant gear. Obviously, rental equipment passes through many hands, not all of them careful, so always give it a close inspection before you hit the trail. Remember, though, that demand during peak season may severely limit choice. Also, anyone who wears especially large or small sizes of clothing should not rely on the availability of such items for rent in or out of season.

ECOGEAR

Your buying decisions might also reflect the environmental connection between trekking and trekking gear. A growing number of manufacturers are supplying ecogear made to high specifications from recycled materials at highly competitive prices. For example, boots and sandals are now available with recycled soles, as are backpacks with recycled webbing, padding, and stays. Clothing made from recycled materials includes jackets spun from recycled plastic soda pop bottles. According to some estimates, the recycled content of outdoorwear sold in the United States represents a respectable percentage of plastics that would have otherwise gone to the landfill.

Another form of recycling is the purchase of secondhand gear. Attentive scanning of noticeboards and magazine advertisements, and similar sources mentioned earlier in this chapter, can net substantial savings. A few years ago in Alaska I snapped up a top-of-the-range tent for almost half price from a backpacker who had used it only once and rejected it for being too small.

TESTING

Once you've narrowed your interest, make sure you give the equipment a good trial. For example, let the salesperson demonstrate the erection of a tent—then try it yourself and see if it's just as easy for you.

If you don't feel the salesperson is competent, try another salesperson or shop: don't lumber yourself with an unsatisfactory, expensive item for lack of advice. Similarly, when trying out boots, take a long hike around the shop, varying the style and tightness of the lacing, trying on thick and thin socks, and testing the feel and flexibility. Ask yourself whether or not the equipment feels large enough, light enough, wide enough—in sum, does it feel comfortable?

Before you clinch the deal, ask about warranties, spares, and repairs. Most of the top manufacturers offer no-quibble exchanges for faulty gear, not to mention lifetime guarantees.

◆ SHELTER ◆

The type of shelter you need will depend on the type of trekking you're undertaking, the weather conditions, and the degree of comfort required at your destination. On some designated routes you'll have the option to lighten the load by staying in bush or mountain accommodation, but even under these circumstances you probably will want to bring a shelter of some kind for emergencies.

A hiking shelter in the Naukluft Mountains, Namibia (**Deanna Swaney photo**)

A tent provides the security of enclosure, whereas a tarp represents no more and no less than basic overhead coverage. For the minimalist, there's the option of sleeping out in a bivvy bag or slinging a hammock.

TENTS

When the weather is balmy, the nights clear, and the furry wildlife and winged insects amenable, you'll scarcely need or want to be under cover. At other times, a tent provides welcome shelter from rain, sun, snow, insects, fauna, and even inquisitive local bipeds.

Choices

Before purchasing a tent, consider the type of traveling you'll be doing, the relevant terrain and weather, the weight factor, the amount of space you'll need, and ease of setup. For trekking solo or with a companion, a dome or single-hoop tunnel tent should fit the bill for all but the most extreme trekking conditions.

Space. The size of your tent will depend on the expected number of occupants and their accumulated gear. In most cases, you can assume that the manufacturer's definition of capacity is of the "tight squeeze" variety, so consider a size rated one person larger than your group. If you camp solo, a two-person tent will give you room to spread out gear or invite a guest. You'll want enough height to be able to sit up without poking your head through the roof and sufficient width to stretch out without brushing condensation off the walls. Tents with a vestibule give you extra space for storing backpacks or muddied gear or for cooking carefully under cover during foul weather.

Rating. All-season models include two varieties. Expedition tents offer heavyweight protection and extra space for the rigors of group camping in wind and snow at high altitudes. Mountaineering tents are for similar terrain, but their space is restricted to reduce weight. A three-season tent is usually adequate for most backpacking or trekking trips at lower altitudes but is not suited to prolonged exposure to snow or heavy wind. In hot climates, your tent requires good ventilation and proper netting to screen out mosquitoes and other bugs.

Weight. If you're traveling with one or more companions, you can share the carrying weight among yourselves by dividing the component parts of the tent.

If you're traveling on your own, an ultra-lightweight bivvy bag (described under "Types," later in this section) provides the minimum of shelter. On the other hand, you could choose a two-person tent, which provides space to stow your backpack inside, shelter from the weather, and perhaps the chance to offer space to a trailmate.

Ease of Setup. If you hate setting up in the rain, look for a tent model that allows you to pitch the flysheet first, before attaching the inner tent.

Construction

In general, tent construction consists of two layers: the inner tent, which is water-permeable (to reduce condensation), and the flysheet (or outer tent), which is waterproof. This system allows moisture, especially water vapor produced by the occupants, to permeate the inner tent, condense on the inside face of the outer tent, and drip down into the ground at the base of the tent. A more recent development is the single-walled tent, made from breathable and waterproof material (Gore-Tex, for example), which is being improved to combat interior condensation. On the subject of condensation, this is reduced with adequate ventilation: look for tent models with effective vents.

Groundsheet. The groundsheet, or floor of the tent, is usually sewn in. As an additional measure, a separate groundsheet laid beneath the tent protects the floor of the tent from wear and tear and can double as a makeshift tarp (described later in this section) or cover. You can save weight by using your poncho as a groundsheet, but don't expect the increased wear and tear to give the poncho a longer life. Whatever you use as a groundsheet, make sure that it doesn't project beyond the tent edges; if it does, rainfall will be channeled back under your sleeping area.

Poles. Tent poles can be either rigid or flexible. Rigid poles are typically made from steel or alloy and connected by springs or elastic shock-cording. Flexible poles are usually constructed of fiberglass or alloy. Alloy is stronger and more flexible, whereas fiberglass can shatter under the stress of severe weather conditions. When dismantling your poles, you can reduce the wear and tension on the shock-cording by breaking them in the middle, starting with the joint in the middle, then continuing outward, joint by joint, to the ends.

Stakes. Give some thought to your choice of tent stakes so that you carry a selection of angled and skewer versions to deal with soft and hard terrain, respectively. Recently introduced plastic (shatter-resistant) stakes can withstand a major rock pounding. Remember, lightweight tents need good staking to keep the flysheet taut and to prevent the whole structure from becoming airborne during storms. Keep your stakes in a separate bag, and, after dismantling the tent, count the stakes back into the sack so that you can search for any stragglers left at the site.

Guylines. Some tent models are simply staked down at regular intervals around the foot of the tent, whereas others are provided with attachment points, lines, and tensioners for guying. Guylines provide greater stability in windy conditions and can be staked into the ground or tied to a nearby boulder, fencepost, or the like—a useful option on unstable ground.

Types

Tents are available in various shapes and forms: ridge, dome, and tunnel.

Ridge. Ridge tents, and related versions such as tapered or transverse ridge tents, are the traditional A-frame shape. Advantages include stability and easy setup, but very few are lightweight and they offer less interior space (and more staking) than other shapes.

Dome. Basic dome, or geodesic, tents, shaped with two or more poles generally crossing at the center, provide plenty of space and are freestanding and easy to move as a unit. In the more complex geodesic model, multiple offset poles provide a spacious structure capable of withstanding extreme weather—hence its popularity with mountaineering expeditions. The quality, however, comes with a hefty price tag.

Tunnel. Tunnel tents, constructed with flexible hoops or poles, provide optimum space but require guying against crosswinds. Single-hoop models are very portable and lightweight but require thorough guying in windy conditions. For increased stability you should consider two-hoop and three-hoop models.

Bivvy Bags. Beyond the definition of tent, but still offering shelter, bivvy bags are waterproof covers (usually supplied in breathable material) for your sleeping bag. The advantage lies in minimal weight and easy storage in a backpack.

Testing

When you try out a tent, rate how easy it is to set up. Do the zippers run smoothly? Is the stitching of even quality? Do the poles offer stability? If the shop won't erect the tent or let you crawl around inside—find another shop. Some shops offer the option to rent a tent. This is a good way to really try out the goods to your satisfaction before handing over a major portion of your budget.

Maintenance

Thoroughly seal the tent as soon as possible after purchase before its first use. Application of sealant to the tent fabric seams keeps their water-repellent properties intact. Silicon spray is good for lubricating flexible poles and zippers. Strong fabric-backed tape is handy as a temporary fix for damaged tent fabric, ripped groundsheets, and holed backpacks. Avoid washing your tent with detergent because this will impair the proofing. If possible, simply sponge off the dirt with water and a mild solution of soap flakes, and dry in the sun. Before storing your tent, make sure it is dry—damp fabric can quickly turn moldy and damage the coating. For tips on tent security, refer to chapter 6, "Look Sharp: Security Basics."

TARPS

As a lightweight, compact, well-ventilated, and inexpensive shelter for the night, a tarp is useful in its own right. It can also double as a groundsheet or extra flysheet for your tent, provide shade in hot climates, or cover your pack during rain or even act as impromptu personal raingear. Bear in mind that the pleasing closeness to nature offered by tarps may also mean less privacy from passers-by, insects, and animals.

Giraffe, Etosha National Park, Namibia (Deanna Swaney photo)

In its simplest form, a tarp consists of a square sheet of material with ties or tabs and grommets that can be tied off in various ways to local foliage. Folded over an improvised roof ridgeline, it can form an A-shaped lean-to. A combination of overhead attachment and corner stakes can create an upright, curved shell shape. If you tie onto local trees, prevent damage to the bark by placing some form of padding between the tie and the tree. If you prefer not to depend on local trees for support, you can buy collapsible poles or use hiking staffs.

For solo use, you can get by with a sheet between 7 and 8 square feet (0.65 and 0.74 square meters); for two people, you need to increase this to around 11 square feet (1.02 square meters).

Recent developments include specially designed, aerodynamically shaped tarps that are sold complete with poles, guylines, and stakes—the overall effect is that of a cut-down tent.

Polyester and coated nylon are durable materials offering good protective qualities. Avoid flimsy plastic that will quickly shred in windy conditions, failing in its protective role and littering the environment. Heavy-duty plastic can provide impromptu survival shelter in tropical rainforests.

In windy conditions, especially in exposed positions, tarps are not dependable for protection—you can maximize their shelter potential by choosing a sheltered spot in the first place. Keep the angle of your tarp pitched steep enough to allow easy runoff for rain or snow. For optimum staking and taut tarps (loose flapping can be irritating and destructive in major winds), use stakes at least 9 inches (23 centimeters) long, and carry enough strong guyline cord for supplementary tiedowns and reinforcement.

◆ SLEEPING GEAR ◆

Your choice of sleeping bag and mat will depend on the climate of your destination coupled with your desired comfort level. You may decide that neither are necessary or a simple hammock will do.

SLEEPING BAGS

If you plan to travel in warm climates or intend to overnight in well-provided local accommodation only, you may not need a sleeping bag. In most other instances, however, you'll find that taking one with you can provide the flexibility to camp as and when the opportunity arises. It also frees you to make your own accommodation arrangements, say, with locals who may not have a bedroom but are happy to let you bed down with your sleeping bag in a vacant part of their home. In the Middle East, local families often invited me to roll out my sleeping bag on their rooftop. At night this was a great spot to catch the cool breeze and enjoy an unobstructed view of the skies; in the morning the sun quickly baked any ideas of sleeping in.

Before purchasing a sleeping bag, run a quick check on the following points.

Temperature Rating. Cast a cautious eye over manufacturers' rating systems, which categorize bags according to season and minimum temperatures. As a general overview, drawn from a selection of manufacturer ratings, the following example should offer a start on this tricky topic: 1 = summer (10 degrees Celsius\50 degrees Fahrenheit), 2 = summer/spring (0 degrees Celsius\32 degrees Fahrenheit), 3 = summer/winter/spring (-5 degrees Celsius\23 degrees Fahrenheit), 4 = four season (-15 degrees Celsius\5 degrees Fahrenheit), and 5 = severe conditions (less than -15 degrees Celsius\5 degrees Fahrenheit). Insulation performance and, hence, the ratings, are tested, but warmth remains a highly subjective topic.

In practice, each individual has a different metabolism and different tolerance or sensitivity to high or low temperatures. Think about the sort of temperature ranges you anticipate on your travels, then seek advice from fellow trekkers and knowledgeable salespersons.

You can uprate your sleeping bag by using a thermal liner (for example, polypropylene or fleece) or sleep inside it wearing your clothes or a set of longjohns.

Design. The shape of a sleeping bag influences your comfort. Rectangular designs provide freedom of movement but also increase the amount of interior space to be warmed and allow heat loss through the top opening. The most popular design is a mummy bag, which narrows at the feet to retain heat, widens at the torso to allow movement, and tapers to a hooded top to restrict heat loss.

Construction. The construction of the bag includes an outer shell that holds the filling in place. Reduced insulation or "cold spots" can occur if the outer shell is stitched, or "sewn through," to the lining. For best results in colder conditions, choose a construction that keeps the outer shell and inner lining of the bag apart.

Filling. Your sleeping gear should reduce loss of heat by insulating your body warmth. This insulation is achieved by packing the sleeping bag with either a natural or synthetic fill.

The best natural source of filling is the soft plumage of geese or ducks, referred to as down, which outperforms synthetic fill for warmth, weight, ease of compression, loft (the ability to expand and trap air), and durability. However, down is expensive, loses virtually all of its insulating properties when damp or wet, and is difficult to dry and maintain, and the feathers may cause an allergic reaction. You can reduce these drawbacks by keeping your down sleeping bag very definitely under wraps: place it inside a well-sealed plastic bag, then insert it inside a stuffsack, which is also placed in a plastic bag. As a protective liner, use an internal cloth or fleece sleeping bag that can be cleaned at more frequent intervals than the down bag. Life expectancy for a down bag in standard conditions is around eight to twelve years.

Usually polyester, the synthetic fill in sleeping bags is inexpensive and easy to clean, continues to provide reasonable insulation when damp, and dries easily.

The down side is that synthetics are heavier, bulkier, and less durable. Life expectancy for a synthetic fill bag in standard conditions is around three to six years.

Features. In colder temperatures, remember that your head is the greatest source of heat loss: a hood with a drawcord retains warmth. A shoulder collar with drawcord will also reduce the amount of heat escaping across the upper body and out of the bag. A padded baffle down the inside of the zipper should also reduce dissipation of heat. In warm conditions, a full-length, double-ended zipper provides an effective means to keep the top or lower half of the body ventilated.

Trekkers looking for more intimacy can purchase a pair of sleeping bags with right-handed and left-handed zippers that interlink to form a double bag.

Liners. Liners are an effective way to uprate the warmth of your sleeping bag and protect it from wear and tear (washing a liner is a lot easier than laundering a down-filled sleeping bag). Silk and polypropylene are good lightweight choices. Pile liners are hardwearing and offer warmth even when wet; some models also function as covers.

Foreign hostels often stipulate the use of a liner to protect blankets and pillows, and for this purpose you can either carry your own or hire one from the hostel for a modest fee.

Stuffsacks. Stuffsacks with compression straps reduce bulky sleeping bags to manageable proportions—remember to use a waterproof liner inside and preferably another waterproof bag outside the stuffsack.

Maintenance. After use, give your sleeping bag a good airing and avoid keeping it rolled up tight for long periods of time—store it loosely. Wash synthetic fill bags at a maximum of 104 degrees Fahrenheit (40 degrees Celsius) with at least five rinses; then either drip dry or tumble dry in a large commercial dryer at a maximum of 104 degrees Fahrenheit. Some old hands favor throwing an old tennis shoe into the dryer with the bag to provide more loft.

Down fill bags should only be cleaned when strictly necessary to avoid gradually breaking down the fill's insulating properties. For best results, use a professional service. If you do the washing yourself, you should gently handwash the bag in lukewarm water using a special down cleaner. Do not wring. When moving the bag, be careful not to let the weight of wet down burst the fabric seams. Dry in a large tumble dryer at a cool temperature. Afterwards gently pat apart any clumps so that the down is lofted evenly again and spread out to complete the drying process.

SLEEPING MATS

Not surprisingly, a major loss of insulation occurs where the sleeping bag touches the ground. A sleeping mat will keep this chill at bay and iron out most of the efforts by ground matter to make an impression on your body.

Sleeping mats come in two forms: closed-cell foam and open-cell foam. Closed-cell foam is inexpensive, provides good insulation, scarcely absorbs water, and resists crushing, but it is bulky to transport. In its standard form, open-cell foam is the stuff of cushions: bulky and eager to soak up moisture. For trekkers, the most practical, albeit expensive, application of open-cell foam is when it is enclosed inside a self-inflating mattress, surrounded by an airtight cover with a valve. Despite being somewhat heavier than a closed-cell foam mat, it can be packed into a compact size and shape and is available in full size or hip-length versions. If you opt for the hip-length design, you can tuck your pack or bunch of clothing under your legs to keep them insulated from the ground.

One disadvantage to the air mattress pad is its susceptibility to puncturing by sharp objects or sparks. This makes it necessary to carry a repair kit and exercise more care, for instance, by placing a groundcloth beneath the mat.

HAMMOCKS
In tropical climates, and especially in South America and Africa, hammocks made from string, cloth, or mesh are a popular, lightweight, well-ventilated, comfortable, and inexpensive way to get some decent shuteye. With a couple of strong hooks and some strong rope, they can be slung in all kinds of places, such as hotel rooms, balconies, forests, boat decks, and beach huts.

◆ COOKING GEAR ◆

STOVES
Unless campfires are expressly permitted, assume you can minimize your impact by using a stove. If you are going on a trekking trip where teahouses, villages, or huts en route provide food, or you purposely take only food that requires no further preparation, you can leave behind the cooking gear and fuel.

If you do carry a stove, your choice of which type will be mostly determined by the kind of fuel it uses. Although dried yak dung pats have been an effective fuel on the Tibetan plateau for centuries, my first attempts to follow this lead with a cowpat created problems.

Trekking with a friend in Nepal on a circuit out of Pokhara, we made impromptu camp around dusk on a steep lakeside slope. Since our fuel had run out, we decided to experiment with a large, basically dry cowpat found in the vicinity. The fire was just starting to smolder into life with olfactory gusto when the pat fell off its bed of kindling and extinguished the flames. Dinner that night was cold, soggy porridge.

When trekking off the beaten track around the globe, for practical and environmental reasons you'll need to consider using a stove.

Types. Trekking stoves fall into two major fuel categories: liquid fuels and gas canisters. Points worth considering include the fuel's availability, price, ease

A stove is for most occasions, but in some cultures, wood has its place.
(Deanna Swaney photo)

of use, heat output, and performance in low temperatures. One way to ensure a wide range of options, especially in remote foreign lands, is to use a multifuel stove, which allows you to burn the local fuel wherever you are.

Liquid Fuel. Kerosene is inexpensive, widely available around the world, provides plenty of heat, and works in low temperatures. The fuel's disadvantages are that it requires priming (preheating with a volatile fuel such as petrol) to vaporize, has a heavy smell, and doesn't easily evaporate if spilled.

White gas (also known as naphtha) is easily flammable and provides high heat output. On the other hand, it is expensive, available only in a few countries, and affected adversely by low temperatures; it also requires priming.

Petrol is widely available at moderate cost, provides decent heat, and requires no priming. It is also notorious for being highly volatile and smelly (toxic fumes) and tends to clog stoves with carbon (either be prepared to manually clear the jet or use a model that does this automatically).

Alcohol, or methylated spirits, is inexpensive and easily flammable, evaporates quickly, and does not require priming, but it provides low heat output and its availability is limited.

Gas Fuel. Gas in the form of butane or a propane/butane mixture is provided in cartridges that are sold in resealable or nonresealable versions. The clear advantage of a resealable cartridge is that you can disconnect it from your stove prior to transport or for storage.

Butane is clean and easy to use and requires no priming. It is, however, expensive and of limited availability and performs poorly at low temperatures. Note also that pressure inside the cartridge drops markedly as the fuel (and the flame) dwindles. To obtain better performance at lower temperatures, use cartridges with a butane/propane mixture. Unlike liquid fuel flasks, gas cartridges are not reusable.

Availability. Unless you've researched the precise availability of fuel at your destination, you'll need to straddle your options by carrying either a multifuel stove or one that runs on kerosene, the most widely available option worldwide. Availability is also a major issue because airline regulations strictly forbid travelers to transport fuel in the plane. This usually means you have to buy your fuel at your destination.

Several years ago, during a visit to Australia, I planned a trek with a couple of friends along the Overland Track in Tasmania. Somehow, during the planning session, where food, fuel, and equipment was organized, we forgot about the short hop by plane from Melbourne to Tasmania. Sure enough, at the airport, the check-in assistant spotted our fuel bottles. With half an hour to go before take-off, we had no option but to dash out to the back of the airport car park, pour out the expensive fuel and watch it evaporate under the stern gaze of security guards.

Stove Safety. Avoid lighting or using stoves inside tents. Not only can tent material go up in flames in an instant, but a stove can easily be knocked over in such cramped quarters. And the buildup of carbon monoxide in such a small, unventilated space can be deadly. If bad weather prevails, light the stove away from the tent and carefully shift to within covered reach of the tent entrance or flysheet.

When handling fuel, never refill a hot stove. Always refill a cool stove at a safe distance from any other heat or flames. Clean up any fuel spills and ensure that you light or use a stove well out of reach of any spillage. I'd recommend using a filter to sift out any impurities in the fuel (thereby reducing clogging and repairs) and to prevent spillage.

Fuel Economy. Fill your stove before preparing your meal: this saves the hassle of interrupting the cooking process. Protect against heat loss by shielding the stove from direct wind. You can save cooking time and fuel by presoaking foods, using a blackened pot (which absorbs heat better than a shiny, reflective one), keeping a lid on the pot, and using a heat exchanger to direct the heat onto the pot rather than around it.

Testing. Be sure to try out a new stove in the shop—first let the salesperson demonstrate its use, then allow the stove to cool as necessary and try it out again for yourself under the supervision of the salesperson. After purchase, read the instructions and learn how to use it. Improve your proficiency by cooking a few meals on it in your backyard, and don't forget to check that it is in working order *before* you go. If you don't, you may end up experiencing any infuriating foibles in the least comfortable weather. Even if your stove is a proven veteran, it still pays to check that it functions properly prior to your trip.

Maintenance. Most of the newer models of liquid-fuel stoves can be dismantled for ease of transport. They may also feature a self-cleaning jet, which typically requires a shake or two to unclog during day-to-day use. For more stubborn clogging, you may need to use a cleaning needle. Use strong plastic bags inside a cloth bag to protect disassembled stove components from dirt, and always carry tools, cleaning needles, and key spare parts as part of the stove kit.

COOKWARE

A prerequisite for trekking cookware is that it should be easy to pack, use, and clean. A minimum cookset for a solo trekker could consist of two nesting stainless steel pots, complete with lids; a stainless steel mug; a spoon; and a multitool pocketknife. Also handy is a pot gripper (a two-piece handle, usually made of metal or aluminum), that clamps onto the rim of the pot to lift it off the stove or fire. To cater for a companion, add a bowl. Chopsticks are a handy addition.

An essential item in your traveling gear is a water bottle with a capacity of at least 1 liter (approximate equivalent of just under 1 U.S. quart and just over 1 British quart) and a leakproof cap, which, to prevent loss, should be attached by a plastic loop. Of course, water bottle designs are numerous:

"Different designs have different virtues. For some years I favored Spanish wine botas, but of course they cannot be filled by immersion and the usual plastic lining springs leaks. Plastic bottles of whatever composition are reprehensible and possibly carcinogenic. The best solution I've found are the French-style aluminum bottles lined with porcelain, with a spring-loaded cap. They have surprisingly good thermal insulating properties but have a tendency to dent easily.

"Amongst my worst moments on the trail, I'd include rolling several hundred meters down a scree slide in Turkey's Aladaglar range, miraculously unhurt but having lost a half hour's excruciating climb, and smashed one canteen—of critical importance in a nearly waterless range in August. We reached a running spring by nightfall, but it was a very near thing."

—Marc Dubin

In addition, a flexible water carrier or bladder water bag of larger capacity than your water bottle is useful in camp, especially if your site is far from your water source. For advice about treating water, refer to chapter 4, "In Good Shape: Staying Healthy."

◆ FOOTWEAR ◆

Take good care of your feet by choosing footwear that matches the terrain and fits comfortably. As a biped, remember that the well-being of your feet can literally make or break your trip.

Before you purchase or pack footwear, you'll want to consider the lightest option that is adequate to protect your feet on the trail and perhaps include another type of footwear to relax your feet in camp. For the easiest terrain in warm climates, it may be sufficient to take running shoes and a pair of flipflops for use in camp, or you may be able to reduce your footwear to just a pair of adventure sandals. For other types of terrain and conditions, you might consider conserving space and weight by only taking boots.

The good news for women is that they no longer have to make do with men's models: several footwear manufacturers produce models for women that provide, for example, a narrower heel.

For tips on keeping your feet in good shape, refer to chapter 4, "In Good Shape: Staying Healthy."

BOOTS

Basic categories of boots include lightweight hiking boots for casual rambling or day hikes, mediumweight boots for backpacking and trekking in mountainous or snow-covered terrain, and heavyweight mountaineering boots for demanding work on ice, snow, and rock.

Purchase boots to match your trekking aims: look for ankle support, robust heels and toes, and the lightest model that can meet your demands. As a rule of thumb, a couple of pounds (1 kilogram) on your foot is the equivalent of carrying over 8 pounds (4 kilograms) on your back. In hot climates consider adventure sandals or fabric boots; leather boots do well for colder climes. If you wear boots, gaiters can offer your ankles and calves some protection against prickly scrub, snakes, and leeches, and they do a good job of preventing snow, rain, or mud from seeping around your ankles and into your boots.

Construction. Boots come in many guises, but the main elements of boot construction are sole, footbed, upper, and lining.

The sole has to be hardwearing and capable of providing a good grip. For lightweight trekking boots, a cut-away heel is common, whereas deep treads and block heels are used in heavier boots.

The footbed, often made from foam or other shock-absorbing material, retains the foot in its optimum position inside the boot. The upper surrounds the top of the foot, holding it in position and protecting against the elements. For upper material, leather has retained its popularity—the best types are made from one piece of leather. A recent development has been a hybrid leather upper with a Gore-Tex inner forming a waterproof breathable lining. Fabric uppers, typically a mixture of nylon and suede, offer reduced weight and are cooler in hot climates. They are available with or without a waterproof, breathable lining.

As the major contact point between boot and foot, the boot lining must be hardwearing, easy on your feet (no folding or stretching to create blisters), quick drying, and able to draw away moisture from your feet. Linings are available in soft leather and synthetic fabrics.

Fit. When trying out boots, use the socks you expect to wear while trekking, perhaps a combination of a synthetic liner and a woolen outer. At the same time, take the opportunity to try on a variety of socks, including thick and thin types that you anticipate wearing during the life of your boots. With the boot unlaced, tap your foot gently inside so that the toes are in the toe area, and then check that there's enough space for you to slide your finger down the back of the heel. This allows for expansion of your foot in hot weather and prevents your toes from scuffing into the front of the boot on steep downhill sections. Once your foot is laced in, check that the instep feels comfortable, that the boot doesn't feel too narrow or pinched, and that your heel sits snugly. Because most people's feet vary in size from one foot to the other, don't part with your money until you've tried boots on both your feet.

The next step after purchase is to break in your boots, wearing them frequently for several weeks on day hikes, in town, or at home. Get used to wearing them with your usual hiking socks and a load equivalent to what you expect to be packing on your travels. Don't wait until your trip starts; otherwise, strife between your feet and your boots might be the most memorable event on your travels.

Maintenance. Always make the effort to care properly for your boots. Check the manufacturer's instructions to see whether or not your boots should be conditioned with silicon, wax, or special tanning agents. Don't dry off boots beside or on top of direct heat—allow them to dry naturally. If they are damp inside, stuff them with newspaper and replace this whenever the paper has absorbed moisture. For a brief list of companies specializing in repair work and resoling, see appendix A.

ADVENTURE SANDALS

Sandals have been popular footwear since ancient times. Adopted by rafters and trekkers in the 1980s, sandals are now professionally designed with these enthusiasts in mind.

The main advantage of this new breed of adventure sandals lies in massive weight reduction compared to boots and excellent ventilation (and quick drying capability) when used barefoot or with socks in warm climates.

One drawback of sandals can be the burrs, vegetation, sand, and so forth that latch onto the straps or lodge in the footbed. Leather or synthetic leather straps offer less grip for burrs, and if the toe space is enclosed make sure there is space to shake out irritants. If you're striding through the day in strong sunlight, use sunscreen to prevent sunburn on your feet.

The design of adventure sandals usually features straps or loops configured to give maximum support for the ankles, heels, and toes; durable, high-traction soles made from Vibram or other materials (some models use recycled vehicle tires); shock-absorbing midsoles; and molded footbeds (raised to keep out stones and grit, and minimize stubbed toes).

◆ CLOTHING ◆

Choosing clothing for your trip involves a fine balance between the size of your pack and the need to keep yourself comfortable and protected from the elements. The best approach to your clothing needs is to dress in layers so that you can deal with cold and warm climates (and the vagaries in between) by adding or subtracting items to regulate your body heat.

Combined with the research you do on your destination, chapter 1, "Prime Time: Choice Trekking," should give you a good idea of what types of temperatures and weather to expect.

COLD WEATHER GEAR

Underlayer. The underlayer should keep your skin at the right temperature for comfort and, most importantly, ensure that it stays dry by drawing away moisture. As an underlayer in cool climates, typically long underwear, the choice of materials for thermal clothes includes polypropylene and polyester, which are less expensive than silk, a natural fiber with a high comfort factor and price tag. Wool is also popular, but not recommended for direct contact if your skin is sensitive. Cotton is to be avoided in cold weather because, as soon as you stop working up a sweat, it does not draw the moisture away but, rather, soaks it up and allows it to freeze against the body.

Midlayer. The midlayer should provide insulation by trapping air inside the material. Popular choices are a heavy wool or polypropylene shirt combined with a fleece or pile-fiber jacket or pullover. In windy conditions you can guard against windchill by adding a windproof jacket or choosing a windproof garment. In cold, dry conditions a down jacket provides excellent insulation but should be worn with a waterproof outer layer in damp climates.

Outer Layer. For your shell, or outer layer, choose a jacket and/or overtrousers to keep wind, rain, and snow at bay. A breathable fabric such as Gore-Tex allows moisture from within the clothing to escape through to the surface where it evaporates. A less expensive and less comfortable option is to wear coated nylon material; however, good ventilation (for example, zipped underarm vents) is essential to allow condensation to exit. If you intend to don your rucksack over this layer, choose a stronger ply material to withstand the added wear and tear.

Gear for Extremities. Your feet, hands, ears, and head are responsible for most of your body's heat loss. Woolen or fiber-pile socks should take care of your feet; woolen or fleece mitts or gloves with polypropylene or silk linings look after your hands; and your head and ears can be kept cozy with a woolen or fleece hat (add a polypropylene or silk balaclava liner for extra warmth).

WARM WEATHER GEAR

Trekking in warm weather, your layering needs may be greatly reduced, but keep at hand a wool shirt or fiber-pile jacket for cooler moments (or rest breaks) and a rainjacket for cloudbursts in temperate regions. Your main concern will be to stay ventilated, cool, and shaded from the sun. Look for materials that are lightweight, easily compressed, and quick-drying. Cotton clothing, ranging from underwear, T-shirt (also doubling as nightwear) or shirt (short- and long-sleeved), shorts or trousers, to socks is a good warm weather choice.

A swimming suit can also double as temporary underwear or night attire. T-shirts and other cotton clothing are a cheap and colorful buy in many countries. Take the minimum of such clothing with you and stock up locally, so you'll then be able to bring back some practical souvenirs.

The simple bodywrap, a long strip of cloth wound round the body, is used in many countries all over Asia, Africa, and beyond, where it is known by names such as sarong, lungi, kikoi, and pareo. Cheap and widely available locally, it is also very versatile. Use it as a sun shade, ground cover, beach wrap, showerwear, towel, head muffler, wrapping bag, makeshift pillow, and lightweight blanket—and don't forget to give it the occasional wash.

CLOTHING GUARANTEED TO GET YOU NOTICED OR JAILED

When trekking in Asia, Africa, and South America, it is best not to wear military surplus or camouflage designs unless you want to be mistaken for a foreign invader, spy, or local malcontent.

◆   REST OF THE PACK   ◆

LIGHTING

Lighting is an essential for moments such as those when you are caught out late on a trail, setting up camp, relaxing in the tent, chasing off intruders, stumbling out in the dead of night to answer nature's call, signaling in emergency, and much more. Carry a flashlight (known as a torch in British and antipodean circles) and select a waterproof design that has a variable focus and an attached strap. A headlamp fits in a harness around your head, thereby leaving your hands free and allowing you to direct the beam along your line of sight. If you find your flashlight suffers from the common problem that jolting during walking accidentally switches it on inside the pack, reverse the batteries after use, or restrain the switch with a strong rubber band.

Always carry extra bulbs and batteries. To spare your batteries, use tub candles or tealights, especially those with a metal casing, which provide enough light in a tent at night to write notes or do some reading. A solar charger reduces environmental impact. The development of polycrystalline cell technology has made solar chargers a viable option for trekkers in climates that are reliably sunny or warm with either clear or overcast skies. A typical solar charger kit weighs less than 8 ounces (224 grams) and consists of rechargeable nickel-cadmium batteries, a charging cradle, and a small solar panel (approximately the size of this book). The panel can be attached with a harness to the back of the pack to charge while you trek. In bright midday sun, a 1.7-watt solar charger can charge a quartet of AA-size batteries in about 2 hours. In overcast conditions, you'd need at least twice the charging time. To achieve optimum output, batteries should be fully discharged before recharging.

If you are trekking in a suitable climate and carry a solar charger, you'll clearly save the additional weight of standard replacement batteries and avoid the associated environmental problem of disposal. However, for cold climates, which make a heavy drain on power, you'll have to rely on standard batteries.

REPAIR MATERIALS

Repair materials are essentials. For running repairs, waterproofing, and general organization, take along a roll of adhesive-backed tape (handy for temporary repairs to your tent, backpack, and sleeping bag), needle and thread, rubber bands, a variety of plastic bags, and about 50 feet (15 meters) of parachute or similar heavyweight cord.

TOILETRIES

Soap, toothpaste, and shampoo are commonly available overseas, so there is no real need to carry more than a small starter supply, although you might not find your favorite brands. Don't overlook the added weight of anything other than sufficient sachets or a tube large enough to last your trip.

Some travelers leave behind toothpaste and brush, preferring to use dental floss (handy as sewing thread too) with a rinse of salt or bicarbonate of soda (baking powder). If you take a toothbrush, you might take a collapsible one or cut down the handle. For taking care of your hair, consider carrying only a comb, or share a brush or comb with a companion.

Towels made from materials such as viscose rayon are small and very light and dry in next to no time. Equally, you could dispense with this and simply use a body wrap, shirt, or blouse instead.

SPECIALIST SUPPLIES

In the developing world, sunblock and specialist medical or toiletry supplies are not usually available unless as imports at a high price, so take them with you. Use durable, lightweight packaging (not glass bottles). A recent introduction to the American market is a three-in-one lotion that functions as moisturizer/ sunblock/insect repellent.

LAUNDRY

Options for laundry day include doing the washing yourself, handing it to a local hotel, or using a local laundromat. If you do it yourself, you'll be well advised to take your own universal plug or squash ball for sinks and baths. Plugs have a habit of going astray in hotels. A length of rope or string will work well as a washing-line. Take care where you hang your washing, because unattended clothing also has a habit of going astray.

CAMPING NECESSITIES

To minimize impact while camping, biodegradable soap, available in a tube or plastic bottle, can serve to wash yourself, clothes, and cooking utensils. As scouring agents, you can also use bicarbonate of soda or sand. For burying waste outdoors while camping, a toilet trowel weighs little and minimizes your impact (for technique, see chapter 7, "Minimum Impact: Trekking and the Environment").

TOILET PAPER

In many parts of the world, especially Asia, use of the left hand and a washdown with water are the norm when using the toilet. As a result, toilet paper is not commonly available there except in major tourist hotels; so if you want to use it you'll have to take several rolls. Extract the inner core from toilet rolls, which then pack flat.

MISCELLANEOUS

The miscellaneous zone is the dangerous part of your pack where wisdom, favor, and weight often conflict. If you are miserable without your Audubon birdcaller, it's got to be there—yes, even if your skills make your tentmate very nervous.

For additional support on the trail, you can use a stick or pole, such as the humble walking stick, modern ski pole, or hi-tech trekking staff. This "third leg" can take pressure off a wobbly knee on downhill stretches, ease the burden of the pack on uphill ones, provide a sounding implement on river crossings, and fend off foliage or irritant dogs.

"The one thing that really seemed to set the Turks off was my reliance on a walking stick. For reasons I could never quite figure out, they found this very threatening and antisocial. Strangers would approach me in bus depots or other public places, give the stick a censorious shake or two and bawl 'Cok fena' (Very wicked!). My stubborn retention of my walking stick(s) was yet one more bone of contention with my Turkish-American colleague who despite being a mountain guide also considered it poor form. In this era of Kurdish PKK guerrillas armed to the teeth, a stick as the hallmark of a brigand seemed an exceedingly quaint notion."

—Marc Dubin

Entertainment, for yourself and for those you meet, is optional. I'd strongly suggest cutting these items down to one or two favorites. You can, of course, bring along your own musical entertainment, such as a mouth-harp, penny-whistle, or harmonica. Depending on your proficiency, you may impress the locals or pique fellow trekkers, especially if tent-bound in foul weather. Other entertainment options include photos or postcards from home, a juggling kit, playing cards, a portable chess or checkers set, or a boomerang.

Minibinoculars are a personal favorite for scouting out the trail ahead and other amateur naturalist pursuits. A compact traveling alarm clock helps for those early departures at the crack of dawn. Your reading matter might include guidebooks, phrase books, and literary coverage of your destination. Remember that you can trade books with other travelers or visit secondhand book stores. Trekkers' haunts sometimes have a book-exchange shelf with English-language magazines and novels.

◆ THE PACK ◆

The "house on your back" not only carries the sum total of your chosen trekking belongings; it also rides on your shoulders and hips for much of your time on the trail. Consequently, you'll appreciate a good fit and soon rue a poor one.

DAYPACK

The function of a daypack is to carry enough gear, food, clothing, and so forth for a day hike or similar excursion from a base hut or camping site. It should also be compact enough to fit into your larger backpack. There are various combinations of padded or unpadded shoulder straps, waist straps, internal and external compartments, loops, and zippers. Daypacks come in many sizes as well as plenty of variation to suit everyone from the ultralight specialist to the kitchen sink fanatic.

BACKPACK

Internal frame backpacks provide a snug fit to your back, ease of movement, and balance. However, lack of ventilation along your back can make you work up a heavy sweat in hot climates. External frame backpacks provide good stability on trails where there is little climbing involved. In hot weather, they also allow better ventilation of your back. A pack capacity in the region of 4,000 to 4,600 cubic inches (65 to 75 liters) should cover most standard treks and allow you to pack up to the recommended one-third of your body weight.

Fitting. When fitting the pack, ensure that the hip belt lies on the pelvis, the back bands fit tight and snug along your back, and the shoulder straps are just above your shoulders or level with them. A well-padded hip belt properly cinched in position transfers over half the weight of the pack away from your back and shoulders to your legs.

Adjusting packs, Namibia (Deanna Swaney photo)

Fill the pack with the weight of gear you expect to be carrying and wear the requisite clothing. If it doesn't feel right, don't assume you'll be able to bend your body to fit—try another model.

Maintenance. Materials used for backpacks are initially water-repellent, but wear and tear can lead to leaky seams or damp patches. A pack cover is handy for the outside, and a garbage bag used as a liner will protect the contents. For hints about backpack security, refer to chapter 6, "Look Sharp: Security Basics."

◆   PACKING FOR WEIGHT AND COMFORT   ◆

Once you've assembled your traveling possessions, perhaps along the lines of the checklists provided at the end of this chapter, think again about ways to cut down weight. Your main concerns when packing are weight, comfort, and protection.

WEIGHT

How many of your items are multipurpose? A capacious poncho, for example, can function as a groundsheet, pack cover, and makeshift shelter. A large bandanna can find use as a handkerchief, bandage, dustmask, sunhat, and much more.

Discard packaging such as glass, cardboard, and bubble packs and, if necessary, use resealable plastic bags or other containers instead. For example, take a look at your toiletries bag: Do you need a monster tube of toothpaste or bottle of biodegradable soap for a one-month trip, or could you decant an appropriate amount into squeeze tubes? Literary iconoclasts may wish to reduce the weight of their guidebook by cutting out the parts that don't relate to the destination. If you take reading matter, a compendium of short stories can easily be split among a group. Discard the core cardboard in toilet rolls and then squash the roll flat.

Retain films in their plastic containers. Before you ditch the paper packaging make a note of the expiration date. Incidentally, when no longer needed for films, these containers are handy for storing all manner of small items from salt and pepper, to fishing hooks, lip salve, toothpaste, and small change (note that there have been reports that chemical residues in film canisters may make them unsuitable for storage of foodstuffs).

COMFORT

Packing for comfort requires placement of heavy gear as close to your center of gravity as possible: in the top section of your pack nearest to your back. Lighter items should be placed below this. Raingear, maps, and other items frequently used during the day should be easily accessible in a top pocket or under the main flap. The upper side pockets can be balanced for weight by inserting fuel bottles and water bottles on opposite sides. Lower side pockets are a good spot for trail

Shapin *(walking fishtrap), Yunnan, China*

snacks, toiletries (toilet paper, foot powder, insect repellent, sunscreen, and so forth), spare laces, gloves, a spare pair of socks, and warm headgear.

On narrow trails, side pockets can jam against rock or scrub. Some backpack models provide detachable side pockets, or you can design your own by attaching fixtures and loops.

Last but not least, your comfort will depend on the weight you carry. If you load yourself beyond your limit, you may cause yourself physical damage and turn your trek into torture. Make sensible demands on your body by matching your fitness and the anticipated demands of the trekking terrain to the weight you carry. If you are carrying a heavy pack, adjust your pace and your daily distances accordingly. One surefire recipe for malaise and dissatisfaction is for an unfit person to attempt to heave a massive load for enormous distances or to great heights.

As a general rule, your load should not exceed one-third of your body weight. Keeping your pack weight to a sound minimum reduces impact on the trail, makes for a more efficient use of your supplies, and promotes enjoyment of the experience.

PROTECTION

A pack liner or plastic garbage bag affords primary protection against rain and dust, while individual stuffsacks and plastic bags help to organize contents and provide another line of defense against seepage. To avoid unwelcome gooey spills of cooking oil or liquid soap, for example, keep containers properly sealed and double-wrapped within their own plastic bag. Freezer bags are extra strong. Protect items susceptible to damp conditions, such as toilet paper or powdered foodstuffs, by using plastic resealable or freezer bags.

A general problem with sealed or closed bags or containers is their tendency to expand with altitude gain. Make allowances for this by underfilling containers. If you don't, flights and other rapid altitude gains may make a spectacular mess in your baggage.

If you wrap sharp or pointed gear in soft clothing, you'll prevent rips in your pack during transit or those repeated jabs in the back while on the trail. Make maximum use of nooks and crannies, such as those inside cooking pots.

If you tie sleeping mats, tents, or clothing on the outside of your pack, beware of snagging on overgrown trails or sideswiping on narrow routes cut against mountainsides. In these conditions, it's best to keep the gear packed inside.

◆ CHECKLISTS ◆

Before you scan the following lists and contemplate hauling everything away with a trailer, run a mental check of climate, terrain, facilities, and length of stay at your trekking destination. To steel yourself for crunch decision time, read through the "Less Is More" section at the beginning of this chapter. If you've learned the sore points of an overweight pack on a previous trip, don't repeat the experience. What did you take that was inapplicable? What was missing when you needed it most? Before you stuff things into the pack, make a pile in the middle of the floor so that you can see the full extent of what's going to be on your back.

Documents and Paperwork
- ❑ Passport
- ❑ Airline tickets
- ❑ Health certificate
- ❑ Driver's license
  (international and resident)
- ❑ Traveler's checks
- ❑ Cash
- ❑ Photocopies (essential documents, reference numbers, and emergency contact details)
- ❑ Visas
- ❑ Travel insurance
- ❑ Passport photos
- ❑ International student identity card
- ❑ Youth hostel membership card
- ❑ Credit cards
- ❑ Address book (duplicate)
- ❑ Transparent resealable document folders

Camping and Sleeping
- ❑ Backpack (and cover)
- ❑ Daypack
- ❑ Tent (with mosquito net and flysheet)/bivvy bag/tarp
- ❑ Groundsheet
- ❑ Inner sleeping bag
- ❑ Mosquito net (treated with repellent)
- ❑ Plastic pack liner and bags (keep contents dry)
- ❑ Tent spares (stakes, poles, pole repair sleeve, cord)
- ❑ Sleeping bag (with stuffsack)
- ❑ Sleeping pad
- ❑ Hammock

Cooking and Food
- ❑ Stove (spare parts, cleaner, primer)
- ❑ Fuel
- ❑ Bladder water bag
- ❑ Mug
- ❑ Pot gripper
- ❑ Scouring pad and dishcloth
- ❑ Multitool pocketknife (wizard item of many uses)
- ❑ Water purification (filter, tablets)
- ❑ Rubbish bag
- ❑ Emergency rations
- ❑ Fuel container and spare
- ❑ Water bottle
- ❑ Dishes
- ❑ Pots
- ❑ Biodegradable liquid soap
- ❑ Matches (waterproof)
- ❑ Chopsticks
- ❑ Spoon
- ❑ Food (fresh, dried, freeze-dried, dehydrated)
- ❑ Rubbish bag

Clothing

- ❏ Socks (polypropylene, wool, silk, cotton)
- ❏ Waterproof jacket
- ❏ Rain pants
- ❏ Shorts
- ❏ Sarong (lightweight bodywrap)
- ❏ Long-sleeved shirt
- ❏ Windjacket
- ❏ Gloves
- ❏ Bandanna or scarf
- ❏ Woolen cap/balaclava
- ❏ Underwear
- ❏ Thermal underwear
- ❏ Poncho (doubles as groundsheet)
- ❏ Long pants
- ❏ Bathing suit
- ❏ T-shirt
- ❏ Woolen sweater or pile jacket
- ❏ Down jacket
- ❏ Inner gloves
- ❏ Sunhat

Footwear

- ❏ Boots
- ❏ Camp shoes
- ❏ Gaiters
- ❏ Sandals
- ❏ Spare laces

Lighting

- ❏ Flashlight (torch) or headlamp (with spare bulb and batteries)
- ❏ Lighter
- ❏ Solar charger
- ❏ Tub candles

Toiletries

Refer also to the medical checklist in chapter 4, "In Good Shape: Staying Healthy."

- ❏ Washbag
- ❏ Toilet trowel
- ❏ Toothbrush/paste
- ❏ Towel
- ❏ Insect repellent
- ❏ Sunscreen
- ❏ Foot powder
- ❏ Tampons
- ❏ Toilet paper
- ❏ Universal bath plug
- ❏ Biodegradable soap
- ❏ Brush/comb
- ❏ Sunglasses and/or glacier goggles
- ❏ Lip salve
- ❏ Contraceptives

Medical

Refer to the medical checklist in chapter 4, "In Good Shape: Staying Healthy."

Security

- ❏ Money belt
- ❏ Combination lock
- ❏ Chain
- ❏ Door wedge
- ❏ Tubigrip (elastic wraparound leg pouch)
- ❏ Chicken wire (pack lining)

Navigation
❏ Compass
❏ Maps
❏ Altimeter
❏ Handheld GPS
  (global positioning system)

Emergency
❏ Survival bag
❏ Medical kit (refer to checklist
  in chapter 4, "In Good Shape:
  Staying Healthy")
❏ Signaling mirror (also for groom-
  ing and finding ticks on body)
❏ Safety pins
❏ Earplugs
❏ Whistle
❏ The Ten Essentials (refer to
  chapter 9, "Emergencies: Prepared
  and Alert")
❏ Spare glasses/contact lenses
  (plus elastic retaining straps)
❏ Sewing thread and needles

Camera Gear
❏ Camera
❏ Filters
❏ Spare batteries
❏ Robust totebag
❏ Lenses
❏ Film
❏ Lens tissues and puffer

Miscellaneous
❏ Walking stick, ski pole, or
  trekking staff (may double as a
  tent pole and dog deterrent)
❏ Adhesive-backed tape
❏ Waterproofing bags
❏ Rubber bands
❏ Books (guides, phrases, literature)
❏ Home country postcards
❏ Star charts
❏ Solar radio
❏ Lightweight radio/tape player
  plus tapes
❏ Calculator
❏ Watch
❏ Minibinoculars
❏ Notebook/diary
❏ Pen/pencil
❏ Plastic bags (thick and thin)
❏ Parachute cord (50 feet/15 meters)
❏ Traveling alarm clock
❏ Family photos
❏ Fun items (boomerang, juggling kit,
  kite, playing cards, travel chess
  set, etc.)
❏ Compact musical instrument
  (mouth-harp, harmonica,
  penny-whistle, etc.)

INVENTIVE MEASURES

Rishiri-to Island lies off the northern coast of Hokkaido in northern Japan. After arriving by ferry late in the day, I spent several hours toiling up the trail towards Rishiri-zan, the island's volcanic summit. As the trail ascended, the snow became deeper and I was pleased to reach the unattended mountain hut at sunset.

As I unpacked my meager items of food and gear, a Japanese arrived in full climbing attire. He unpacked an impressive array of sleeping pads, cooking gear, reading lamp, and a radio. I made short work of my supper rations purchased hastily in the village below, and gratefully took up the offer of a hot cup of coffee from my hutmate before we both turned in.

The night was cold and became even colder as the wind blew around and into the hut. Having mentally kicked myself for thinking a sleeping mat too much weight to carry for the season, I made do with a nest of newspaper scrounged from around the hut. I soon found this was insufficient to keep the piercing chill out of my down sleeping bag. In time I had donned every piece of my clothing—balaclava hat, thermal longjohns, sweater, windcheater, rainpants, and several pairs of socks which were distributed around my extremities. In the morning, after a modicum of chilled sleep, I noticed the Japanese watching curiously as I stirred from my sleeping bag—hands suitably insulated with plastic bags and several pairs of socks!

4

IN GOOD SHAPE
Staying Healthy

 AMID ALL THE OTHER PREPARATIONS FOR A trek, it's easy to overlook health precautions. Although losing gear is an annoyance, it rarely dictates a speedy return home; illness, however, can seriously affect the quality of your travels or even bring them to a halt.

At first glance, the number of possible ills and woes lurking overseas seems daunting, but with appropriate information and forward planning, simple precautions, and a touch of good fortune, the vast majority of travelers experience little more than a case of traveler's diarrhea.

Useful addresses and suggestions for further reading are provided in appendices A and B.

Warning: Please note that the information supplied here is in no way intended as a substitute for the advice or attention of a medical doctor.

◆ PREPARATION ◆

Prepare for a healthy trip before you go: glean as much information as possible from your doctor, specialist services qualified to advise on travel health overseas, background reading, travel agents, and national tourist organizations. Remember that your doctor may not specialize in tropical medicine or travel medicine in general, so cast a wide net for the most up-to-date and qualified information. For a brief outline of sources, refer to appendix A.

Think ahead for inoculations, some of which may have to be taken several weeks or months in advance. Brush up on your first-aid skills or enroll in a course. Although the aim of precaution and prevention is primarily to keep yourself

---

Symbolic spirit: **Unkatahe, Goddess Against Disease;** North American Indian

Local refreshment: Plantation workers eating a cacao *lunch, Savai'i, Western Samoa* (Deanna Swaney photo)

healthy, in an emergency you may find yourself able to offer assistance and a medical kit to a doctor treating other less fortunate (or less prepared) travelers.

Visit your doctor, dentist, and optician for a checkup and talk about your past medical history, current level of fitness, the destinations you have in mind, and the activities you are planning. If you have a specific or long-standing illness, you might want to take along a letter from your doctor translated into the language of your destination. Consider your possible requirements for prescriptions—for medicines, spare glasses, contact lenses, and oral contraceptives—and carry a second supply of glasses or contact lenses.

A spare pair of glasses would have set things right in the following instance:

"Several years ago I went for a hillwalk in Scotland with a friend. As this was my first walk with her, I was a little surprised that she was not wearing her glasses, but assumed she had contact lenses. However, after seeing her stumbling badly while trying to cross a stream, my anxious enquiry revealed that she had none and that she'd left her spectacles behind to avoid breakage. In fact her eyesight was such that the surrounding scenery was out of focus and, as a result, she was not too steady on her feet!"

—*Graeme Cornwallis*

IMMUNIZATION

If you are traveling outside the United States, Canada, Australia, New Zealand, Japan, and Western Europe, check carefully with a qualified medical source (such as those listed in appendix A) on the required and recommended vaccinations for the prevention of illnesses prevalent at your destination.

Most authorized medical centers and consultants will provide an international health certificate to record the date, place, and type of your immunizations. This is highly recommended as a compact personal record and as official proof, for example, of the yellow fever vaccination, which is a mandatory entrance requirement for visitors to certain African, Asian, and South American countries. As a result of worldwide eradication, no immunization is required for smallpox.

INSURANCE

You are well advised to take out a travel insurance policy that covers medical problems. Check the small print carefully prior to purchasing your policy. Are "dangerous activities" excluded and if so does the relevant description specifically exclude, for example, trekking? In this case you should look for another policy. How does the insurer settle claims: do you pay first and claim later, or do you call a number in your home country for clearance on the course of action? If you have to claim back from the insurer, be sure to ask for and retain receipts for any payments you make for overseas medical assistance. Does the insurer provide emergency repatriation? This is essential if you fall seriously ill in a remote place without the required medical services. For additional hints on insurance, refer to chapter 2, "First Steps: Travel Arrangements."

FITNESS

A couple of months before departure, assess your fitness in relation to your planned trip and start getting heart, lungs, joints, and muscles into shape. Prepare for trekking—don't expect your body to leap out of an office routine one day and into a grueling trek the next. One regime followed by a doctor acquaintance of mine is to walk up and down flights of stairs several times a week with a pack on his back, at least six weeks before he leaves.

◆ FOOD AND DRINK ◆

A large portion of the fun in travel lies in discovering foreign food and drink. Curries in India, gado gado (vegetable salad with spicy peanut dressing) in Indonesia, couscous (semolina with meat and vegetables) in Morocco, sake (rice wine) in Japan, juices of exotic fruits in Brazil, and yak-butter tea in Tibet are just a few of the novelties waiting for your palate. Once you've arrived at your destination, it will take a couple of weeks for your digestive system to acclimatize to the new fare, and throughout your trip you should heed the following advice on hygiene.

AVOIDING CONTAMINATED FOOD AND DRINK

Given the link between contaminated food and a number of diseases, you should keep an eye on your food and drink. In practice, you'll have to compromise between what is desirable and what is possible.

The risk of food contamination is much higher if you stray from well-cooked and freshly served food. Beware of raw vegetables, peeled fruit, salads, fish (especially shellfish), and meat (unless well cooked and served piping hot); food left

Well-packaged alfresco dessert: Fresh coconut, Manono, Western Samoa (**Deanna Swaney** photo)

lying around or reheated; dishes or ingredients populated by flies; and open table condiments, sauces, and relishes. Some travelers dodge possible hygiene problems with local food implements by using their own chopsticks or cutlery.

If you are in any doubt about the quality of the water you encounter on your travels, be sure to treat it—most of the illness experienced during foreign travel is related to contaminated water. Consume treated water within 24 hours unless it is in a properly sterilized and sealed container. This advice extends to water used for local ice cubes or ice cream, washing vegetables or fruits, and brushing your teeth. If you are buying bottled water or bottled carbonated drinks, take a look at any sell-by date and check that the seal is intact—in some countries locals have found a lucrative income by refilling bottles from the tap. Cups or glasses washed in contaminated water should also be avoided (some traveling folks carry their own mug).

There are three basic methods for decontamination of water: boiling, filtration, and disinfection. It may seem obvious, but you can greatly improve the purity of your water if you head up and away as close as possible to its source; as far as possible from human habitation, pasturing animals, stagnant or discolored pools, and industrial pollution.

Boiling. At sea level, bringing water to a full boil for at least 2 minutes at 212 degrees Fahrenheit (100 degrees Celsius) will kill most major microorganisms, especially *Giardia*. If ingested, this nasty cyst lurks in your intestines for a few days before unleashing a noxious bout of explosive diarrhea lasting many weeks. As you gain in altitude, remember to allow at least 1 extra minute for every 1,000 feet (300 meters) above sea level. Boiling doesn't remove debris, and it necessitates the use of fuel and requires a subsequent wait for the liquid to cool.

Filtration. Filtration devices are available in various designs to pump water through a filter with pores small enough to block organisms. The standard used to measure these tiny critters is 1 micron, equivalent to 1 millionth of a meter. Filters should be able to block organisms larger than 0.5 microns (including *Giardia*) and ultrafine models are also available to a specification of 0.2 microns, enough to knock back yet more microbeings, including some viruses.

With pore sizes as small as this, clogging is to be expected, and filters should normally be self-cleaning or provided with a cleaning device. A simple preliminary method to remove coarse impurities before proceeding with full filtration is to use a coffee filter.

Filters vary considerably in price. Points to consider are your intended use; rate of flow and, hence, amount of water; weight; cost of internal elements and spares; robustness; portability; and reliability.

Disinfection. There are several chemicals used for the treatment of water, the most common being iodine and chlorine. Iodine preparations (liquid, tablets, or crystals) are faster acting (around 20 minutes) and more effective against cysts than most other chemical treatments. Iodine does not remove solids suspended in water; and it imparts a recognizable taste that you may want to disguise with a drink flavor mix. It is not recommended for extended use because it can produce side effects in pregnant women or people with thyroid problems.

Chlorine, available in tablet form, also has a strong taste and is considered less efficient against cysts than iodine. Dosage should be carefully matched to the anticipated contamination. Allow at least 30 minutes for sterilization, longer if the water is very cold.

COMMON PROBLEMS ASSOCIATED WITH FOOD OR WATER

For travelers, the usual source of an upset stomach lies in a reaction to contaminated food or water.

Diarrhea/Gastroenteritis

Travelers' diarrhea, also known as Montezuma's revenge, Delhi belly, and a host of other names, usually only lasts 3 to 4 days before the symptoms subside without the need for treatment with drugs. During this time, you are recommended to rest and eat lightly. Keep up your intake of fluid by using a proprietary rehydration solution or make up your own—8 level teaspoons (40 grams) of sugar and 1 level teaspoon (3.5 grams) of salt to just over 1 U.S. quart (1 liter) of treated water. Because diarrhea has a strong flushing effect on the body, be aware that it may impair absorption of the contraceptive pill.

If diarrhea persists, seek medical advice.

Constipation

Constipation can also be caused by dehydration, reaction to new surroundings, or cramped travel conditions. Keep up the fluid intake, and include fibrous foods, such as fruit and vegetables, in your diet.

Giardiasis

A frequent infection in many parts of the world, giardiasis is transmitted through contaminated water and causes chronic diarrhea, pungent gas, and a general feeling of bloatedness. Refer to the section on water purification in this chapter for ways to keep *Giardia* out of drinking water. If you wonder why many trekkers discuss this ailment with awe, here's an extract from Mike Ford's journal:

"Waking up in the middle of the night in Kagbeni (Annapurna Circuit), I had an extraordinarily strong urge to vomit. As I sat bolt upright the pressure in my abdomen changed, releasing an almighty yellow sulphuric burp which nearly took my head off. Within seconds the urge became critical, and as I attempted to stand up, another fetid burp arose and passed away, a large yellow bubble in the

candlelit room. The first fart woke up the other trekkers who accused me of having stuffed their pillows with dead animals during the night.

"Burp! Nausea! Fart! Deoxygenation of the room. I had become the worst of trailmates, harbinger of giardia. . . ."

—Mike Ford

◆ DISEASES TRANSMITTED ◆ BY INSECT OR ANIMAL BITES

MALARIA

Malaria is a parasitic infection transmitted by the bite of the female *Anopheles* mosquito. Of the four types of malaria, the vivax and falciparum forms are the most common. Falciparum can kill within days. Initial symptoms may seem like flu, with headaches, chills, joint pains, fever, and diarrhea. The vivax form, though rarely fatal, is extremely unpleasant and can remain dormant in the liver and cause relapses months or even years later.

Malaria is a serious, potentially life-threatening illness. If you think you may be coming down with it, consult the closest professional medical opinion immediately.

Taking preventative action greatly reduces the risk of malaria but does not totally exclude the chance of catching it. Prevention works on two levels: stopping the mosquitoes from biting you, and taking a course of pills as a prophylactic measure

Remember that mosquitoes bite between dusk and dawn. Cover up exposed parts of the body with long-sleeved shirts, trousers, enclosed shoes, and hats and use a strong concentration of repellent, which can be applied to clothing and exposed skin. Note that some repellents can melt certain types of synthetics and plastics. When not in use, treated cotton clothing, such as shirts or bandannas, can be kept in a sealed plastic bag for longer lasting protection.

At night, use a mosquito net that has been professionally treated with a strong insecticide. Pretreated nets can be bought from retailers and manufacturers who will also provide reapplication service. Treatment of this kind usually lasts for around three months and can be reapplied. Look for a portable net that's easy to set up, with vertical sides offering enough space between the inside and biters trying to lunge from the outside. If left draped on your bed during the day, treated nets will also deter other insects, such as bedbugs.

For a knockdown of mosquitoes and other insects already in the room, you can use insect spray or spiral coils of pyrethrum (a natural insecticide), which are placed on a holder and ignited to burn slowly like incense.

Preventative drugs should be taken as prescribed by a specialist medical advisor for a particular country. Up-to-date advice is especially important because some species of malaria in some countries have already become or are becoming resistant to some drugs. You should also remember that full treatment involves a complete drug regime before, during, and after your trip. It generally starts at least one week before departure and ends at least four weeks after leaving the malarial region. See "After the Trip," later in this chapter.

Finally, in case you do contract malaria, you may want to carry a course of antimalarial drugs. These are available on prescription and should be thoroughly discussed with your doctor or equivalent specialist advisor.

YELLOW FEVER
Yellow fever is a serious viral infection transmitted from monkeys to humans by mosquitoes. In some countries in South America and tropical Africa, visitors are required by law to be immunized against yellow fever—without the certificate you may be refused entry. Vaccination is valid for ten years and must be given only at authorized medical centers, which will then issue an official international certificate.

SLEEPING SICKNESS (TRYPANOSOMIASIS)
Sleeping sickness occurs commonly in Central and West Africa and is transmitted by the bite of the tsetse fly, which inhabits the periphery of rivers and lakes. Symptoms include swelling of the lymph glands, fever, lassitude, and general debilitation. As a protective measure, apply insect repellent and use accommodation away from the tsetse fly's usual habitat. Prescription of drugs for treatment should be left to a qualified doctor who can diagnose the specific type of sleeping sickness. Immunization is not available.

LEISHMANIASIS
The *Leishmania* protozoan is transmitted between dusk and dawn via the bites of tiny sandflies in South America, Africa, Asia, and the Middle East. The external version of the disease attacks the skin and may leave severe scarring. The internal form, known as kala-azar, attacks the liver, spleen, or bone marrow and can cause organ enlargement and anemia as well as other infections. Symptoms include painful, inflamed bites that do not heal. If you suspect infection, seek medical treatment immediately. Prevention requires the same environmental precautions as for mosquitoes (see "Malaria," earlier).

JAPANESE ENCEPHALITIS
A viral infection spread by mosquitoes, Japanese encephalitis occurs mainly in rural parts of Asia. Symptoms include headache, a stiff neck, fever, and vomiting. If these occur, seek medical attention immediately. Prevention of infection

requires environmental precautions against mosquito bites, as detailed in the section on malaria earlier in this chapter. Vaccination is available from specialist medical centers.

RABIES

Rabies is a viral infection contracted from animals. It occurs in most parts of the globe except the United Kingdom, Ireland, New Zealand, and Australia. If you are bitten or scratched by an animal that you suspect due to its erratic, aggressive behavior or copious saliva around its mouth, thoroughly clean and disinfect the wound and immediatley seek medical assistance. Ideally, if no risk is involved, the offending animal should be trapped and examined to see if it is rabid—in practice the critters are unlikely to prove willing examinees. You should stay away from stray animals and refrain from petting them.

Vaccination is available and recommended for long-term travelers in endemic or remote areas. If you know you will be handling animals, rabies vaccination is a must.

◆ DISEASES TRANSMITTED BY CONTAMINATED FOOD OR WATER ◆

CHOLERA

Contaminated water and food are the source of cholera. This disease, which rarely affects travelers, causes acute diarrhea and, unless properly treated, can lead to death. The standard immunization consists of two injections administered at least 10 days apart, but the World Health Organization considers the efficacy of these jabs to be inadequate. If you suspect you have contracted cholera, seek medical attention immediately.

In some countries, if you cannot supply a suitable piece of paper, officials may ask for a certificate of immunization against cholera as a ploy to extract a bribe or fine. Your medical advisor may agree prior to your departure to issue you an "International Certificate of Cholera Immunization" created with an impressive stamp, date, and title, but bearing a small annotation such as "unnecessary," in the margin.

HEPATITIS A

Hepatitis A is a common virus infection of the liver. It is transmitted through contaminated food and drink or when bathing in infected water. After an initial incubation of three to six weeks, symptoms may include aches and chills, fatigue, fever, and subsequent loss of appetite, with a yellowish discoloration of the skin and eyes. If you contract hepatitis A, seek medical advice and take plenty of rest, keep up proper intake of liquids, and eat what you can stomach.

There are two options for immunization. For travelers off on a short trip, a gammaglobulin jab just before departure offers limited protection for up to six months. If you plan to stay abroad for longer or intend to make frequent trips, there's the expensive option of a recently introduced vaccine. This can be given in one dose, providing immunity for one year or more if a booster dose is given up to a year later.

For information on hepatitis B, see "Sexually Transmitted Diseases," later in this chapter.

TYPHOID

Typhoid fever is a bacterial infection transmitted by contaminated food and water. Symptoms include abdominal pains, fever, and delirium. Treatment is with antibiotics. Vaccination is available as two shots or a recently introduced single-shot version, offering three-year immunity. If you are averse to needles, an oral vaccine, offering immunity for one year, has also recently become available.

POLIOMYELITIS (POLIO)

Transmitted by contaminated water and food, the polio virus causes untreatable paralysis. Although it is much less common in industrialized countries, it still poses a major threat elsewhere. Initial vaccination is available in live-virus or killed-virus form, and a booster dose is recommended if you have not been immunized within the previous ten years.

DYSENTERY

Contaminated food and water cause two types of dysentery: bacillic and amoebic. Symptoms of bacillic dysentery include heavy abdominal cramps, diarrhea, and fever. Amoebic dysentery produces similar, longer-lasting symptoms with blood or mucus in the feces. If you suspect you've contracted dysentery, consult a doctor as soon as possible for a stool test and diagnosis. Medical opinions on dysentery are constantly being updated.

◆   COMMON BACTERIAL DISEASES   ◆

Bacteria are microorganisms found in soil, water, and the digestive tract of animals. Although many types of bacteria are beneficial, some may cause disease.

TETANUS

Tetanus germs occur in the soil and can enter via skin wounds or scratches. The disease attacks the nerves and produces muscle spasms. If you suspect infection, seek medical treatment immediately. The germs responsible for tetanus disease, also known as lockjaw, are found all over the world, hence the importance of

Enjoying "paradise" at Papase'a Sliding Rock, Western Samoa (Deanna Swaney photo)

keeping your immunization up to date. Vaccination, providing up to ten years' protection, is usually supplied as two jabs given one month apart in combination with diphtheria immunization. Regular booster shots are advisable to maintain protection.

DIPHTHERIA

In developed countries, mass immunization has virtually eradicated diphtheria, but the disease is widespread elsewhere, especially in heavily populated tropical countries. Diphtheria is caught through contaminated dust or close contact with an infected person. Symptoms may begin as a skin infection or simple sore throat but can quickly develop into dangerous illness. In developed countries, most people receive vaccination in combination with tetanus immunization. Regular booster shots are advisable to maintain protection.

MENINGOCOCCAL MENINGITIS

Meningococcal meningitis produces symptoms such as fever, headache, and stiff neck. Epidemics occur frequently in sub-Saharan Africa and parts of Asia (especially in India and Nepal). Transmission takes place through close contact, such as coughing and sneezing. If you suspect infection, seek medical attention immediately. A vaccination is available and recommended if you are traveling to an area experiencing an epidemic or at risk of such.

◆ SEXUALLY TRANSMITTED DISEASES ◆

AIDS

Acquired immune deficiency syndrome, or AIDS, is caused when the body is infected with the human immunodeficiency virus, or HIV. Travelers should be aware that AIDS occurs globally. Always take appropriate protective action. For the latest advice, consult qualified medical sources (see appendix A).

In most cases, transmission of AIDS occurs through sexual intercourse with an HIV-positive partner. Although gay men and intravenous drug users are commonly perceived as the groups most affected, worldwide comparisons show that in the majority of cases infection occurs through sex between men and women. Prostitutes of either sex are likely to pose a high risk of infection—in some countries, estimates show some 80 percent or more of prostitutes are infected with HIV. Other sources of infection include shared needles and syringes and unscreened blood products.

Protection against infection should include the following measures.

Avoid casual sexual encounters, and *always* use a condom when having sex outside a monogamous relationship. *Do not* inject drugs or share needles or syringes, and *avoid* all body piercing, including your nose and ears, and tattooing unless you witness the proper sterilization of the equipment to be used. As a precaution, some travelers carry a sterile medical equipment pack (available from specialist medical centers) containing needles, syringes, and an enclosed multilingual description of the pack's purpose for foreign customs personnel.

Current medical opinion states that HIV cannot be spread through everyday social contact, such as kissing, dirty eating utensils or food, insect bites, toilet seats, coughing, or sneezing.

HEPATITIS B

Although similar to hepatitis A, hepatitis B is caused by a different virus transmitted through sexual contact (refer also to "AIDS"), unscreened blood transfusion, and use of improperly sterilized medical equipment. Hepatitis B exhibits similar symptoms to hepatitis A, although it can be more severe and permanently damage the liver. If you catch hepatitis B, you should seek medical advice immediately.

Protection through vaccination requires a series of three jabs given over a period of six months prior to departure.

For information on hepatitis A, see "Diseases Transmitted by Contaminated Food or Water," earlier in this chapter.

VENEREAL DISEASE

Apart from AIDS and hepatitis B, other sexually transmitted diseases causing serious infections are gonorrhea, syphilis, and chancroid. Abstinence from casual sex is clearly the most reliable protection; failing that, always remember to use good-quality condoms.

The symptoms of gonorrhea, a common infection, usually appear 2 to 10 days after sexual intercourse. Men experience an uncomfortable or painful discharge when urinating and sometimes, but not always, there are similar early symptoms for women.

Syphilis usually commences as a painless ulcer on the external sexual organs and develops into lumpy swellings of the lymph nodes. The first appearance of symptoms occurs between one and twelve weeks after sexual intercourse. If symptoms are untreated they will disappear, but syphilis will continue to spread and cause serious problems several years later.

Chancroid, a disease prevalent in Africa, presents similar symptoms to syphilis, but the incubation period is reduced to between 3 and 14 days.

Treatment for these three diseases requires antibiotics; however, they should not be used to prevent infection.

♦   PARASITIC PROBLEMS   ♦

Parasites are widespread worldwide and can find their way into or onto the human body via food, water, or direct contact with the skin. The best way to prevent infestation is to watch what you eat and drink, take care where you swim, and keep your body and clothing clean.

WORMS AND FLUKES

Parasitic worms and flukes come in all shapes and sizes. The main sources of infection are food, water, and walking barefoot. To minimize the risk of infection, make sure water is adequately treated; food properly cooked, especially meat; and wear shoes or sandals at all times, even around your accommodation. If you suspect you have been infected, get a stool sample analyzed by a doctor—most worm infections are curable.

Bilharzia (schistosomiasis) is caused by blood flukes, which are acquired when washing, bathing, or wading in freshwater. The flukes are hosted by freshwater snails, which are found in many parts of the Middle East, Africa, Asia, and South America. In high-risk areas (the Nile, for example), as a preventative measure avoid contact with freshwater—swim only in saltwater and chlorinated pools. Incubation of bilharzia can take several months or years. A common symptom is a skin irritation or rash within the first 2 days, and one or two months later fever and debility with periodic, bloody discharge in urine or feces. If you have been exposed to possible infection, get a medical checkup.

BODY BUGS

Body bugs are a common annoyance encountered by travelers and trekkers in basic types of accommodation and in backcountry areas. As a general rule, you'll keep these parasites at bay by attending to personal hygiene. Ask your doctor for recommended treatment.

Bedbugs. These large, brown bugs are wingless and very common throughout the world, especially in seedy hotels, where they hide in the walls during the day and visit guests during the night. Their bites produce painful itching for a week or longer. The simplest form of prevention is to find uninfested accommodation, but if you discover you're being targeted during the middle of the night, you can slow down bedbug activity by leaving the light on.

Lice. These tiny insects can infest the hairy parts of the human body and continue their life cycle by laying microscopic eggs. Infection occurs through close contact with infected persons, bedding, or clothing.

Scabies. A skin infestation caused by mites, scabies can multiply rapidly and cause serious irritation.

Fleas. These insects generally find their way onto humans via mattresses, sheets, and blankets. If you think fleas are likely partners in your accommodation, use an insecticide and sleep away from the source of infestation. You can also cover it with a groundsheet, tarp, or similar cover to provide a temporary barrier.

Ticks. These minute insects live in undergrowth and attach themselves to passing creatures, including trekkers. Once the tick reaches your skin, it quickly pierces an entrance for its head before sucking blood, which inflates its body to an impressive size. Ticks can spread other diseases, so check regularly for their presence in your bodily nooks and crannies. If spotted at an early stage, when still crawling rather than embedded, the whole insect can be removed by hand.

Once the head is embedded, the most important thing is to extract the entire tick, preferably by carefully holding it by the head with a pair of tweezers and rolling it gently up and out—otherwise, a portion of the head may remain to cause infection.

Chiggers. These insects, common in South America and Africa, are usually found in bush areas, where they penetrate the toes of passing walkers, especially those wearing sandals or treading barefoot. Within a few days, female chiggers lay eggs. During this time you'll notice a painful, itchy bump—disinfect a needle in a flame and extract the offender and its brood of eggs, and then carefully disinfect the wound.

Leeches. Leeches wait patiently in undergrowth, overhanging foliage, swamps, and streams. A common nuisance for trekkers, they attach themselves to clothing or limbs, and then seek skin contact to suck blood. Leeches inject an anticoagulant to promote blood flow. Because their bite is barely felt, it can be quite a surprise to discover a heavy trail of blood emanating from such a small creature. Remove leeches by applying salt or a lit cigarette, then thoroughly disinfect the wound to prevent secondary infection.

◆   VENOMOUS BITES AND STINGS   ◆

SNAKES

If snakebite occurs, stay calm. The bites of many snakes contain no poison, some are painful but not life-threatening, and some species of venomous snakes may not inject venom (for example, they've just had a meal or temporarily run out of venom).

The first stage for treatment is to reassure the victim and reduce the shock from the surprise and any initial pain. In most cases, snake bites won't kill within the proverbial 2 minutes; usually there are several hours' leeway to counter the effects by seeking medical help. Keep the victim still and the affected limb cool, wrapped tightly (enough to compress the tissue but not constrict blood flow) with a crepe bandage, splinted, and slightly raised. This slows down the absorption of venom. Don't use a tourniquet, don't try to suck out poison, and don't cut into the bite. Antivenin is matched to a specific species of snake; hence, it is not recommended unless you have a reliable identification of the culprit and a doctor to administer it.

SCORPIONS

Although rarely lethal, a scorpion sting can cause searing pain. Application of an ice pack may slow the spread of venom. If the sting produces severe reaction, seek medical advice on appropriate antivenin treatment.

At Petra in Jordan, having walked through the narrow entrance defile late

Watch that sting: Don't impede the megapede, Seychelles

in the evening, I unfurled my sleeping bag in a cave, folded my sweater as a pillow, and soon fell asleep. Next morning I rose early to fetch water and returned to pack up my gear. As I lifted my sweater, out scuttled a sizable scorpion that had clearly found itself a warm spot beneath my pillow. Not my favorite bed companion!

SPIDERS

The number of species of spiders is estimated to exceed 40,000, and their body size can vary from less than a millimeter to the megaspecimens of the Amazon rainforest, which are almost 100 times larger. However, it's comforting to know that only a few dozen of these creatures are potentially dangerous to humans, the most well known being the various species of black widow spiders occurring worldwide and the funnel-web and redback spiders found in Australia. Most spider bites produce local irritation and swelling, which can be relieved with the application of ice. If the victim suffers an allergic reaction, seek medical help.

BEES, WASPS, AND HORNETS

If you've been stung by a bee, remove the stinger using a needle or sharp knife edge to carefully prise it out without exerting pressure on the venom sac. Relieve the irritation of stings with a cold compress, calamine lotion, aspirin, and/or antihistamine tablets. If you know you react allergically, always carry an antiallergy kit.

◆ ENVIRONMENTAL AND ◆
CLIMATIC HEALTH PROBLEMS

One major attraction of adventure trekking is the opportunity to experience different environments and climates. It is most important to take proper precautions to deal with the effects of the elements, which are often far stronger than those experienced in the traveler's home country.

ALTITUDE SICKNESS

When traveling or trekking it is essential to be aware of sickness that may result from the body's adjustment to high altitude, where the air is thinner and the oxygen density lower. To adapt to this reduced oxygen, we breath faster and deeper; our blood is pumped harder through our lungs; and, as a result of dehydration, our blood becomes thicker, with less water and more blood cells to carry oxygen.

Other changes occur over a period of several weeks, these processes being known as acclimatization. The effects you will notice are shortness of breath, pounding of the heart, and tiring more easily. These are all normal adjustments. The rest of this section advances beyond acclimatization to outline acute mountain sickness (AMS).

AMS can be divided into two categories: benign and malignant. Benign AMS is the more common, milder form of AMS, but it can herald the onset of the severe form. Symptoms include headache, loss of appetite, dizziness, sleeping difficulty, cloudy head, nausea and vomiting (especially in children), or perhaps just feeling unwell.

If you feel sick at high altitude or have any symptoms of benign AMS, rest for a few days until the symptoms pass. If you feel worse and the symptoms will not go away, then you must consider descending quickly.

Malignant AMS is very serious and can be rapidly fatal. It may occur without warning, or it may be preceded by symptoms of benign AMS. Both the lungs and the brain may be affected. In high-altitude pulmonary edema, fluid accumulates in the lungs, causing the person to drown in their own lung fluid with symptoms such as extreme breathlessness, cough, white frothy sputum, and blue lips.

In high-altitude cerebral edema, fluid accumulates in and around the brain causing symptoms such as severe headache, separate or combined problems with nausea, vomiting, vision and speech, drowsiness, unsteadiness, disorientation, abnormal behavior, and a progressively reduced level of consciousness leading to coma and death. Someone suffering from this form of altitude sickness may initially seem to be drunk or very antisocial. Make the effort to find out what is going on.

There is great variation in the altitude at which people are susceptible to AMS. Some people get it at altitudes as low as 8,000 feet (2,450 meters); others feel fine at 20,000 feet (6,000 meters). In general, AMS is rare below 8,000 feet (2,450 meters).

Most cases of AMS occur in the most commonly visited altitude range of 8,000 to 14,000 feet (2,450 to 4,300 meters). People usually reach altitudes of 14,000 to 18,000 feet (4,300 to 5,500 meters) only in the Himalaya and Andes mountains—for example, trekking to Everest base camp (Tibet) or skiing at Chacaltaya (Bolivia). Only experienced mountaineers would usually be found

Essential elements: Llamas packing salt from Salar de Uyuni to Tarija, Bolivia (Deanna Swaney photo)

at 18,000 to 29,000 feet (5,500 to 8,800 meters). A prolonged stay at altitudes greater than 18,000 feet (5,500 meters) results in a loss of physical conditioning rather than increasing fitness.

It is never possible to predict who will get AMS. Even experienced climbers who have been at high altitudes many times before may get AMS upon returning to high altitudes. Everyone is at risk.

Treatment of AMS

The best treatment for any form of altitude sickness is descent. If the symptoms are not severe, then rest at that altitude for a minimum of 24 hours before going any higher.

In extreme cases, descent should be immediate, even if it's the middle of the night—every minute counts and it is easier to help an unwell person walk down than to carry an unconscious person. If someone is unconscious and vomiting, then place them on their side so their vomit does not get into their lungs. If oxygen is available, then immediately administer it, preferably at 4 to 6 liters per minute with a close-fitting mask.

Drugs for acclimatization and treatment of high-altitude pulmonary edema and high-altitude cerebral edema are only available through your doctor.

A recent development is the Gamow Bag, available in solo and two-person models, which looks like a large bivouac bag and functions as a portable compression chamber. By inflating the bag, it is possible to achieve compression equivalent to a descent of several thousand meters. The Gamow Bag is now used by groups and expeditions as an emergency measure.

How to Minimize Your Risk of AMS

Ascend slowly. Rising to about 9,000 feet (3,000 meters) usually presents no problem, but above this your body needs time to acclimatize. It's advisable to ascend only 1,000 feet (300 meters) per day and give yourself a full rest day every 3,000 feet (1,000 meters). Remember—climb high, sleep low!

Try breathing only through your nose while walking; this slows down your pace and the amount of oxygen you need, reduces the amount of moisture you exhale, and makes the air you inhale more moist.

Drink extra fluids. Trekking at high altitudes dehydrates you because you sweat more and lose the moisture in your breath to the cold, dry air. Avoid fatty foods—eat light, high-carbohydrate meals because carbohydrate is more efficiently turned into energy.

Avoid tobacco because smoking produces carbon monoxide, which reduces the amount of oxygen your blood can carry. Avoid alcohol as it increases urine output and will further dehydrate you. Do not take sedatives to help you sleep; you may be masking a symptom of AMS.

If you trek in a group, you can compare judgments on problems or symptoms as they arise. If you trek solo, you'll have to make such decisions for yourself: beware of your better judgment being lulled into neglecting changes in behavior or missing obvious signs of physical discomfort.

Do not ignore the symptoms. If you are suffering from any symptoms of benign AMS, avoid heavy exertion and don't go any higher until they have disappeared. Light outdoor activity is better than bed rest.

HYPOTHERMIA

Hypothermia occurs when the body is unable to maintain its temperature by replacing lost heat with its own heat production. The transition from feeling chilled to becoming dangerously cold can take place rapidly, even in cool weather, if you are tired, hungry, soaked, or without shelter.

To prevent hypothermia, dress in layers using good insulating materials such as polypropylene, pile, silk, or wool. For your outer layer, use an adequately waterproof and windproof garment. Because your head can account for over 75 percent of the body's total heat loss, one of your best forms of protection is to wear warm headgear. Keep your body fueled with plenty of fluid and food to maintain your blood sugar, which aids heat production.

Symptoms of hypothermia include shivering, slurred speech, fatigue, staggering, exaggerated outbursts of energy, and strange behavior (sufferers emphasizing how warm they feel or the need to strip off clothing).

Treatment in the initial stages should consist of bringing the sufferer into shelter, donning dry clothing, encouraging warming exercise, and providing hot food and drink (not alcohol). Advanced stages of hypothermia may require the sufferer to be placed inside a sleeping bag together with a companion to boost warmth.

FROSTBITE

Frostbite occurs when skin and flesh are frozen and usually affects the extremities or exposed parts of the body, such as the toes, ears, chin, fingers, or nose. Symptoms often commence with a prickly feeling, skin turning waxy, painful and progressing to numbness.

Frostnip, an early stage of frostbite, leaves the affected skin numb and white. In this instance, it can be thawed by placing it against a warm part (mouth, groin, or armpit, for example) of your own or someone else's body.

Frostbite goes beyond the skin and into tissue, presenting symptoms of blistering and redness. The affected part should not be rubbed with snow or exposed to a direct fire. Once frostbitten and partly rewarmed, body parts should not be allowed to refreeze. For example, if feet are frostbitten, it is better to walk out for treatment than risk worse problems through inadequate thawing. The patient should seek medical attention, which usually consists of thawing the affected parts in water at a temperature of 104 degrees Fahrenheit (40 degrees Celsius).

Prevention is the best cure: wear proper clothing, keep circulation active (wiggle toes and fingers and stamp your feet), and don't ignore loss of sensation.

SUNSTROKE AND HEAT EXHAUSTION

The effects of overexposure to sunlight, especially in the tropics or at high altitude, should not be underestimated. Apart from sunburn, sunstroke, and heat exhaustion, there is also a risk of skin cancer.

Be aware of the effects of dehydration, especially in hot, humid climates. Maintain an adequate intake of fluid and salt to match the weather, humidity, and any energetic activity—10 liters or more a day is not uncommon. Check that the color of your urine is pale; if not, you need to top up with water, soups, tea, and drinks rich in mineral salts.

Always have a hat handy to shade your head. To protect your face, make sure it has a brim or peak. A neck flap or bandanna keeps the back of the head protected.

Protect your eyes from ultraviolet (UV) light with sunglasses. For high-altitude and glacier travel, side-shields, a noseguard, and extra-dark lenses are recommended. An advantage of shield models is the exclusion of most airborne dust particles, air currents, and small insects.

High-protection-factor sunscreen is essential for the skin. Make sure that the sunscreen you use specifically protects against the two types of UV light: UVA and UVB. While UVB rays cause sunburn, especially in hot climates and at high altitudes, UVA rays enter deeper into the skin and are implicated in premature aging and wrinkling.

The sun protection factor (SPF) of a cream is given as a number that indicates approximately how much longer the sun will take to burn you than if your skin was unprotected. Choose the SPF to suit your skin type, anticipated altitude, and depth of desired tanning. Remember that snow, water, and sand reflect the sun's rays and you can burn just as easily on an overcast day as on a bright one. Apply the cream liberally and reapply in good time before it is worn away by sweat, water, or wind.

Heat exhaustion occurs through lack of fluid and salt. Symptoms include headache, fatigue, heavy sweating, irritability, and nausea. Heatstroke is a serious medical condition when the body becomes unable to regulate its temperature. Symptoms include high temperature; cessation of sweating; dry, hot skin; headache; uncoordinated behavior; and unconsciousness.

Shade, rest, and rehydration are recommended treatment for heat exhaustion. Treatment for heatstroke, preferably administered under medical supervision, restores the body's normal mechanism for temperature regulation. Shade, gradual rehydration, and thorough cooling are essential.

PRICKLY HEAT

Prickly heat is a skin rash caused by sweat glands becoming inflamed in a warm, humid climate. Keep the skin clean, dry, and covered with light clothing. Medicated powder or calamine lotion can also help.

FUNGAL INFECTIONS

Fungal infections, such as athlete's foot and dhobi itch, thrive in hot, humid climates. Bathe and dry the affected area several times daily and apply antifungal ointment and powder. Frequent washing, thorough drying, and ventilation of the previously affected parts should ward off reinfection.

◆   GENERAL TRAVEL HEALTH TOPICS   ◆

While traveling you'll have to be prepared to maintain your general health. This applies especially to jet lag experienced after a longhaul flight, foot care on the trail, health for women travelers, novel forms of sanitation, and first-aid skills to deal with emergencies.

FOOTCARE AND BLISTERS

Forgive the pun, but keeping your feet in good shape does keep your trek on a sound footing. Blisters result from friction of the skin and can rapidly cause excruciating discomfort at every step.

Prior to your trek, try to toughen up the feet by walking barefoot or wearing boots in and around the house. Rubbing alcohol applied morning and night can also help roughen the skin.

Easy preventative measures, often overlooked, include keeping your socks worn properly (without blister-inducing creases) and clearing your boots of grit, seeds, and other irritants.

As soon as you notice the development of hot spots with reddened skin, apply moleskin or a dressing around the blister. Placing plasters directly over fully formed blisters can often cause even more friction. Airing your socks and feet once or twice a day during a break on the trail gives them a chance to dry for a moment. Foot powder counteracts softening of the feet caused by sweating.

Opinions vary on the desirability of pricking blisters. If you puncture, be sure to clean the patch of skin, disinfect the needle or pin in a flame, and pierce at the edge. Keep the blister clean, dry, free of infection, and cushioned from further friction.

Carry a blister kit in a side pocket so that it is close at hand for running repairs during the day's trekking.

CRAMPS, SPRAINS, AND STRAINS

A muscle cramp is brought on by a combination of exercise and lack of water and salt. Treatment consists of rehydration, preferably as an isotonic drink to restore the body's electrolyte level; light massage; and the application of warmth to the affected muscle.

Sprains need prompt attention, especially if the problem zone is an ankle joint. If there is light swelling and tenderness, apply cold water to the affected part and provide support. Wrap an elasticized bandage round a sprained ankle in a figure-eight pattern. A more severe strain, typically presenting impressive rainbow coloring within a day of occurrence, should be treated by resting the affected joint in an elevated position and applying a cold compress.

Strains involve torn or stretched muscles. Treat by resting the affected part, applying a cold compress, and taking appropriate painkillers as necessary.

TOILETS

Where would travel be without the never-ending supply of toilet stories? The sit-down model is the one most Westerners recognize; however, squat toilets, as commonly found in Asia, allow the user to place feet on either side of the bowl and hunker down. One hygiene advantage is the lack of contact with a seat; another is, reportedly, the additional downward pressure. Holes in the ground, with or without a shelter, are the most basic version.

My favorite establishment is a musical restroom at the tip of Sukoton Peninsula on Rebunto Island, Hokkaido, Japan. In the middle of nowhere stands this gleaming, windswept restroom. As you enter, an electric eye starts a tape, which plays classical guitar music or the recorded swishing of the sea, which is outside the door.

In many countries, especially in Asia, use of the left hand and a washdown with water are the norm. Maintain scrupulous hygiene and be aware that the associated stigma of uncleanliness means that the left hand should not be used for daily contact in these countries. If you want toilet paper, you'll have to supply it yourself. Apart from the extra expense of toilet paper, the local plumbing system may not be able to deal with resultant clogging. Usually the local solution is to place a basket next to the loo. Used paper is placed in the basket, and then the contents are emptied and burned.

Before you squat, make sure the contents of your pockets are secure. Small change, wallets, and other items can easily tumble into oblivion. Keep your eyes open for other occupants of the toilet: in Australia, the venomous funnel-web spider is known for its love of toilet seats; and in India, if you hear strange noises coming from the bowl it could well be a family of frogs.

For many Westerners, sheltered from the nitty-gritty of waste disposal for most of their lives, the first encounters with pits can have amazing effects: tears, feelings of faintness, and shrieks of laughter. Just do your utmost to avoid the ultimate nightmare: falling in. Yes, a friend of mine half-fell into the abyss at the bottom of a field during a sodden camping trip in Wales; and I've known worse to happen in China.

There are a few ways of minimizing your risk of earning your own unique toilet story. Always take a flashlight. An Australian doctor friend of mine told me an illustrative tale. Once when he was sleeping by the fire in a very hospitable Tibetan family's kitchen, he felt mother nature's call. Not familiar with the maze of rooms that formed their cozy domicile, he found what he believed to be the adjoining livestock room and was just about to begin micturition only to be greeted by screams of protest—he was actually in the main bedroom. Now he carries a flashlight with him everywhere.

The same doctor also recounted how one dark, windy night, a strange batlike creature flapped up through the hole and scared the hell out of him. In fact, a gust of wind had blown his toilet paper back up and out the hole.

Never go barefoot to the toilet—you can imagine for yourself the consequences you risk.

To resist nausea, before you enter dab something aromatic under your nose, or breathe lightly and calmly through a partially opened mouth (thus temporarily excluding the olfactory sense).

HEALTH FOR WOMEN TRAVELERS

Don't count on the availability of tampons at your destination, where they may also be more expensive—take a supply from home. Also, note that irregular menstruation, even cessation of the period, can be the natural response of the body to the upheavals of travel.

In warm, moist climates, vaginal infections can pose problems. Wear loose-fitting trousers or a skirt and cotton underwear. Because dehydration can be a contributory factor, drink sufficient liquid, especially in hot climates. If you have had one or two urinary infections in the past, consider asking a doctor to provide you with antibiotics before you leave, just in case.

If you take birth control pills, remember that absorption may be partially or totally stopped by the bodily disruption of diarrhea and that hormonal rhythms can be temporarily upset due to jet lag after long flights.

JET LAG

Flying across time zones disrupts the natural rhythms of your body, producing symptoms of jet lag: fatigue, insomnia, and erratic appetite and digestion. For reasons unknown, the effect is more pronounced when traveling eastward.

General advice for the flight is to drink plenty of fluid (avoid alcohol, tea, and coffee), wear loose-fitting clothing and footwear, and during long flights take a few strolls to keep the muscles from cramping. There are indications that doses of melatonin (a natural hormone that balances reaction to darkness and light) may ease jet lag. Some travelers also use aromatherapy oils or homeopathic pills for this purpose. Plan for jet lag at the end of the flight by setting aside 24 hours of adjustment time.

◆ **AFTER THE TRIP** ◆

After your trip, you'll hopefully feel fitter and feistier than ever. If you don't, go and see your doctor for a checkup. If you didn't visit before you left, be sure to tell him or her that you went overseas and the specific places visited—some diseases, malaria for instance, take several weeks or months to appear. As long as the doctor is alerted to the possibility of a disease having been picked up overseas, there'll be a much better chance of nipping it in the bud.

◆ **SUGGESTED MEDICAL SUPPLIES CHECKLIST** ◆

Though not exhaustive, the following checklist will be useful when collecting supplies for your medical kit. Your first-aid kit should be separate from the rest of your medical kit, which should be neatly and clearly packaged for quick identification. Use strong, resealable plastic bags to prevent spillage. Avoid glass bottles; use plastic ones instead. For toiletries, refer also to the checklists in chapter 3, "Gear to Go: What to Take." Note that some of the following medicines are only available by prescription.

General

❑ Oral rehydration salts	Diarrhea—rehydration
❑ Loperamide	Diarrhea—plugger!
❑ Painkillers	Fever and aches
❑ Antihistamine tablets	Skin problems, itching, and allergic reactions
❑ Antiseptics (choice of powder, spray, liquid, cream, or wipes)	
❑ Lacto-calamine lotion	Heat rash, minor sunburn, and prickly heat
❑ Blister kit (moleskins, second skin)	
❑ Cream and powder	Athlete's foot, thrush, and ringworm
❑ Tiger Balm	Nausea, congestion, and muscle aches
❑ Cold sore ointment	Cold sore
❑ Sunscreen lotion or sunblock	

Prescriptions

Discuss preparations for your trekking destination with your health advisor.

❑ Antibiotics for infections of the
    skin, nose, ear, and throat
❑ Metronidazole or tinidazole   *Giardia* and amoebiasis
❑ Chloroquine, mefloquine, or   Malaria prophylactics
    proguanil
❑ Quinine, fansidar, or mefloquine   Treatment of malaria

First Aid

❑ Plasters	Minor cuts and light grazes
❑ Wound dressings	Deep cuts
❑ Sterile nonstick dressings	Large wounds
❑ Hypoallergenic surgical tape	To secure dressings
❑ Zinc oxide tape	To tape dressings
❑ Sterile strips	To hold cut skin edges together
❑ Crepe bandages	To support sprains and weak joints
❑ Gauze swabs	To staunch bleeding
❑ Tweezers	To remove splinters and infected hairs
❑ Sturdy scissors	
❑ Thermometer	
❑ Emergency kit (syringes, needles) with multilingual note for customs	

Dental

❑ Cavit	For temporary treatment of lost fillings, crowns, and so forth
❑ Floss	For sewing, flossing, and so forth

A CAUTIONARY TALE FROM TIBET

Finally, a tale about a woman who was caught short in the freezing hours of the early morning, in a room on the roof of a guest house, deep in the heart of Tibet:

As the night was as cold as an iceberg, the need urgent, and the toilet pit a long trek away, she decided to use the roof. Meanwhile, down in the room below, the Chinese cook was preparing to wash in a basin of hot water. Unfortunately, the roof of stamped earth was porous and the cook was dumbfounded by the deluge of what was quite clearly not rainwater. Within seconds, the enraged cook was demanding that the foreigner be thrown out, on the instant, by a sleepy, but secretly amused manager.

Somehow the cook was placated and everyone went back to bed. By the morning, the roof had absorbed all trace of evidence.

5

SETTING THE PACE
Trek Preparation, Technique, and Navigation

PREPARATIONS FOR THE TREK AND RELATED decisions can be your sole responsibility, a combined effort with local support, or delegated to a trek organizer. You'll need to assess the difficulty of your trek and any special requirements. Before you set foot on the trail, you'll have to decide if you need to hire guides, porters, and pack animals and purchase provisions in advance. Once on the trail, careful preparation will help you match your pace and your trekking technique to your surroundings and use basic navigation techniques to keep you on the right track.

As part of your planning, include sufficient time for access to the trailhead—often an adventure in itself. Add a delay factor to cover late starts, mechanical breakdowns, blown tires, landslides, and other major and minor mishaps. Buses may have a notional departure time, and they may also drive around town for an hour or so picking up passengers before starting on their route. Planning for a short first day can compensate for delays and get you mentally and physically eased into the rhythm of the trek.

◆ PREPARATION ◆

PERMITS

In some countries, permits are required to trek in certain areas or to enter national parks. The requirement may be in place as a means to balance the

---

Magic amulet: **Makes traveling safe**; origin unknown

Hiking at Sössusvlei in the Namib Desert, Namibia (Deanna Swaney photo)

number of visitors with the available facilities and regulate sustainable environmental impact; or it could be funding conservation and preservation measures, common considerations in a national park. The fees you contribute probably will benefit trekkers and locals alike, perhaps by financing local enterprise, paying salaries for park rangers and anti-poaching patrols, or improving the environmental quality of life.

Trekking permits are usually issued at an administrative center close to the trekking area; park permits are usually obtained at the entrance. Remember to allow time in your pretrek schedule to complete application procedures (anywhere from an hour to half a day). At some places, no payment is required; elsewhere, fees vary from country to country and again according to selected areas within the country. Daily fees range, for example, from a few dollars per week in the core trekking areas of Nepal, to around U.S.$20 per day for admission to Mount Kenya National Park.

TREKKING OPTIONS
Independent Trekking

If you travel independently, you are the boss: you organize the trip yourself and learn as you go. At the same time, you take responsibility for equipment, advance planning of routes, finding maps and guides, overnight stays, provisions en route, judging the weather, and avoiding trouble. You also have an open choice on pace and progress: when to join up with others and when to keep your own company. In general, arranging things yourself rather than through an organized tour keeps down the overall costs and provides more flexibility.

Assisted Trekking

As an intermediate stage between being independent and fully organized, you can opt for assisted trekking, which means you will engage local resources, such as guides, porters, and pack animals, to assist you with routefinding and carrying. With this approach you interact with the local people, contribute funds to the local economy at ground level, and increase your range by reducing the weight on your back. On the other hand, you will need to set aside several days for negotiations. You'll also have the responsibility of looking after your group, directing operations, and sharing decisions.

Organized Trekking

Organized group trekking can be useful as an introduction to trekking or as a means of access to regions where independent travel is restricted. In some cases, it may be cheaper to join a group so that you can take advantage of group bargaining power for visas or block booking of transport, guides, and accommodation. Trekking companies keep a constant eye on the vagaries of politics and transport. Most will also be keen to cultivate reliable and knowledgeable local contacts and guides.

If you travel in an organized group, the price you pay should reflect the planning, equipping, and provisioning work done by the organizer who takes care of the logistics and leaves you free to get on with your trip.

If you decide to join a group, take time to assess the programs of several companies. If you don't like what is offered, you may be able to assemble your own group and have a company tailor a trip for you. Apart from telephone advice and mail-order catalogues, many companies organize slide shows and encourage prospective clients to talk to trek leaders and participants in previous tours. Some adventure trekking companies now provide on-line information over the Internet.

Ask about the number of years the company has been operating, membership in trade associations, the number of trips already organized to your prospective destination, the maximum numbers per group, age range, experience, route grading, comfort level, and health requirements. Once you deduct the time spent getting to and from the trekking region, how many days are you spending on the trail?

At the same time you can ask about the company's environmental approach to your prospective destination. Who benefits at local level? Are local accommodation, food, and transport used? Are local staff employed? How much use is made of alternative fuels, such as solar heating? Is litter packed out?

Find out the costs involved, including equipment hire, airport taxes, supplements for singles, surcharges, and insurance. If the price is quoted as "land only," you'll clearly need to budget for the flight fare.

TREK ASSESSMENT AND SELECTION

It is important to gauge the demands that your trek is going to put on you and your resources so that you are prepared for and can meet the challenge. Your assessment will be refined with maps, guidebooks, and local advice, but remember that careful evaluation of your abilities and stamina are equally important for preparation of your trek. One way to make the transition from an easy trek to a more difficult one is to link up with more experienced trekkers in a group, which can be independent, assisted, or organized.

Throughout the planning, consider the focus of your interest: there is more to a trek than "bagging" the route. Be flexible with your expectations en route and accept that part of the appeal of the outdoors is the unpredictability of the elements. If you feel it's unwise to continue, trust that feeling and turn back or seek safety.

Categories and Contributory Factors

Few treks will fit exactly into one category, but as a rough guide there are those that are easy, moderate, and strenuous. At the gentle end of the spectrum, there are treks that follow tended footpaths along mostly level ground, traveling daily for some 10 miles (16 kilometers) and a maximum of 5 or 6 hours. A grade beyond this are moderate treks, covering some 15 miles (24 kilometers) in up to 8 hours of daily hiking, which includes ascents and descents along marked trails. The strenuous category packs in more hiking miles and hours per day and requires previous experience of moderate treks to deal with altitude, rough terrain, and absence of marked trails. Beyond this category, you'd be edging into the domain of scrambling, semitechnical, and mountaineering routes, which require equipment such as ropes, ice axes, and crampons.

Trek categories mean little unless you bring several other factors into the picture. Carrying a heavily laden pack will have a pronounced effect on your progress; on the other hand, hut-to-hut hiking (in the European Alps) or teahouse treks (in Nepal) can cut down on pack weight and reduce the effort required. Good physical fitness, such as that maintained by simply hiking regularly at home, will stand you in good stead. A strenuous trek is not for those who are out of shape; a moderate trek or two will help to regain form.

"My walking career really began in 1980, when I started 'Munro Bagging,' a peculiar and addictive Scottish sport which involves visiting the summits of all Scottish hills over 3000 feet (914 meters) high. Munro Baggers will climb in any weather just to 'bag' their peak: to get another tick on the list. Lesser, and perhaps more interesting summits, will almost certainly be ignored, as the mad Bagger blindly crusades towards 'completion,' a state of nirvana where his or her name is entered in the ultimate list, namely that of the Baggers themselves. This list of Baggers is kept in the book of 'Munro's Tables,' a revered tome often seen on the parcel shelf of Baggers' cars when parked in mountain-road lay-bys."

—Graeme Cornwallis

Planning Daily Stages

Gauge the number of days your entire route will take, and then look at the days in more detail, subdividing them into stages, if possible alternating long hard days with a shorter one. Using your map, mentally cover the route, assessing and selecting primary and secondary campsites suitable for short or long days. If there are few water sources on your route, you will have to plan your stages precisely so that you always have sufficient water. Plan overnight stops spaced close enough so that you don't have to race through the day or risk losing your way after nightfall. Consider the location in relation to possible weather changes, such as snowfall on exposed sites or flash floods near streams. During your trek, keep an eye on alternative routes and sites in case you need to change your plans during an emergency.

Rest Days and Acclimatization

Most importantly, build in a rest day every 2 or 3 days to give you time to physically relax and mentally appreciate the contrast between movement and rest. As an extension of this concept, for high-altitude trekking you will need to spend several days, preferably a short trek, acclimatizing at a lower altitude before attempting high elevation. This is essential to guard against altitude sickness (refer to chapter 4, "In Good Shape: Staying Healthy").

It's quite easy to become obsessed with the target and fail to absorb the points en route. What you do on your rest days depends on your fitness and interest. You might want to write up a journal, delve into plant life with macrophotography, loll in a hot spring, or take a gentle hike into the surrounding area. Some routes are simply point to point; others are more complex, perhaps with side valleys inviting exploration from a base on the main route. If you are using a popular trail, these side options can be a good way to lose the crowd.

Weather Reports

Your planning must always consider the potential fluctuations in weather conditions at your destination. Make use of weather reports broadcast over the radio or TV, featured in newspapers, displayed in outdoor equipment stores, or available for computer download, including weather satellite images, via the Internet. Try to assess the weather conditions that will occur along your trekking route while you are there. Once you arrive, be sure to check park headquarters, huts or mountain resorts, or other trekker haunts for the latest forecasts. Find out if there's a local weather bureau at your destination, and call direct for the latest weather forecasts before you leave and after you arrive.

PROVISIONING

Unless you are planning daily treks between huts, teahouses, or villages with food and water, you'll need to plan your provisions. On long treks you may have to balance the expense of importing lightweight food with the advantage of being self-reliant, or you can hire assistance to help carry your supplies.

Quantities

To determine the amount of food you'll need, calculate the number of days for your trip, add a backup of a day or two for delays, and then multiply by the number of meals (breakfast, lunch, and dinner). Add an extra 1 to 2 days' worth of rations for emergency, which, to resist temptation, should be stowed in a package separate from the main meals. As your trip progresses, the food you eat reduces the weight you carry. In warm climates you'll need to ensure an adequate supply of water, and in colder climates you'll be burning plenty of calories to provide energy for warmth.

Assuming two simple meals are cooked each day on a multifuel stove (with windshield), as an approximate estimate, you'll need around 1 liter (approximately 2 U.S. pints) of fuel per week for one person. You'll require possibly twice as much fuel if you anticipate extreme weather conditions or expect to be melting snow for water. For hints on ways to economize on fuel, refer to chapter 3, "Gear to Go: What to Take."

Lunch on the trail, Naukluft Mountains, Namibia (Deanna Swaney photo)

Nutrition

An essential element for healthy travel is a balanced, nutritious diet to cover your requirements of carbohydrates, fats, proteins, vitamins, and minerals.

When trekking, the bulk of your calorific intake should be carbohydrates, which provide an easily digested source of energy for those busy muscles. Short-term energy, useful for boosting vigorous activity, is derived from simple carbohydrates, such as sugar products like candy bars, jam, and honey. Complex carbohydrates, however, offer more in terms of sustained energy yield, fiber, and bulk: aim to base some 50 percent of your diet around the common types of complex carbohydrates in the country visited.

Fats yield a substantial amount of energy, but the body requires considerable time to break them down for use. Eaten as part of the evening meal, fats provide heat through the night. As a general rule, they should constitute no more than 30 percent of your daily calorific intake.

Protein is used to build up and repair your body after the day's exertion. An adult's daily protein requirement rarely exceeds a couple of ounces. Eggs, nuts, beans, meat, milk, cheese, and fish are major sources of protein.

Vitamins and minerals round off your nutrition, keeping you fresh and fit. In general, they need to be replenished daily. Useful sources include fresh foods, such as fruit and vegetables. If these are lacking on your trip, you may want to supplement with multivitamins.

Choice

When choosing your food for a trek, bear in mind the length and type of trek involved. Foods should be assessed for their nutritive value; packaging bulk and weight; ease of preparation; cost; and, last but not least, tastiness.

Fresh foods are obviously healthy, but a tendency to spoil quickly means they are generally best consumed within a few days of purchase—exceptions include onions, garlic, and potatoes. Most fresh foods also have a high water content, which results in additional weight.

Canned foods, often containing even more water, are also heavy to carry in and out—keep the trails clear of empty cans. They are inexpensive, however, and offer a quick way to prepare a meal.

Dried foods, having had around 90 percent or more of their water removed, are lightweight, compact, long-lasting, and easily prepared. At high altitudes, however, avoid dry foods, which require long cooking times and consequently more fuel. Most trekkers fill the bulk of their meals with food and drinks in this category, such as beans, lentils, peas, pasta, rice, oatmeal, vegetables, soups, sauces, puddings, milk, tea, coffee, herbs, and spices.

Freeze-dried foods have the lightweight advantages of dried foods, but usually cost considerably more and are not widely available.

Watch where the locals buy and how they deal with prices, quantity discounts, and bargaining. This is also a good way to see what makes a culture tick. For shopping errands and purchases of provisions en route, you should have local currency in small denominations. It's unwise to produce large notes and often difficult for traders in remoter regions to find change. Imported foods are often very expensive due to freight costs and taxes. Make savings by purchasing the local fare.

Although local fruits and vegetables may not keep, they can provide a welcome vitamin boost for the first couple of days on the trail. Cooking at altitude takes longer and requires more fuel, a point to remember if you are thinking of buying foods that require long cooking times, such as dry lentils and beans.

When arranging an assisted trek locally, ask how the food quantities and types are being calculated. Find out whether the price you are being quoted for food is per person or for the group. There is less confusion and less scope for creative accounting if the food element of a quoted trek price is calculated per individual then multiplied into a block figure for the group.

Packaging

Once you've bought supplies, remove excess packaging. Either cut out and keep the cooking instructions or write them with an indelible marker on the bag. Package the foods so that they are easily identifiable and group them for specific meals. Make sure they are secure against spillage and sealed against inquisitive fauna.

GUIDES AND PORTERS

Trekking with a guide may be compulsory in some national parks or highly advisable if there is little or no trail to follow and you lack experience in the area. The best guides will provide a wealth of local trail knowledge, possibly tracking skills, and deliver insight into their country's culture and the region's wildlife— a worthwhile reward for what is usually a modest fee. Conversely, you will have less control over decisions for the trip and will be dependent on your guide and vice versa. I've had mixed luck with guides. One character in the Andes led us on a trip that started inauspiciously with his attempts to solder our jeep's leaky petrol tank with a blowtorch. At the other extreme was a brilliant duo of Indians in the Bolivian Amazon who took us out to river camps to track wildlife at night and trek the undergrowth in search of flora during the day.

Whereas guides expect to take care of your direction-finding, for long treks requiring substantial loads of supplies, you or your guide may engage porters. Occasionally one person may assume both functions, but there is usually a hierarchy and distinction between the two. Porters have their own preferences for carrying their load; in Nepal, for example, it's a basket on the back with a strap around the forehead. Pack your gear in a secure duffel or sack and carry fragile items yourself. As your trek progresses, the porter's load of supplies is consumed, and you then have the option of releasing the porter.

Before the porter pads off with the daily load, make sure you have extracted the things you need for the day. It's tiresome for both parties to have to unpack again en route, and the odds are that just when you discover you need something the porter will be either miles ahead or miles behind.

Hiring

You can find out about guides and porters in the area by contacting local trekking companies, park headquarters, hotels, and traveler haunts. Talking to other trekkers is a good way to get feedback about individual reliability. These word-of-mouth recommendations on the spot will help you to steer clear of guides with unsavory reputations ranging from poor service to petty theft, violent robbery, or sexual misconduct. Sadly, recommendation in guidebooks is no guarantee of enduring probity. I've known a few isolated instances where a local guide acquired popularity and success in this way and then developed into a thoroughly corrupt character.

During peak season, you may have trouble finding assistance. This can be compounded by factors such as the need for villagers to work in the fields during harvest season, local construction projects, and whether or not your trek leads out of the prospective guide's familiar territory. In mountainous terrain, it's quite common for communities in valleys just a few days away on foot to be wary of each other.

When selecting guides, take time to talk about their background. Find out where they have traveled and how far their trekking experience extends in the region. Perhaps they are also good with languages and can organize treks with porters or pack animals and animal minders. If you're uncertain about your choice, you might suggest a short trek first just to see how you all get along.

Agreement and Payment

Once you start discussing an itinerary, you have to establish who provides food. If it is your responsibility to provide for yourself and the guides and porters, then you may decide to purchase in advance or, when food is available en route, agree in advance on a daily rate so that the bill for the whole team is a known quantity. For high-altitude treks, you should see if your team already owns suitable clothing and tents for high passes. If not, you may need to rent or purchase these locally. You are also expected to organize help if one of your guides or porters encounters medical problems. If you plan to release porters en route, they may expect payment for their return trip.

Address camping guidelines for minimum impact. Agree how you want to deal with rubbish, sanitation, and fuel; and explain why you think this is useful. The logic can be reinforced by offering an increment on payment at the end of the trip if the agreement is kept.

Calculate the payment sums before departure, and if practicable write them down. Separate the calculations so that it's clear for everybody. If you are to make stage payments, be sure you agree on what constitutes a stage or section of the trek. Don't pay more than a small portion in advance, and the rest on completion of the trek.

Where tipping is the established local practice, follow it, or if you are not sure stick to the 10 to 15 percent rule. Elsewhere, it's best to avoid introducing the concept of tipping, which can be confusing for people used to negotiating a fixed price.

Pack Animals

Pack animals, such as ponies used on Himalayan treks in northern India, can extend the range of your trek, but you'll have to keep to their pace. They are usually accompanied by a paid minder who takes care of their grazing or fodder and water. During harvest season, when working animals (such as yaks, llamas, ponies, and burros) are in demand, you may find owners reluctant to spare their time and their animals for a trek.

◆ PACE AND WALKING TECHNIQUE ◆

In daily life, most of us barely notice the way we walk when performing our errands. In contrast, on a trek we focus on the act of moving through the land on foot. Pace and timing are important so that we can assess our progress and complete the day's trek without unnecessary stress.

PACE

Your pace will depend on various factors, such as your fitness, the weight on your back, the steepness of the trail, the conditions underfoot, and your general mood and interest in the surroundings.

If you haven't trained in advance, the first day or so of a trek can be especially taxing, all the more reason to take things steady and conserve energy. Once the rhythm of the days has set in, you'll find your body adapting to the new demands.

At the start of a trek, the load of supplies on your back will be extra heavy and put more strain on the body, which will slow your pace.

A route that leads up and down steep gradients will slow you down and require more effort and energy. Slogging over boggy marsh will have a similar effect.

If you are in a tired state, you'll naturally slow your steps and drag your feet to the end of the day's trek. Give yourself time to regain energy, shortening the route or adding the occasional rest day. If you are continuously stopping to look at the view, take photos, inspect the vegetation, or observe wildlife, then, rather than fall into a stop–go routine, make adjustments to your itinerary.

Steady Tread. Keeping a steady pace gives your body the chance to deal with constant demands on joints, muscles, and breathing. If you are out of breath or constantly needing to take a break, the body is jarred by a confusing rhythm. Try slowing your pace and shortening your stride to the stage where you can breathe steadily; this will also balance your body temperature.

Resting. When resting, your body can quickly lose the warmth generated by movement. Try and keep breaks short, say, 5 or 10 minutes every hour or at whatever interval fits into your rhythm. In cold conditions, find a sheltered spot, sit on your pack to avoid being chilled by the ground, take off sweaty clothing and replace it with warm, dry clothes; and keep up energy levels with a snack and a drink. Space out snacks throughout the day and eat well at lunch, but avoid a "blowout," which will leave you feeling sluggish while the body copes with digestion. Use the rest to make adjustments to your pack, to treat any foot problems, such as burgeoning blisters, and to check your position on the map.

Taking a break, Cirque de Mafate, Réunion

Uphill and Downhill. When climbing uphill you can take the strain off your legs by walking in short zigzags rather than straining to stride straight up the slope. Adjust your stride to a shorter length. On uphill (and downhill) stretches, a trekking staff acts as an extra support and can take weight off a sensitive knee or ankle. The exertion of grinding upward encourages sweating; by removing layers of clothing while on the move (and replacing them when at rest) you can help the body to regulate its temperature.

The "rest step" is a useful technique for steep ascents. This requires you to raise the left leg and place it forward on the ground while keeping the weight on the right foot. Pause for a brief moment, then shift your weight forward onto the left foot. Maintaining the weight on the left foot, bring your right leg forward, pause briefly, then shift your weight to the right foot. Continue with the technique, alternating brief pauses with forward motion.

Descending requires plenty of goodwill from your knees, which you should keep sufficiently bent to absorb the downhill jolts. Keeping your weight over your feet will prevent you from slipping backward.

If you are descending a steep, rocky slope in a group, proceed with members of the group spaced apart, moving diagonally so that any dislodged rocks don't fall onto the person in front.

TIMING

For some treks you'll have maps and guidebooks that will give timings. These may be calculated as an average derived from the times of fast and slow walkers, or they could relate to the times achieved by a local who knows the track inside out. Whichever case applies, you should consider the timing as an approximate guide. Note that the timesetters will have given you the route times—it's up to you to add time for your wayside stops for photos, cloud-gazing, snack breaks, and so forth. Once you've completed a few stages of the trek, you can compare your times with the published ones, and compute your own average.

If you are following your own route without given timings and want to make an approximate estimate of the time it will take, you can measure the distance off the map (as discussed later in this chapter, under "Navigation") and employ Naismith's Rule, named after a Scottish climber in the last century. According to this rule, you cover 3 miles (5 kilometers) per hour plus 30 minutes for every 928 feet (300 meters) of height gained. Traveling with a heavy pack, this would be adjusted downward to 1.9 miles (3 kilometers) per hour and an additional 45 minutes for the same height gain. Although this is a general rule of thumb, which should be modified in line with the factors described earlier in this section, it provides a figure to get your calculations off to a start.

RIVER CROSSINGS

Where there's no bridge, you'll have to cross a river. Before deciding to cross, carefully consider the best place, time, and method. The power of even a modest-looking river or stream should never be underestimated, and a tumble into freezing water can come unpleasantly close to hypothermia.

Places to Avoid. Avoid places where the river narrows and cuts deep channels with powerful currents, and look for wide sections with shallow, riffled water. Boulder-hopping across deep channels is dangerous—doubly so if the boulders are slippery and you are carrying a heavy pack. Beware of slippery rocks on the riverbed; scout along the river to see if you can find a gravel or shingle section. Avoid the treachery of river bends, which have shallow gravel beds on the inside and swift deep channels gouged on the outside. Don't cross just above waterfalls; if you lose your footing, you could be flipped over the edge.

Times to Avoid. Don't cross a river during a flood; if necessary, prepare to wait a day (or longer) for the water to subside. Also, watch out for storms in the mountains, which can produce flash floods and turn a trickling stream into a raging torrent. Glacier-fed streams and rivers are supplied by ice melted in the heat of the day. Consequently, they are at their fullest in the late afternoon, and in normal weather conditions should only be crossed in the early morning.

Crossing Technique. As a general rule, water flowing deeper than your lower thigh is the limit for stability, and even this may be too high if the riverbed is unstable. Never cross barefoot. Either cross in your boots or use your camp shoes or a pair of adventure sandals. Remove clothing, such as trousers, to prevent the

River crossing in the rainforest, Bolivian Amazon

current dragging at your legs. Waterproof the contents of your pack with several garbage bags. To avoid being dragged under by the weight of your pack, before you enter the water release your hipbelt and carry your pack lightly on one shoulder so that you can ditch it rapidly if you run into trouble.

If you are hiking solo, a trekking staff or stick will be useful to give you extra support and to probe the riverbed. Face upstream, then proceed carefully as a "tripod," moving no more than one point of contact with the riverbed at a time. Avoid the mesmerizing effect of the rushing current by keeping your eyes on the far river bank. If the current is fierce, you should face downstream and reduce your resistance to the current by cutting across the river diagonally.

If you are crossing with a partner, face each other and lightly rest arms on the partner's shoulders before entering the water with one hip facing upstream. Proceed at a slow shuffle. With three or more crossing partners, you can form a wedge to face upstream. You can also use a tree branch or link arms, aligning the group *parallel* to the flow (not against it).

If you do fall, release your pack, then roll onto your back with feet facing downstream and let yourself go with the flow until you can maneuver to the shore.

Mighty rivers are impressive but streams can be more deceptive:

"A couple of days before Christmas I took time off to head for a Scottish mountain hut. By the time the bus had dropped me off at the trailhead it had been dark for hours and the weather had degenerated into cold rain and strong wind. By rapidly fading torchlight, I followed the shore of the loch. Whilst crossing a feeder stream, I stepped into it by mistake—and was astounded to be almost instantly submerged. Although only 18 inches (45 centimeters) wide, the stream turned out to be about 5 feet (1.5 meters) deep! By the time I reached the hut, I was so heavily soaked that it took two days to dry out. Needless to say, there was no firewood at the hut, so that was indeed a damp Christmas!"

—**Graeme Cornwallis**

◆ NAVIGATION ◆

Good navigational skills keep you in control of your trek and can steer you away from impending danger. In fine weather on well-mapped, waymarked trails, there's rarely a problem finding your way from point to point with the aid of the occasional glance at a good map. Once you strike off into wilderness or encounter sudden changes in weather, worsening visibility, the absence of trail markings, or confusing terrain, your orientation will rely primarily on map, compass, and observation. Depending on the terrain, an altimeter or global positioning system may also be suitable.

If you are in a group, don't rely on one person for navigation. Make sure all the group members have the skills and tools for navigation so that they can take over in an emergency.

MAPS

Maps are a practical tool to give you a feel for an area while planning the trip at home and as a detailed reference to orient you in your surroundings when you are on the trail. They are produced in a wide range of specialist or combination formats. For example, general political, background, and sightseeing series may concentrate on specifics such as a country's administrative divisions, historical perspectives, and sites of cultural or tourist interest.

The most suitable format for trekkers is the topographical map, which represents landscape features such as rivers, streams, lakes, roads, tracks, trails, and paths, and provides contour lines.

In some countries, such as the United Kingdom, maps adhere to a grid reference system that divides the map into squares of equal size, each of which is subdivided by numbered lines running on a north–south axis and an east–west axis. A point on the map is designated by the numbers of its position, given as a combination known as a grid reference.

Aside from their functional purpose, maps also have aesthetic appeal—some guard their own stories of bureaucratic intrigue, whereas others may have been commissioned by a local enterprise to please with their advertising artwork rather than spatial accuracy. You'll probably be surprised how quickly maps amassed on your travels develop into a small library of cherished mementos at home.

Map Components

The following components should be considered when using a map.

Scale. Because it is impracticable to carry around a full-scale map, a ratio is used to present the information in miniature form. So, for example, a scale of 1:20,000 indicates that each single unit (an inch, for example) on the map represents 20,000 of the respective units in the outdoors.

If you have a choice of maps for your destination, for trekking purposes opt for a scale of 1:50,000 (an approximate equivalent of 1.25 inches to the mile or 2 centimeters to the kilometer) or, preferably, 1:25,000 (approximately 2.5 inches to the mile or 4 centimeters to the kilometer). If you are following clearly marked trails, you'll still be able to use maps on a scale of 1:100,000 (approximately 1 inch to 1.6 miles or 1 centimeter to 1 kilometer), but beyond this you'll lack sufficient accuracy for the map to be useful.

You can make a rough distance estimate by measuring along the map using a piece of string or dental floss or your compass baseplate (if supplied with a scale).

North. Topographical maps indicate true north, which refers to the earth's North Pole. More importantly, they show the magnetic declination (also known in Britain as variation) to the earth's magnetic north pole, which varies its position in northern Canada. Wherever you are in the world, you'll need to know this variation so that you can make the appropriate correction, adding or subtracting degrees, when using your map with a compass (as described later in this chapter). On grid maps, for example Ordnance Survey (or OS) mapping in Britain, you'll also find grid north, which is aligned with the vertical grid lines.

Contours. Contour lines, drawn to connect points of equal height above sea level, indicate a three-dimensional view of terrain. The interval, or distance, between adjacent lines can vary according to the format and scale of the map in use. A small interval, such as 32.8 feet (10 meters) or 164 feet (50 meters), is a lot more useful for detailed interpretation of the land than a large interval, which may not reveal what lies between adjacent lines. By studying the patterns and density of contours, you'll be able to visualize the undulations of the actual feature—a crowding of lines, for example, indicates steep ground, whereas more even spacing indicates a gradual slope.

Keys. Most maps represent features such as heights, land, water, roads, and trails, with symbols or abbreviations, which are explained in a key or legend on the side or base of the map.

Publication Details and Names. On the margin of the map or close to the legend, you'll find publication details. Look at the dates to establish the age of the survey data. Surveying and printing are costly ventures that may only be repeated occasionally. This can mean that older maps no longer reflect the full story on the ground where you may find features changed by, say, bush fires, landslides, logging trails, roads, utilities, or abandonment.

On foreign maps, you should also be prepared to deal with the language factor. Towns and villages may have several names given by different ethnic groups. For example, much of the local mapping of Tibet includes Chinese names in Mandarin characters and phonetics, which may or may not be an approximation of the original Tibetan name. You may also come across old and new names, which may be used interchangeably on maps and by the locals. In border towns and villages, it is quite common for locals to refer to the same place with different names in their respective languages.

Keeping Your Map at Hand

There is little point in having a map if it falls to bits or is kept out of easy reach at the bottom of your pack. Crumpling, soaking, jabbing with fingers, scribbling, pawprints, and coffee spills are just a few of the rigors suffered by maps. If possible, have your map sealed in clear plastic or keep it in a plastic pocket; if you hang it round your neck with a strap, remember to tuck it out of the way in high winds or risk being throttled. Some jackets have a useful built-in map pocket.

Map Sources

Maps are essential planning tools, so the sooner you can get to grips with the appropriate ones for your destination the better. Pick them up in advance and consider anything else you can find on the spot as a bonus. You should not be totally reliant on obtaining mapping when you arrive overseas—sometimes there simply are no detailed maps for your destination. Those that do exist may be out of print or the local sales outlet may be out of stock or closed for a holiday. See appendix B for select map sources.

Specialist international mapsellers negotiate with governments and mapmakers to obtain an amazing variety of maps for trekking destinations—in some cases, they may hold stock long since unobtainable in the original country. These companies are also able to close a commercial deal with obscure state agencies that may have scant monetary incentive to deal with individual trekkers. The extra cost to the purchaser reflects the time and effort invested in the search. For a brief selection of international map sources, refer to appendix A.

If you are drawing a blank with mapping, local reference sources may solve the problem. Depending on the sensitivity of the area, the local library may prove an excellent source of out-of-print titles, and you may be able to photocopy relevant details for your trek. Similarly, local hiking clubs are likely to have a collection of maps and advice that they may be happy to share with you.

Government and military survey agencies or commercial enterprises produce most of the world's mapping. Some countries are very sensitive about maps, particularly with regard to the way a disputed border zone might be portrayed. The Indian government, which has several long-running border disputes, routinely requires maps to be printed with a statement regarding their authenticity and correctness. If you are in a country engaged in territorial disputes, it's wise to use maps, especially small-scale ones, discreetly and avoid attracting official suspicion of your motives, which might prompt confiscation. If you are hauled in, remember that at first sight your motive does seem strange—opting to travel an immense distance from home to walk in remote areas—but once it's established, there'll be an obvious reason why you carry such detailed mapping.

Although spy-satellites can deliver startling accuracy, some governments restrict access and sales for the best of their terrestrial mapping because it is considered of national strategic importance. In the former Soviet Union, much of the cartography available to foreigners was deliberately doctored with built-in errors to mislead the user. Superbly detailed Chinese military mapping, marked *nei-bu* (internal use only), sometimes slips into the local bookshops.

Most state mapping agencies have commercial outlets to derive an income from their national and international work. If the outlet is quasi-military, you may have to register or seek permission before obtaining your maps.

Maps supplied by hotels, tourist offices, or tour operators, and maps in guidebooks—and often trekking guidebooks as well—should all be treated with caution. The pocket-guide format rarely allows more than an overview of large areas such as national parks, acting more as illustrative reference for the text than as a route map. As for hand-out maps, in many cases they have not been compiled for dedicated use on the trail, but rather for decoration or as rough orientation only.

Setting the Map

Setting the map requires you to locate your position on the map and then look around the landscape and identify a feature, such as a bridge or lake. Match this to its depiction on the map, which can then be rotated so that it is set or oriented in close relationship with other features of the landscape in view.

COMPASS

Whether you are spending a day in the hills or a month in the high peaks, it is essential that you pack a compass and know how to use it before you go. In fine conditions, you'll seldom need to use your compass, but when you encounter sudden foul weather and loss of visibility, you'll want those techniques literally at your fingertips, guiding you in the right direction toward your destination. Make a point of keeping in practice.

It is beyond the scope of this book to cover the full variety of compass techniques, which are best learned through further reading of manuals and reference works, a few of which are mentioned in appendix B. Most outdoor stores can tell you where to take a local class in backcountry navigation.

Compass Components

The basic principle for the function of a compass, known and used for many centuries, is that a thin magnet (needle), when lightly suspended, will align itself to point north along the earth's magnetic field. This is the basis of its value for direction-finding.

The standard baseplate compass is a popular workhorse for regular trekking use. It consists of a baseplate with built-in magnifying glass and edge scales (to measure map distances) and a needle enclosed in a circular housing filled with liquid to dampen movement. The rotatable housing has an outside rim marked with the four compass points (north, east, south, west) and a scale dividing the dial into 360 degrees, usually in 2-degree increments. Painted inside the housing on its base is an orienting arrow, which points to the North/360-degree mark on the housing. A large arrow close to the front edge of the baseplate is the direction-of-travel arrow.

The needle is usually tipped with red at the north end. Luminous paint on key points of the compass is useful for nighttime use. The dial should rotate smoothly but should not slip from a setting if jolted.

At altitudes above 2,000 feet (600 meters), a drop in atmospheric pressure or low temperatures may cause a bubble to form in the housing fluid. This should disappear once the compass is back in normal conditions.

Declination (Variation) and Inclination (Dip)

As already noted, a compass operates on the principle that a magnetized needle will align itself to the north. The north-pointing arrow of the compass needle (usually tipped with red) will point to magnetic north (as explained in the previous section on maps) rather than the geographical north pole.

You will need to compensate for this magnetic declination, subtracting or adding degrees as indicated, whenever you use your compass with reference to a map. Because declination varies over time and place, when available always use more recent maps with updated declination data. Some compass models are supplied with a declination adjustment feature.

Another factor affects the use of a compass in different parts of the world. The earth's magnetic forces vary from straight vertical at the magnetic poles to horizontal only at an irregular line, known as the magnetic equator, which encircles the earth in the region of the equator. Due to these differences in magnetic forces, the north or south end of a magnetic needle has a tendency to "dip," or incline, downward in the areas between the magnetic poles and the magnetic equator.

This means that for proper functioning compasses should be balanced for the area in which they are used—the manufacturer Silva, for example, identifies five zones: magnetic north (MN), north of magnetic equator (NME), magnetic equator (ME), south of magnetic equator (SME), and magnetic south (MS).

If you buy a compass in the United States or Europe, it will be balanced for MN; whereas in Australia or New Zealand, the applicable zone will be MS. The amount of dip varies in strength and importance; before you pack your trusty compass from home, check with the supplier to see if its balance is applicable for your intended destination. A neat solution to the problem in most parts of the world is a recently developed Swiss design, the Recta Turbo 20, which separates the magnet from the needle, thereby allowing compensation for tilt up to 20 degrees.

Deflection and Reversed Polarity

Bear in mind that electromagnetic fields and iron or metallic objects can deflect a compass, so don't use it to objects such as flashlights, radios, pens, watches, cooking pots, or belt buckles. If you are trekking in an area of magnetic rocks, your compass readings will be unreliable.

If you notice the needle becomes sluggish or slow to settle, appearing to stick or be out of balance, then its polarity may have been partially or completely reversed. In the case of complete reversal, the normally north-seeking (red-tipped) end of the needle will be pointing south. A quick solution is to obtain a strong magnet and drag its "south" pole outward along the "north" end of the needle; then repeat vice versa. Finally, check for accuracy against a compass known to be correct.

Basic Compass Techniques

The following are examples of basic techniques using a compass.

Setting a Bearing. A bearing is the angle between the direction of your travel destination and magnetic north. Bearings are measured on the rim of the compass housing in degrees from 0 to 360, which start at the north and increase in clockwise direction.

If you already know that your destination lies, say, on a bearing 75 degrees from north, you keep the compass level in the flat of your hand in front of you and then align the 75-degree notch on the rim of the housing dial with the direction-of-travel arrow on the baseplate. Then swivel the entire compass so that the north tip of the needle is aligned with the orientation arrow. You can then follow the direction-of-travel arrow along your bearing to your destination.

Taking a Bearing. If you know your destination, but not the requisite bearing, you can take a bearing by sighting along the direction-of-travel arrow toward your destination and rotating the dial until the north tip of the needle aligns with the orienting arrow. As a precaution in case you jolt the compass setting, your bearing should be read off the dial and remembered.

Taking a Back Bearing. This is useful if you've followed a bearing and decide to backtrack to your starting point. With your original bearing still set on your compass, turn the circular housing until the south (white end) of the magnetic needle is aligned with the orienting arrow. The direction-of-travel arrow on the baseplate indicates your back bearing. Now turn around, align the orienting arrow with north, and follow the direction-of-travel arrow. Note that back bearings can be found by adding or subtracting 180 degrees (if the original bearing was less than or more than 180 degrees, respectively).

Rounding an Obstacle. If the route for your bearing is barred by a major obstacle, such as a hillock or stone outcrop, you may want to skirt round it and then resume the route.

A simple technique is to stand before the obstacle with the compass set to the original bearing and then walk (either to the left or right) along a line at 90 degrees to the top of the baseplate and count the number of paces until you have cleared the edge of the obstacle. Follow the original bearing until you are past the obstacle and take the same number of paces (at 90 degrees to the top of the baseplate in the opposite direction) so that you return to your line of travel on your original bearing.

Basic Map and Compass Techniques

The following are examples of basic techniques when using a map and compass.

Setting a Bearing. If you can pinpoint your current position on the map and wish to take a bearing to walk to another point, then place the compass on the map with the long edge of the baseplate connecting the two points (note that the baseplate direction-of-travel arrow points toward your next intended position).

Rotate the dial until the north–south lines on the transparent base of the dial are parallel with the grid lines of the map and the orienting arrow points to north on the map. Make the declination adjustment as recorded on the map.

Then take the compass off the map and, without altering the dial position, turn the entire compass horizontally until the red tip of the needle is aligned with north on the orienting arrow. Holding the compass level, you can sight along the direction of travel to your destination. If this lies out of your line of sight, you can choose an intermediate feature that is visible, such as a tree or rock, and once you've reached it look for the next intermediate point, repeatedly sighting for intermediate points along your route until you reach your destination.

Aiming Off. This a useful technique if you think you might miss your intended objective—for example, a small encampment beside a stream. If you take a bearing to the stream, rather than the encampment, you will be aiming for a more readily recognizable feature, which you can follow to the smaller objective.

Finding Your Way If Lost. While it is always best to know where you are, aided by the map contours you can use a map and compass to locate your position on sloping ground in nil visibility. When standing on a slope, take a bearing along your current level: this gives the direction of the contours. If you know your approximate position and altitude, you can usually use the contour direction to refine your position on the map. Exceptions to this include the sides and tops of straight ridges, but perfectly straight- and smooth-sided ridges are most uncommon.

You can also use the gradient of the ground and the map contour intervals to help locate your position: just compare the map to what you are standing on. If you are unsure of your location walk a given distance (say 500 yards or 500 meters) and chart the variation in gradient and contour direction. Then compare with the map. If you are lost on a large area of flat ground, just walk until you find a slope.

NATURAL SIGNS

Apart from using the essential skills of map and compass navigation to keep on track, you may want to sharpen your directional perception through observation of natural signs.

In the southern and northern hemispheres, the sun stimulates more abundant growth on the northern and southern sides, respectively, of plants. If you look at tall vegetation or trees in exposed regions, you'll usually notice a pronounced sweep in the branches away from the prevailing wind, which will also provide moisture and thus stimulate growth of lichen and moss on the exposed side of vegetation. If you know the most frequent winds for the area, this will give you an approximate indication of direction.

In northern Australia, the compass or meridional termite usually builds its slablike nest to point north–south; and in North America, the compass plant aligns its leaves along a north–south axis.

If you are trekking with a traditional analog (face and two hands) watch, you can make an approximate estimate of direction. In the northern hemisphere,

Winter walk in Daisetsuzan National Park, Hokkaido, Japan (Deanna Swaney photo)

hold your watch horizontal and point the hour hand at the sun. A line bisecting the angle between the hour hand and the 12 o'clock mark will point along the north–south axis. In the southern hemisphere, point the 12 o'clock mark toward the sun and the line bisecting the angle between this and the hour hand will point along the north–south line.

At night in the southern hemisphere, the alignment of the five-star constellation of the Southern Cross can be extrapolated to indicate the direction of south; while in the northern hemisphere, the lowest two stars in the seven-star constellation of The Plough (also known as The Great Bear or Ursa Major) point to the Pole Star, located almost directly over polar north.

THE GLOBAL POSITIONING SYSTEM

Introduced to the general public in the 1990s, the global positioning system (GPS) was originally developed by the U.S. Department of Defense to provide the military with worldwide positioning and navigation information. Later it was used by civilians for surveying, marine position-finding, aviation, vehicle tracking, and outdoor recreation. The development of lightweight, compact GPS receivers as handheld navigation devices has expanded its use from commercial shipping and aviation to mountain rescue services as well as anyone venturing off the beaten track.

GPS devices have reached the top of the world on an ascent of Everest, tracked traffic in Tokyo, and helped map the bed of the earth's deepest lake.

How the System Works

The GPS consists of satellites (twenty-four at the time of writing) circling the earth twice daily at a speed of 6,000 miles (9,660 kilometers) per hour in a configuration of six geostationary orbits at a height of 10,898 miles (20,183 kilometers). Each satellite constantly transmits its position and keeps track of time courtesy of the U.S. military atomic clock, which loses just 1 second every 70,000 years—no point waiting around to check!

By taking a "fix" from three or more satellites, the receiver computes the distance from the satellites before displaying the user's exact position, speed, and direction. All handheld GPS-based devices require open sky to receive data—without access to open sky for a few minutes, they may not be able to operate accurately. Consequently, reception is obscured or impeded in thick rainforest, underground, under snow, and inside a vehicle or aircraft (an external antenna is recommended).

For military reasons, accuracy of position and velocity for civilian users has been tweaked, or "degraded" to use the official term. Velocity degradation is still under discussion, but position accuracy is officially degraded up to 984 feet (300 meters); the average, however, is closer to 328 feet (100 meters). You'll have to join up if you want to pinpoint within just a few feet, as demonstrated in Operation Desert Storm!

On the other hand, a civilian user scrambling around craggy peaks in misty weather should remember that leeway of 328 feet can be the difference between a trusting drop into the next world and a cautious foothold retained in this one! It's worth pointing out that the GPS was not designed for use against a mountainside. When visibility drops below 656 feet (200 meters), do not rely on it for navigation.

Using the GPS

Current handheld devices are approximately the size of a Walkman, weigh barely 1 pound (453 grams), and can run for some 5 hours of continued use (or longer in power-saving mode) on a few AA batteries.

A "cold" start, when the system has to acquire a full set of data, can take some 15 minutes. A "hot" start, when the system acquires a quick update, may require a couple of minutes or less, so you should be prepared to accept a relatively short battery life and plan for the extra weight of spares.

The user punches in position coordinates, which can then be used in a variety of ways. For example, you can enter the coordinates of your intended destination and then be guided directly there while the device automatically displays the distance remaining and your speed, direction, and course. Backtracking allows you to reverse your route back to your starting point. Locations can be displayed as latitude/longitude coordinates or using local systems, such as the British National Grid System.

Conclusions

For trekking, the GPS has proved especially useful in featureless wilderness as a means to get you into the general area. To use the system properly, you must know the coordinates of your destination.

Current limitations for civilian users include delays in availability of digital mapping data for certain regions and various gaps in satellite coverage. GPS technology advances rapidly, so expect to see solutions and refinements coming thick and fast within the next few years.

Given the hi-tech status of these receivers, it's not surprising that they have a high price tag and strong fascination for gearheads. Equally, if you aim to trek in wilderness regions, the GPS could be a boon and provide vital backup in an emergency. In regions where tracks, features, and maps are easily ascertained, and you can trust to your usual orientation methods, you may question such an additional expense or fork out for a GPS system anyway for use as emergency backup. Any comments from readers about the pros and cons or joys and pitfalls of GPS would be welcome.

ALTIMETER

An altimeter measures and converts barometric pressure into an altitude reading. It can be a useful backup tool to correlate your position with the contour lines on a topographical map. As a bonus, at constant altitude it acts as a barometer, forecasting weather changes.

Altimeters are available as mechanical and electronic models. Mechanical types require no power source and perform well at low temperatures. Electronic types are robust, compact, and capable of storing and recording data (or even triggering time or pressure alarms), but their power is sapped in extreme cold.

Altimeter designs include compact, palm-size models and the ultralight option of a wristwatch with built-in altimeter. Readings for the newer models are digital whereas traditional designs are analog (with pointer and dial). Depending on its features, your altimeter will indicate current altitude, altitude gain and loss in 20-foot (6-meter) increments or less, rate of ascent or descent, sea level barometric pressure, temperature, and barometric trend.

A mechanical altimeter calculates barometric pressure by measuring changes in the volume of air inside a miniature sealed container; electronic models perform the calculations with an electronic sensor and circuitry. Because the volume of air varies according to pressure and temperature, manufacturers calibrate

Chain to assist hikers on a steep section, Naukluft Mountains, Namibia (Deanna Swaney photo)

altimeters for maximum altitude and compensate for temperature changes. Your chosen altimeter should be temperature-compensated for the climate and calibrated for the altitude range at your trekking destination.

◆   TEN POINTS FOR TREKKING PREPARATION   ◆

1. Don't embark on a long trek without preparation and some initial training.
2. Let someone know where you are going and when you expect to be back.
3. Watch the weather and make use of weather reports.
4. Heed the advice of experienced local trekkers or mountaineers.
5. Accidents and extreme weather conditions can happen even on short treks: equip and prepare yourself properly.
6. Take a map and a compass—and know how to use them.
7. Trek alone only if you are extremely experienced and know the area and the vagaries of its weather well—it is up to you to make a responsible, objective decision.
8. Trust your intuition to turn back or abandon the attempt in good time: the mountains and the trail will be there for another attempt.
9. Always pack emergency gear: clothing, food, and survival equipment. Always be equipped to help yourself and others.
10. Don't panic; conserve your strength; seek shelter in good time.

6

LOOK SHARP
Security Basics

FOR MANY TRAVELERS CONSIDERING WHERE TO GO, concern about safety and security is one of the major reasons for feeling apprehensive about traveling. Sometimes an entire country has a reputation that it deserves; at other times media attention can turn a local incident or series of incidents into a total write-off for a country that really isn't high risk in all areas.

For most of us, security can be analyzed in terms of our person and possessions. The commonest threats are posed by theft, mugging, and indecent assault or rape. The important point to bear in mind is to be in control of the situation, to counter fear or apprehension with awareness. Some travelers may already have extensive experience with crime in their own countries, whereas others may have encountered nothing more than petty crime. The detail in this chapter is provided to heighten awareness and indicate how travelers can control much of the risk.

Don't assume that the potential for nefarious deeds is exclusively local in its nature. Some travelers finance their wandering urges by stealing from gullible fellow travelers.

◆ PRECAUTIONS BEFORE YOU GO ◆

"Travel light and you can sing in the robber's face."

—*Juvenal, X.22*

Remember the simple dictum: the less you have, the less you lose. A basic rule before departure is to take only those things that are expendable—in other words, pack what you are consciously prepared to lose or replace.

Magic amulet: **Protection**; Japanese

Look ahead: Crossing over, Cirque de Mafate, Réunion

Another worthwhile strategy is to disperse the risk: distribute your valuables about your person and your baggage, thereby reducing the chances of losing everything in one fell swoop at any stage of the trip.

Travel insurance is essential if you want to replace rather than lose valuables. A good insurance policy offers more than financial restitution: it also offers peace of mind when faced with the high level of stress and emotional upheaval caused by petty theft or violence. For basic money precautions and advice on insurance, refer to chapter 2, "First Steps: Travel Arrangements."

Before you leave home, prepare for the worst. Make copies of all your important documents and records. This applies to your passport—including issue and expiration dates—and any visas, traveler's check numbers, credit card numbers and relevant emergency loss numbers, transport tickets, and a short list of important contact addresses. Although a European or American passport is not the first thing that springs to mind when one thinks of valuables, in some parts of the world they are highly valued by thieves for immigration dodges or other rackets. A copy of a birth certificate can be handy to expedite clearance for a new passport if your old one goes missing.

Make four copies: keep one on your person and one with your belongings and exchange one with a traveling companion. A fourth set left at home provides increased backup if you need someone at home to act for you in an emergency.

◆   SECURING YOUR BELONGINGS   ◆

There are several ways to protect your backpack or daypack from the unwelcome attention of casual pilferers or even those with more determined interest.

If you are using a backpack, make sure it has sturdy zippers that can be secured with combination locks. If double zippers aren't fitted, you can also improvise by sewing an extra tab on the end of the zipper. This poses a tempo-rary hindrance and tends to deter opportunistic thieves who prefer quick and easy spoils. Most of the small, mass-produced padlocks are easier to pick whereas combination locks need more effort and don't require keys.

For your daypack, double zippers are also recommended. To deter light fin-gers, secure the zippers with combination locks or at least safety pins. A bicycle combination lock or padlock (steel or chain) is handy for securing baggage to fixtures in your lodgings or to seats or racks in buses and trains.

A modified canvas sack or backpack cover made from heavy material should reduce wear and tear and make your baggage look less appealing to handlers and onlookers. It may also deter pilfering and the "planting" of incriminating items (such as drugs). Mail bags provided with my parcels courtesy of the Australian postal system have proved excellent for the job. If you have farming friends, they may have some spare sacks of the right kind.

This heavy cover is good to prevent hip belts from ripping off or straps from snagging when checking baggage onto planes, trains, or buses. In addition, when you are walking around with your pack on your back, it can also provide basic protection against pilfering or razoring. With judicious tailoring, I have man-aged to cut "slits" for backpack straps and reinforced them with strong tape. On one trip to Bolivia and Brazil, I became quite fond of a heavy-duty plastic fertil-izer sack, which spent many months being dragged through dust, frost, and rain.

In some parts of the world—South America and Asia are frequently cited by travelers—thieves ignore padlocks on your backpack or daypack and expertly use a razor to make a slit in the material. In this manner, nimble fingers can get at your belongings while you walk down the street or slumber in your bed. To prevent the loss of contents, you can make a lining from plastic-coated chicken wire (available cheaply from do-it-yourself shops) or, reportedly, from ballistics nylon or similar material such as Kevlar (very expensive!). This way, if your pack is slit, you can at least have the satisfaction of thwarting the thief, although there's no denying that the cesarean damage and subsequent stitch-up job for your pack is annoying.

YOUR ROOM

If you find yourself in a dodgy hotel with a suspect lock on your room door, you can increase peace of mind by using your own lock. A rubber wedge is useful to jam windows or doors from inside your room. Recently developed options include a lightweight, portable, electronic motion-sensor (with banshee alarm) and a small, portable lock that jams the inside door-frame against outside access.

YOUR TENT

Tent theft is rare, but pilfering of its contents is more common, either by humans or by cheeky wildlife. Simple precautions include basics such as picking a site

Meeting a policeman on patrol, Niuafo'ou Island, Tonga (**Deanna Swaney photo**)

that doesn't invite constant local scrutiny and keeping valuables out of sight of curious onlookers.

To improve security of a tent and its contents, you can carefully prepare holes and insert grommets in the fabric of the inner tent and outer fly prior to your trip. When you're on the trail, thread a padlock and chain or bicycle combination lock through the holes before attaching it to a post, tree, or suitably heavy object. Emblazoning your name on gear makes it distinctive and, thus, less attractive for resale by thieves. A motion-sensor alarm or pin-activated alarm could also be useful—position it securely inside the tent so that it will be triggered by violent movement rather than an innocent gust of wind. A pressure-sensitive pad for use in conjunction with this type of alarm has recently been developed for tents. A simple deterrent for casual prowlers is to secure double zip tabs with a safety pin. Leave them zipped up at the top of the zipper, as close to the top as possible, where they will be less obvious.

VALUABLES ON YOUR BODY

As a practical option to carry some of your cash, traveler's checks, credit cards, photocopied records, and other small items of value, the original "money belt" idea has been expanded to cover a wide variety of security contraptions.

Individual money belt designs are available as a flat pouch to fit around your neck or waist, as a holster clipped around your shoulder, and as an elasticized bandage strapped around your leg. Other models clip onto a belt and can be tucked inside trousers or a skirt.

Although many of these products are made from nylon with a soft backing material, travelers who dislike the feel of synthetics in a humid climate can choose cotton or leather versions.

Before you fall for snazzy looks, take a good tug at the stitching. Many years ago I bought a heavy green canvas, army-issue money belt as surplus stock for the equivalent of a couple of dollars in England. A short while ago I bought two nylon belts. After one came unstitched within days, the other soon suffered from elastic strap fatigue and buckled clips. Meanwhile, the original canvas purchase lives on.

Remaining true to the money belt concept, specially designed belts with a discreet zipper along the length of the reverse side are available in many forms. Just make sure that the belt doesn't look too much like a glamorous designer accessory worth stealing by a chic felon!

Some travelers prefer to sew their own money belts. A nifty trick is to sew your own cloth pouch and attach it with a safety pin inside trousers or appended to a trouser pocket. Parallel Velcro strips sewn onto the lining of pockets make it tough for pickpockets to dip into the contents.

Remember to always, always wear your money belt *under* your clothing. Pouches or belts worn outside clothing attract thieves who gladly assume the traveler has considerably concentrated valuables where they can be swiped in one fell swoop.

In Lhasa I observed teams of pickpockets darting in and out of the crowds of passengers pushing to board early morning buses. These light-fingered experts were unzipping and emptying waist pouches (and camera pouches) of foreign travelers distracted by the boarding chaos, then disappearing into the morning mists—but not before one pickpocket had been caught and dispossessed of his booty.

Bearing in mind the need to distribute valuables, it can be beneficial to use more than one money belt. Practiced thieves have long since become wise to concealed money belts, so it pays, for example, when threatened with violence, to be able to "sacrifice" one belt and thus convince the thieves that they've got your valuables. If you're lucky, your other concealed stashes will at least prevent your loss from being total.

◆ STREET WISDOM ◆

Without condoning crime, it's amazing how often I've seen foreigners strolling the streets of a poor area, for example in South America, with gold watches on their wrists, cameras dangling around their necks, and video cameras in hand. Flaunting wealth can invite envy and loss if you fail to appreciate that in some countries a simple item such as a camera can represent considerable wealth.

If you are a foreigner in a strange place, you can attract the attention of criminals through various means: how you act; what you do or say; what you wear; and, in places with a clear tourist trail, where you go. Observe how things operate locally and do as the locals do.

Know Where You Are. A simple rule is to make sure you have a map or at least a rough idea of orientation before arriving in a new place. If you are entering a known high-risk area, consider using a taxi and try to leave enough time in your travel plans so that you don't arrive there at night. In a high-risk area, it is unwise to conspicuously study a map, thereby signaling that you are both foreign and lost.

Seek Local Advice. Follow local advice on times, places, and people to avoid. Approached in the right manner, many news agents, shop owners, hotel managers, and other locals close to events on the street may feel proud to impart some street wisdom.

Buddy Up. If you are traveling solo, distraction is easier. It can be beneficial to find a companion so that at least one person can watch what's going on, look after baggage, or keep an eye out whilst the other discreetly checks a map or asks directions.

Dress Sensibly. Wherever you go, pick a style of dress that blends with local standards and keep to casual wear. Inexpensive clothes bought at your destination will reduce your profile. A plastic bag from the local supermarket or a copy of the local newspaper can signal that you are not a total stranger to the district.

Watch Your Daypack. Get into the habit of wearing your daypack strapped to your front, thus giving you maximum overview. Worn in the conventional manner, with contents behind your back, daypacks are much easier targets for furtive theft or razoring, especially during an "arranged" distraction. If you have to take your daypack off and place it on the ground, make it a reflex action to put your foot through one of the straps. It's amazing how quickly you can be distracted in a bus station, restaurant, or market, giving a thief the chance to make off with your pack in a flash.

Conceal Your Camera. If you carry a camera with you, using a flashy pouch will clearly identify it as a valuable item. When you're not actually taking a photo, get in the habit of keeping your camera tucked away out of sight. If you sling it around your neck or shoulder, it is more obvious and easier to heist. In major cities in South America I found it less obtrusive to carry a camera inside a plastic bag emblazoned with the name of a local supermarket. Obviously it is best not to expose the carrier bag to hot sun; otherwise, your precious film may cook.

Organize Your Money. Take care how you pay for daily expenses. If you use a wallet, keep it buttoned away in an inside pocket—flashing around a bulging wallet can invite envious thoughts. For minor payments, keep small denomination notes and some coins in an easily accessible outside pocket. This saves the hassle of extracting your wallet, is convenient when paying for public transport, and can act as rapid appeasement for a mugger.

Avoid High-Risk Areas. It may seem obvious, but just as bears go for the honeypot, thieves congregate around tourist sites, car rental agencies, currency exchange offices, banks, and any plush spots that cater for those with money. By avoiding looking like a foreigner, displaying wealth, and tempting with easy pickings, you'll be encouraging thieves to seek an easier target.

Observe. If you notice that you are being followed or closely observed, stay calm while you pause to look straight at the person(s) involved and to assess the situation. If you're not alone, point out the person(s) to your companion. This at least shows the followers that they have lost the element of surprise.

Stay Alert. The commonest ploy for thieves is to distract their target person with a diversion, preferably in a crowded or busy place (market, bus station, train station, airport), before pickpocketing or making off with baggage.

Working singly or in a gang, the thieves might simply "bump" into you, perhaps also knocking you off balance, before "assisting" you to your feet again with an expert riffle through your pockets or a grab for your daypack.

The same effect can be achieved in various ways: staging an argument or fight around you; approaching you with a request or sales pitch; or throwing or dropping something (even lifelike baby dolls) onto or in front of you.

The "smear" technique, widespread in South America, involves the use of colorful, odorific, or sticky substance, such as ketchup, mustard, dog muck, or chocolate. Thieves spray the stuff unnoticed onto you or your belongings, then draw your attention to the "mishap" and kindly invite you to place your bag on the ground whilst they help you wipe away the mess. Of course, the instant you let go of your bag it's whisked away. Difficult as it may be to ignore your sullied state, recognize the situation and concentrate on getting off the street into a safe spot away from the willing "helpers."

Be Cautious With Authority. If an official stops you and explains that he is with the police, immigration office, or similar organization, be wary of a request to see your passport or money, doubly so if the official is in plainclothes. Colleagues may coincidentally appear on the scene to confirm the impression that the "officer" is bonafide. Don't be duped into following the lead of those around you who may be part of the scam. Once the impostors get a chance, they'll want to relieve you of valuables under the guide of "confiscation" or "inspection."

When you notice this type of situation developing, don't hand over anything. Follow the general rules of caution. Ask to see identification first, taking time to look at the number, photo, and seal. Then offer to go, not in a vehicle, but on foot with the person or persons to the police station where you will be ready to answer questions.

MUGGING AND THREATENING WEAPONS

As mentioned in the preceding section, it's always wise to have a small sum of money easily accessible to appease a mugger. Carrying weapons is not advisable: in some instances this can make the situation much worse. Resistance is not recommended, although knowledge of self-defense may be useful if you, rather than your valuables, are targeted (see appendix A for details of self-defense courses). Muggers can be highly nervous, on drugs, or plain violent. The best solution is to let the money go, let the moment pass.

If you have prepared yourself along the general lines mentioned in this chapter, the loss will either be recoverable through insurance or an expendable experience to be measured against the daily pluses and minuses of travel.

◆   WILDLIFE PRECAUTIONS   ◆

In most cases wildlife makes a special effort not to be around you. Where it has become attracted to trekkers and their sites, you can follow simple precautions to minimize problems. Refer also to comments on wildlife in chapter 7, "Minimum Impact: Trekking and the Environment."

When camping, you can lessen the attractions for wildlife by keeping food out of your tent; cleaning your hands, face, and cooking utensils thoroughly after meals; and suspending food from a suitable tree—20 feet (6 meters) up the tree, and 10 feet (3 meters) out on a limb—if bears or other mammals are a potential problem. If small rodents are a problem, leave pack pockets unzipped, so that they can investigate freely without the need to gnaw entry holes. Deter casual intruders by keeping your tent zipped up.

"While camping in the bush near Derby, Western Australia, I feasted on bread, honey, and a can of pineapple chunks. Attracted by the sweet smells, local termites quickly hurried to visit, and I had to seal up the tent rapidly to keep them out. Shortly afterwards, the proceedings attracted the attentions of larger and larger wildlife, culminating with the arrival of a lizard measuring some 3 feet (one meter)."

—Graeme Cornwallis

SNAKES

Snakes generally give humans a wide berth. To avoid close encounters with them, practice preventive action. Because snakes almost always strike from ground level, in snake country wear sturdy footwear, socks, trousers, and canvas gaiters. Vibrations can warn snakes to move out of your way: on overgrown trails, use a staff or stick to rap the ground and shake the ground vegetation ahead.

Beware of placing your hand into a crevice, behind a rock, or under a log—favorite basking sites or living quarters for snakes. Similarly don't shift rocks or logs or sit on them before having a quick look, and learn to step *onto* a log rather than straight over and into a possible blind spot on the other side. Use a flashlight and be particularly alert for snakes on trails at night. Always shake out boots or shoes before stepping into them. For information on snake bite treatment, refer to chapter 4, "In Good Shape: Staying Healthy."

Lounging dogs at a Lhasa meat market

DOGS

When you meet man's best friend on the trail, don't assume you are the chosen partner. Many dogs in remote regions are not pets: they are trained to sound the alarm, keep out predators and strangers, and generally guard home and livestock. If you enter their territory or approach their flock, especially at night or in murky weather, you may provoke an attack. In remote parts, dogs can also be spooked simply by the strange smell of foreigners and their baggage. If you are being challenged by a dog, try to attract the attention of the owner, and carefully back away to a point where the challenge slackens. For information on rabies and treatment of bites, refer to chapter 4, "In Good Shape: Staying Healthy."

There are various dog deterrents to smooth your path. Small, handheld devices that zap dogs with an ultrahigh electronic tone are reported to be effective (if used frequently, carry a spare battery or two). Yet another use for a stout walking staff or stick is to fend off dogs. In many cases where a dog has been blustering, I've found the widespread method of shying a stone close to the dog's nose is dissuasion enough; and even if no stone is at hand often just the pretense of stooping to pick up a stone and holding back the hand as if ready to throw will get the right message across to the dog.

BEARS

Bear attacks are given dramatic press coverage but are not common (in comparison to the number of bears and hikers) and almost always occur when the animal feels trapped, such as during a surprise encounter in thick bush; threatened, for instance, when a mother bear perceives a threat to her cubs; or obstructed in its search for your food.

You can give due warning by attaching bells to your pack (or an empty tin can filled with stones), loudly yodeling, chatting (to yourself if necessary), or finding another way to make your presence known. If you come across bear cubs, the mother may well be close by—leave the area as soon as possible to avoid posing a potential threat.

The bear's strong sense of smell attracts it to the food at campsites. In bear country, be sure to camp away from bear trails along riverbanks or lakeshores—look for evidence of bear activity such as bear scat. Set up your tent at least 50 yards (55 meters) upwind from where you eat. At night, never take any foods or odorous items (such as toothpaste and suntan lotion) into your tent, and wash off odors from your clothing, face, and hands before you sleep.

Keep your food wrapped and sealed in several plastic bags. At night you should store it in bearproof boxes or containers (if available) or suspend it from the limb of a nearby tree.

Bears are very agile climbers and easily capable of outrunning humans. If you are confronted by a bear at close range, don't charge it or run from it; these moves may respectively trigger a defensive reaction or a predatory response. Talk calmly (to advise the bear of your presence) and back off slowly—don't run. Although bears often only bluff charge, in the event of full attack, drop to the ground and then adopt a fetal position, hands interlinked around the neck, and play dead.

7

MINIMUM IMPACT
Trekking and the Environment

THE SEARCH FOR ALTERNATIVES TO STANDARD tourism products and activities has stimulated the growth of ecotourism, which, as its name implies, emphasizes the ecological and environmental aspects of a destination. The drive to promote these interests, as the following examples illustrate, has had a mixed impact on the countries and peoples involved.

In Costa Rica, the country's tropical forests and spectacular wildlife have become one of the world's top ecotourism attractions. As the word has spread, the increasing numbers of visitors have in turn attracted developers keen to introduce large-scale resorts for mass tourism. Some of these resorts were constructed on nature reserves, where they made a severe impact on the environmental resources and wildlife. In Belize, the lure of major money to be made from the development of islands renowned for their wildlife has caused similar problems. As a solution for this negative effect, one suggestion has been to downsize facilities to a scale that balances the numbers of visitors against their impact on the natural environment.

In Africa, ecotourism has funded the establishment of national parks to protect biodiversity. Setting aside this land has caused conflicts with the local people, who are angered at exclusion from their traditional homelands and the loss of their traditional means of support, such as herding, hunting, and gathering wood. Those affected include the Maasai pastoralists of Kenya, the Barsawa people in Botswana, and San (Bushmen) in Namibia.

The challenge of this dilemma is to find a compromise so that the locals retain the right to use their lands, overgrazing is avoided, and diverse stocks of wildlife are preserved. At the same time, ecotourism can provide funding for

---

Symbolic spirit: **Yo-He-Wah, Spirit of the Grass;** North American Indian

An endangered species: Hyacinth macaw, Pantanal, Brazil

participatory management of the land and act as an extra source of income for locals. However, if local income were completely dependent on tourism, there would be the loss of dignity derived from traditional livelihoods. On the other hand, an obvious crisis would result should the revenue from tourism, a notoriously fickle business, suddenly stop.

In Europe, the Alps attract some 100 million visitors annually in pursuit of outdoor recreation, ranging from skiing and hiking to rockclimbing and mountaineering. As a result, the region's ecosystem faces enormous pressures on a variety of fronts. The ski industry has created a vast network of thousands of miles of graded slopes, runs, and lift systems; and new developments require yet more bulldozing and dynamiting of an environment already stressed by problems, especially refuse disposal (when the snows clear in the summer, the winter litter comes back into view). Meanwhile, the region's forests are expected to shrink to two-thirds of their present size by the year 2010 as a result of acid rain which is itself caused as a side effect from exhaust emissions of more than 11 million vehicles (commercial and tourist traffic) passing through transalpine routes each year. The loss of tree cover leaves unstable slopes that are more prone to avalanches. Small wonder that most mountain farmers have sold out and left for the cities.

In 1991 seven nations from the Alps region signed the Alpine Convention and agreed in principle to counteract the decline with a raft of proposals, including the encouragement of rail transport as an alternative to transalpine road routes, the designation of special zones to remain unspoiled, restrictions on ski slope development at high altitudes, and the implementation of proper waste treatment at ski resorts. While the international impetus to make these proposals work will take many years, another organization, Alp Action, has already launched schemes for nature trails, reforestation, environmental education, and wildlife conservation.

The search for answers continues. Meanwhile, turning to the effects of trekking, the most productive long-term strategy will be a cooperative effort to attract as many trekkers as possible to address their impact and contribute ideas for solutions.

◆   ECOTOURISM–THE TREKKING PERSPECTIVE   ◆

When you trek in a country you are a guest, sharing the environment with the locals. It's only fair that you do your best to minimize your impact on their land and resources by carefully choosing the path you follow, where you stay, and what you take into or out of your destination. Aim to leave as little evidence as possible of your passage through the area, and avoid disturbing the natural balance.

Nepal, a country with a long tradition of receiving trekkers, serves as an example of environmental crisis. Rapid population growth there is accompanied by environmental problems ranging from air pollution in the capital, Kathmandu, to deforestation and erosion in the hills. Popular trekking regions, such as Annapurna and Khumbu (Everest), attract some 50,000 trekkers annually, a sizable percentage of the estimated 300,000 tourists visiting the country each year.

In the hills, trekking contributes to the economy but it also adds to existing problems with garbage disposal, sanitation, hotel facilities, and fuel. According to some estimates, an individual trekker (including related fuel and construction requirements) consumes between five and ten times more wood per day than a Nepali. Because this wood is obtained through deforestation, and used mostly for fuel, there is now a concerted effort to reduce such environmental impact by encouraging the use of solar energy and fossil fuels, such as kerosene. Trekkers are also being asked to observe minimum impact rules (described later in this chapter) for garbage disposal and sanitation. In the long term, it's hoped that by supporting these measures trekkers will provide an incentive for local traders to switch to minimum impact themselves. This, in turn, will take some of the strain off the country's environment.

If you are trekking with guides and porters, let them know you want to conserve resources and minimize impact; and explain how and why it is of benefit. If you are thinking of joining an organized trekking group, ask the company about its conservation and impact policies before you book (for suggested questions, refer to chapter 5, "Setting the Pace: Trek Preparation and Technique").

Interaction with local people and the cultural impact of trekking are discussed in chapter 8, "Foreign Cultures: Meeting the Locals," and useful addresses are given in appendix A.

Fragile ground: Trekking in the Naukluft Mountains, Namibia (Deanna Swaney photo)

◆ MINIMUM IMPACT ◆

CAMPING

If you are camping, it's advisable to set up camp more than 100 feet (30 meters) from the closest water source, preferably using a previous site rather than contributing to an expanding "honeycomb" site, which gradually erodes the surrounding area. Choose a site with natural drainage rather than digging runoff trenches, which can seriously damage the natural drainage pattern.

Avoid hacking down vegetation for use as bedding; use a sleeping pad. If you have to use a site beside a river, select a spot below the high-water mark, preferably on a beach or sandspit. Traces of your stay will be erased with the next high water.

When you've finished hiking for the day, wearing lightweight camp shoes rather than heavy-soled boots around the campsite will make less impact on the ground.

As a general rule, don't sweep aside ground cover, such as pine needles or leaves; instead, pick out uncomfortable stones or twigs and set them aside to be replaced when you leave. The overall effect should be as close to no-trace camping as possible.

Garbage. Out of sight, out of mind, is not an effective means of garbage disposal. Estimates assess decomposition time for plastic bags at between one and two decades, aluminum cans at eight or more decades, and glass considerably longer than humans.

Any rubbish you bring in, make sure you pack it out—if there's space in your pack, take along other people's detritus too and feel a righteous glow. In remote regions, although there may be bins for garbage collection, the lack of disposal facilities may mean that the contents are simply dumped down an adjacent hillside (out of sight, out of mind). If possible, pack your detritus to the largest communities with adequate disposal facilities. Providing there's no fire risk, a convenient solution for paper packaging, toilet paper, and other easily combustible items is to burn them. Always carry matches and a spare lighter or two.

One way to minimize garbage and save space in your pack is to buy food with less packaging, or repackage food efficiently when preparing for your trip. Use a water bottle and water purification (as outlined in chapter 4, "In Good Shape: Staying Healthy") rather than purchasing plastic bottles of mineral water, which are becoming a persistent source of litter on trekking trails in the Himalaya and elsewhere.

You can reduce the impact on local rodents, insects and other wildlife by placing a tarp or similar sheet under your eating area to collect food scraps, which are then either burned or packed out. Don't bury food remains—once wildlife has unearthed leftovers, it quickly identifies campsites as a food source and will return regularly for more pickings.

Hygiene. Toilet choices may include a locally provided hole in the ground, or you may have to dig your own. For the latter, make sure you are more than 200 feet (60 meters) from any water source, preferably downstream of campsites or settlements. Take a trowel and dig a hole 4 to 5 inches (10 to 12 centimeters) deep or, preferably, ease up a large divot. Assuming there's no fire risk, burn toilet paper, or pack it out in a sturdy, sealable plastic bag. When you're done, replace the earth or divot and tamp down the surface.

If you want to go a step further, special collector/container bags (made from lightweight plastic with a reinforced base for stability) enable you to pack out human waste. The bag is placed on the ground on its base; you then unfurl the top wide enough for clear aim, hunker into position, and roll up the bag upon completion. An additional heavy-duty refuse bag is provided for final packing. More information on this product is available from Intelligent Products, P.O. Box 626, Burlington, KY 41005, USA.

What not to do in a hot spring, Land-mannalaugar, Iceland (Deanna Swaney photo)

When washing clothes, pots and pans, or yourself, keep 200 feet (60 meters) from a water source. It is important to wash or dispose of waste water (soap, suds, dishwater, toothpaste, and so on) no closer than this, allowing it to filter through soil rather than exposing the water source to concentrated pollution.

There are also ways to cut down on soaps and detergents. For the time that you're on a trek, flossing does a reasonable job of cleaning your teeth, and sand or pot scourers (and dishcloth) deal with most pots and pans. Hot water is often enough to wash off the worst caking of body dirt—and you can follow that up with a small dollop of biodegradable soap for the remainder.

Fires, Fuel, and Power. Although the rosy glow of a campfire is instantly associated with camping, it isn't always necessary or appropriate to light fires, especially in regions where deforestation and erosion are a problem.

Where fires are permitted, it's preferable to use an existing firesite in a position sheltered from the wind and at a safe distance from surrounding vegetation. Use only dead and downed wood, rather than maiming live trees, and keep the fire small to conserve fuel. Do not throw aluminum foil into the fire because it will disintegrate into flakes and pollute the site. Always keep an eye on the fire; and before you turn in for the night or depart the site, douse it thoroughly several times with water, stirring the coals between each dowsing, until you are satisfied that it is out.

Smokers should take care that cigarettes and matches are properly extinguished. Don't fling stubs into scrub or grind them out on the ground; pack them out. If you use a lighter, use the refillable kind rather than a disposable.

If you're trekking with local guides or porters, insist on using fuel-efficient methods (for example, kerosene stoves) rather than scarce local firewood. Give some thought to the use of hot water and its consequent drain on fuel resources. Can you make do with a shower once every few days rather than every day? Do you need the water to be piping hot, or will just warm do the job? Less fuel is required if meals for the group are eaten at the same time, and further reduction can be achieved if cooking is restricted to simple fare. A well-maintained stove burns less fuel, causes less pollution, and costs less to run.

If you use batteries in a flashlight, radio, tape player, or other electronic device and are traveling in a warm climate, consider switching to rechargeable batteries combined with one of the new range of lightweight, portable solar chargers.

TRAILS

Although the act of one individual may seem a drop in the ocean, if you multiply it over months and years through hundreds and thousands of visitors, the resultant impact can rapidly change the landscape.

Don't uproot or pick plants or take away rocks at campsites or along the trail. Leave all religious artifacts, such as prayerflags and prayerstones, in place and untouched, and do not destroy traditional waymarking, such as cairns.

Consider the footwear you are using and where trails have been laid out—keep to them. Heavy boots with deep-cut treads can quickly churn up fragile ground; if conditions permit, change to lighter footwear.

Mountains. In mountain terrain, it is particularly important to reduce trail erosion by keeping to the track and resisting the temptation to take shortcuts (a common cause of dramatic trail damage on steep mountainous sections).

Reduce impact on the fragile vegetation of an alpine meadow by taking a detour and not camping directly on it. If it must be crossed and you're in a group, spread out to avoid the erosion of single-file walking.

Where alternative routes are available, avoid crossing talus or scree slopes, which often host intermittent vegetation built up over decades. If this covering is dislodged, the rocks on the slope are more likely to fall, the slope is eroded, and the vegetation lower down undergoes the same process of destruction. Don't deliberately shove boulders or throw rocks down steep slopes; apart from the cumulative damage to the slope, any persons climbing below may be placed in serious danger.

Deserts. In the desert, remember that the landscape may undergo little change over decades or centuries because vegetation grows very slowly. Equally, tracks, firesites, and campsites can remain in evidence for many years unless you make a special effort to leave no trace. Given the complex interdependency of species in the desert, it's important to leave everything in place so that, for example, dead plants can be broken down naturally to create the basis for new vegetation.

Coastlines. In coastal areas watch out for crumbling trails along cliffs, and avoid extending the erosion by keeping to the trail rather than its shoulders. Beach fauna and flora, including objects such as shells, which provide shelter for other living species, should be left in place.

Marshland and Tundra. In marshlands and boggy tundra regions, keep to the trail, even if it means going straight through a section already heavily churned—this will concentrate the mess rather than widen the whole problem. Make use of any boardwalks or other designated trail conservation measures that reduce the tendency of the trail to turn into a quagmire.

Forests. If weather and trail conditions permit, such as fine weather on easy forest trails, consider switching to lighter footwear. Poisonous plants and fungi should be left in place to serve their purpose in the environmental balance; don't hack them down just because they are inedible.

WILDLIFE

For many trekkers the highlight of a trip is the chance to see wildlife, large and small. Remember that the trail you tread and its surroundings are shared with many other creatures that form part of nature's complex system. In most cases, wildlife steers well clear of human contact; only when surprised, touched, trodden on, or otherwise disturbed or cornered will it seek to defend itself.

When observing animals, give them space and respect. If they show agitation, withdraw to a distance that is comfortable for both them and you. One way to be close without confrontation is to use binoculars.

Don't feed wild animals. This can encourage otherwise reticent species to abandon their normal foods and jeopardize their health. Once an animal has made the association between humans and food, it may also exhibit deviant behavior, attacking or threatening humans as a means to scavenge food.

In Tasmania, the Lake St. Clair cafe at one end of the Overland Track is attended by a number of very savvy and aggressive crows and birds of prey. As hungry trekkers troop out of the door to take a seat under the trees, the birds dive-bomb diners and plates, scooping up cream teas and sandwiches in their talons.

As a form of indirect feeding, litter and food scraps attract wildlife that quickly associates campsites with food. You can reduce the impact on local rodents, insects, and other wildlife by placing a tarp or similar sheet under your eating area and burning or packing out the food scraps.

At a campsite on the Overland Track, I was woken during the night by the sound of scrabbling and clicking. As I shined my torch out of the tent, it met a circle of glinting eyes: pademelons and other furry creatures keen to continue tinkering with backpack pockets and zippers. In Africa, baboons and hyenas are well known for their interest in buried litter.

During breeding season, animals are protective of their breeding sites and young. If you intrude you may be attacked and if you handle the young they may be abandoned. Mother bears with cubs are well known for challenging any perceived threat, and birds such as the great skua will relentlessly dive-bomb any intruder (including hikers) on their clifftop territory.

Lost or injured wildlife is best left alone. Although you may want to help, it's best to let nature look after its own. Sometimes an injury may be caused by a less than obvious reason. A bird might feign injury to lure you away from a nest, or a young animal might be lying motionless waiting for the emergency (your presence!) to pass.

Finally, abetting extinction is maximum impact: resist the temptation to purchase animal or plant products made from endangered species. To quote Douglas Adams and Mark Carwardine from their excellent book, *Last Chance to See:* "It's easy to think that as a result of the extinction of the dodo, we are now sadder and wiser, but there's a lot of evidence to suggest that we are merely sadder and better informed."

◆   THE HIMALAYAN TOURIST CODE   ◆

The following set of guidelines has been developed by Tourism Concern, a network promoting awareness of the rights and interests of people living in the world's tourist areas. Although this code was written specifically for the Himalaya, its general points are applicable anywhere you may find yourself trekking. For Tourism Concern contact details, see appendix A.

By following these simple guidelines, *you* can help preserve the unique environment and ancient cultures of the Himalaya.

PROTECT THE NATURAL ENVIRONMENT
Limit Deforestation. Make no open fires and discourage others from doing so on your behalf. Where water is heated by scarce firewood, use as little as possible. When possible, choose accommodation that uses kerosene or fuel-efficient wood stoves.

Remove Litter. Burn or bury paper and carry out all nondegradable litter. Graffiti are permanent examples of environmental pollution.

Keep Local Water Clean. Avoid using pollutants such as detergents in streams or springs. If no toilet facilities are available, make sure you are at least 30 meters away from water sources, and bury or cover wastes.

Plants. Plants should be left to flourish in their natural environment—taking cuttings, seeds, and roots is illegal in many parts of the Himalaya.

Help your guides and porters to follow conservation measures. The Himalayas may change you—please do not change them.

AS A GUEST, RESPECT LOCAL TRADITIONS, PROTECT LOCAL CULTURES, AND MAINTAIN LOCAL PRIDE

Photographs. When taking photographs, respect privacy—ask permission and use restraint.

Respect Holy Places. Preserve what you have come to see. Never touch or remove religious objects. Shoes should be removed when visiting temples.

Gifts. Giving to children encourages begging. A donation to a project, health center or school is a more constructive way to help.

Follow Local Customs. You will be accepted and welcomed if you follow local customs. Use only your right hand for eating and greeting. Do not share cutlery or cups and so forth. It is polite to use both hands when giving or receiving gifts.

Respect Local Etiquette. Respect for local etiquette earns you respect—loose, lightweight clothes are preferable to revealing shorts, skimpy tops, and tight-fitting action wear. Hand-holding or kissing in public are disliked by local people.

Observe Standard Charges. Observe standard food and bed charges, but do not condone overcharging. Remember when you're shopping that the bargains you buy may only be possible because of low income to others.

Value Local Traditions. Visitors who value local traditions encourage local pride and maintain local cultures—please help local people to gain a *realistic* view of life in Western countries.

Be patient, friendly, and sensitive. Remember—you are a guest.

TAKING SUPPER WITH TIBETAN NUNS

In the following extract from *Walking to the Mountain*, Wendy Teasdill describes her meeting with Tibetan nuns during ritual perambulation of Mount Kailash:

"Before tea was taken, one of them took a ladle and offered some of the hot liquid to each of the four points of the compass, with special attention to the direction of Kailash. Clouds drifted off the mountain and swam up the valleys, to

be followed always by more. The silt of the tsampa tea ran down my throat with all the joy of coming upon hot springs in a cold place, and wallowing in them. One of the women found a tiny fly in her cup, and removed it with floury fingers. 'Om mani padme hum,' she said as she did so. Never had I seen the principles of ahimsa (non-violence) enacted so naturally nor so particularly.

"There was a squall of rain, and we retreated into their white canvas tent, in which elongated triangles had been sewn together so as to flare out in every direction. The central pole was made from a natural branch, and the open doorflap was tucked up over a guy rope along which hung coloured prayer flags. The walls of the interior were shored up with sacks of tsampa, roots, yak dung, sheepskins, noodles, dried meat and a few treats. At the base of the pole a stone made a small altar. One of the nuns brought out a tin of brilliant synthetic orange sugar crystals. We all had to stretch out our hands, and into them she poured an even mountain each. We lapped up the stuff with quickly stained tongues, and by the time the rain had gone we all had an orange sun in the centre of our palms, and emerged marked as if by initiation into some feral rite."

—Wendy Teasdill

153

$\bullet$ 8 $\bullet$

FOREIGN CULTURES
Meeting the Locals

 THE TRAVEL AND TOURISM INDUSTRY IS RESPON-
sible for an enormous share in total world trade. With pro-
jected figures for the year 2010 envisaging almost one billion
tourists generating around U.S.$3,000 billion in turnover, it's
not surprising that this industry lays claim to being the largest in the world. Even in 1993, almost 500 million tourists generated a revenue
of some U.S.$300 billion.

While mass tourism is inundating ancient monuments, museums, and parks,
virgin land is being developed to cater to leisure pursuits, and local labor is being recruited to provide services.

Clearly, the expansion of this industry is set to have an enormous impact
on living standards, the environment, and local cultures. Chapter 7, "Minimum
Impact: Trekking and the Environment," discusses environmental choices and
ways for you to make a positive contribution to the protection of the environment at your destination.

Trekkers experience foreign cultures at ground level, sharing the trails with
the local community. However, the experience encompasses more than new scenery, food, language, and currency. It will also include different, perhaps profoundly different, cultural values and social interaction where life within
communities and families revolves around basic religious beliefs and social customs evolved over many centuries. Tradition may shape social etiquette, the rules
governing life within families and society, so that there will be acceptable (and
unacceptable) behavior for young and old, for male and female, in private and
public, and at religious sites.

Oriental symbol: **Noshi, Humility in Gifts;** Japanese

In this situation, the foreign trekker needs to be observant and respectful or risk indignation or worse. In theory, the list of "dos and don'ts" poses a minefield for the foreign visitor; in practice, as long as you make an effort to be courteous and learn as you go, locals will return your respect. For an idea of what to expect, take a look at the appropriate title for your destination in the excellent *Culture Shock* series published by Kuperard (see details in appendix B).

In many cases, your tact may be rewarded with fulsome hospitality and insights into local culture. What you learn—the differences you encounter—may change your view of life at home.

♦ CULTURE SHOCK ♦

Your reactions can be understandably confused when faced with a barrage of new experiences: climate, food, transport, accommodation, language, and customs. Once you touch down in a foreign culture, you are suddenly cut loose from your previously accepted points of reference in almost every sense. Perhaps the signs you see may be in an unintelligible script; the food stalls in the street market may serve dishes with spices or ingredients novel to the tongue; homes and temples may reek of incense; chatter and street noise resound yet you may comprehend very little; and greetings may be exchanged in novel ways.

There is a great deal of stimulation to absorb as you ease yourself into local life. You may relearn or encounter so many things you take for granted at home, such as dealing with currency, making do with acquired snippets of language, leaving shoes at the door before entering the house, using squat toilets instead of sit-down ones, or drawing the attention of crowds simply because of your foreign features.

One reaction to this overload of change can be an irritation that things are not the way they are at home. There can also be feelings of isolation and homesickness. Within a couple of weeks, most travelers have come to terms with the initial flurry of novel elements and can focus on aspects of particular interest.

As a trekker, you'll probably pass briefly through an urban center for a few days, then continue to the trailhead before starting the trek. Depending on the chosen route, your main contacts in the developing world may be villagers, farmers, and pastoralists in rural areas, or nomads in wilderness regions. Although English is spoken in more countries in the world than any other language, its use does not generally extend into remoter regions. A knowledge of local language or a willingness to communicate in basic phrases, however skimpy, can draw you into the homes and hearts of the locals and add a new dimension to your trek.

◆ LANGUAGE AND COMMUNICATION ◆

The skills for communicating with the people you meet can come from several sources. If you have the time, you'll do well by finding a native speaker for conversation practice in advance, or you can pick up what you need as you go and supplement with nonverbal cues (for instance, miming a request).

Don't feel put off by the apparent complexity of language. With an observant eye and attentive ear, you can pick out the essentials that will do the job for you, perhaps glowing inside with triumph when your greetings are returned or you get the numbers right when buying fruit at the market. The important issue is that you have a go. An interpreter or a companion with knowledge of the language will certainly provide insights, but if you relinquish all your direct language contact you'll be experiencing at least a portion of your trip at one remove.

LEARNING LANGUAGES

The complexity of language is an endlessly absorbing topic, ranging from the cursive grace of Arabic script on the dome of a mosque, to the staccato of Chinese street market chitchat, to breezy African greetings.

Learning before you go might entail taking night classes, attending a short immersion course at a language school, using a CD-ROM course on your computer at home, borrowing language courses at the local library, or finding a national of the country you intend to visit and asking him or her to engage in conversation. Even if you don't learn an enormous amount of book knowledge, the last method can still be useful because you learn first hand from an insider about the country.

Once you've arrived at your destination, another option is to ask around for someone (teachers or students at universities or schools are obvious choices) prepared to share a few hours with you and provide a basic view of the building blocks of their language: script, alphabet, pronunciation, stress, intonation, and common phrases you'd like to use. If you have already delved into the language in its written form in books such as "teach-yourself" primers, you'll lack the dimension of the spoken language, which is what trekkers will use repeatedly on their trek. Some countries, particularly those in Latin America, have specialist language schools where foreigners can learn the language for a few weeks or several months before setting off on their travels.

LANGUAGE ASSISTANCE

A phrase book provides ready-made questions and answers, which are fine as long as you wish to limit your queries to the scope of such phrases, which may be of limited application for trekkers. As long as you can read the script or the phonetics, I've found compact, pocket dictionaries to be very effective at supplementing stock phrases with customized words on the spot. If you can convey to locals you meet the fact that you have a particular interest or hobby, then you'll probably find them more responsive.

As a rule of thumb, most languages (English included) use a small proportion of their linguistic stockpile very heavily. As a stopgap measure to get started in a new language, assemble in a notebook your own skeleton vocabulary of some 100 words or phrases that cover the basics, such as greeting, thanking, apologizing, declining, accepting, requesting, route-finding, eating, drinking, sleeping, purchasing, and traveling. It won't win you awards for rhetoric, but it will make you dig deeper into the world around you and build your confidence.

USING LANGUAGE ON THE TRAIL

Once you are on the trail, you'll be using language to greet those you meet, chat about where you are going, and organize food and lodging. Learning to deal with local languages, dialects, and slang adds interest and color to your trek.

In many cultures it is considered bad form to disappoint a visitor's request or admit outright to a lack of information. If you seek directions, avoid questions that require a yes/no answer; otherwise, the dictates of propriety may mean that you receive an obliging confirmation for each direction you point out and every question posed.

It's best to phrase the question in general terms—for example, asking where (is the village), how (far is it), and what (is the trail like). If you already know the direction for a particular place you've just come from, such as village *X*, you can test the likely reliability of the information by asking directions to village *X;* then, assuming the response is clear, ask for directions to the village you wish to visit.

Stopping for a chat is a common social need all over the world. Guidebooks have their place for reference, but don't keep your nose buried in them all day and miss out on the enormous satisfaction to be gained from using language to make your own way.

The names adopted by cartographers may not be easily recognized by locals, who may very well use a different name or an abbreviated form. Also, just as you may find your way around your neighborhood without a map each time you go out the door, don't assume that those you meet, farmers, for example, wander around with more knowledge at their fingertips than is necessary for their needs.

NONVERBAL LANGUAGE

Words have no monopoly on the conveyance of meaning. Smiling not only exercises dozens of muscles in your face, but it also has a powerful effect on those around you, softening icy bureaucracy, reassuring suspicious villagers, and

Vaqueiro *(cowboy), Pantanal, Brazil*

possibly lifting flagging spirits. Equally appreciated is politeness, the accordance of equal respect, toward the families and possessions of those who follow different ways of life.

As a response to curiosity about your home life, you can show postcards or photos of home. Games, such as playing cards or chess, can keep kids (and adults) amused in playful cooperation for ages. Music and songs are good for cultural interaction. When you are tired or hungry or need information, summon your creative instincts and allow mime skills to come to the rescue. Drawing pictures with pen and paper can also get the message across, assuming your drawing skills are up to the task.

◆   MEETING, GREETING, AND VISITING   ◆

Traveling and trekking overseas you'll meet people of various beliefs and cultures in official and private capacities. One of the reasons for going in the first place is to experience a change of scene and culture. Initially you may feel rebuffed by the striking differences in dress, behavior, and social attitudes, so different to your life at home. You may also feel like a bystander, but this will change once you start mixing socially with the locals and are invited to join them. At the same time you'll learn in closer detail about different approaches to social interaction.

TIME

In *Brazilian Adventure,* an account of exploration in Brazil in the 1930s, the British author Peter Fleming mused about time: "Delay in Brazil is a climate. You live in it. You can't get away from it. There is nothing to be done about it . . . a man in a hurry will be miserable in Brazil."

If you are used to punctuality, deadlines, appointments, and the trappings of time management, the developing world will stand much of this on its head. Be prepared for very flexible timetables, buses that leave soon (enough), invitations for a meal on a day (not at a time), and bureaucratic procedures that grind and grind. On analysis, as long as what is to be done is eventually done, this relaxed attitude about time is considerably healthier than a blind hurry to save time for its own sake. Be patient and drop your mind into neutral while you adjust—or be miserable.

GREETINGS AND INTRODUCTIONS

In many cultures it is essential good manners to greet someone, for instance, to wish good health or peace when you meet and a safe journey when you leave. Take your cues from those around you, and follow their gestures (for example, bowing in Japan) and speech (such as the phrase *salaam aleikum* ["peace be upon you"], used in Islamic countries).

Learning and using the appropriate language for these occasions is generally well received by older members of the community (whose accumulated years merit greater deference) and, in conjunction with modest dress, by officials (who like their standing to be recognized). In rural areas, a visit to the chief or head of a village is advisable to establish your credentials before making camp nearby or drawing water from the community supply.

Temple lodging, Koya-san, Japan

The shaking of hands, common in the Western world, is often replaced elsewhere with other gestures that do not involve touching, such as the folded hands greeting in India or Nepal or placing your right hand over your heart in Islamic countries. The best approach is to watch for the norms of behavior. If the men do not shake hands with women, as is often the case in the Islamic world, then follow suit. Children are accorded less formal greetings, but they should not be patted on the head, especially in Buddhist countries, where the crown of the head is considered a spiritual locus.

VISITING AT HOME

If you are lucky you'll be invited to visit or even stay in someone's home. Just as you are interested in your host's life and surroundings, you can expect similar curiosity about your own home life. I cannot recommend too strongly the benefit of foreign language skills as a means to win friends. However rudimentary your skills, the fact that you have made the effort will instantly raise your standing in the eyes of locals. A home visit is an excellent opportunity to have a go with the language and tap into local goodwill.

Don't be afraid to ask for guidance on correct local etiquette or for instruction in the use of household objects. The usual reaction is for the entire family to beam with delight and energetically give you a crash course in being a local.

Part of the learning process may require a new perspective on etiquette we may take for granted at home. For most Japanese, it's a mysterious and distasteful sight to see someone blowing their nose into a handkerchief. Why does someone blow the contents of their nose into a piece of cloth and then carry this around in their pocket? If part of a room is devoted to a shrine, you can assume it deserves respect and ask your host about the specific ways in which this is expressed.

Conversation may quickly settle on topics such as your employment, family, marital status, possessions, and earnings. In many cases, these questions are asked as a ritual politeness, not necessarily out of a desire to know the exact details or figures. You can choose to answer in lengthy detail or in general terms or simply move to another topic. Photos from home always offer good scope for conversation.

Be tactful with indications of wealth and possessions because they can distort your image. Calculation of your earnings may seem very high when translated into local currency, but it's worth pointing out the high cost of living in your home country and the much smaller amount remaining once expenditures have been deducted.

When your host shows you around the house, it's fine to show your admiration of furnishings, crafts, and produce, but overly effusive appreciation can prompt the owner to feel obliged to present you with the object of your admiration, even if it is of considerable value. One way to politely decline such an offer is to indicate the small size of your pack (if the object is large) or tactfully convert the offer to something less costly and bulky, such as a small handicraft item or food.

Don't forget to express your thanks for the hospitality as you leave and perhaps write a note when you return home. A small gift of a local delicacy or fruit is often better appreciated by wealthier hosts who might be offended by payment, but use your discretion.

Eating and Drinking

Some of the best meals on your travels will be those shared with fellow travelers or by invitation to a private home.

As explained in the health section in Chapter 4, "In Good Shape: Staying Healthy," in many parts of the world, especially Asia, use of the left hand and a washdown with water are the norm after using the toilet. For this reason, where food is eaten with the fingers, you'll find that the *right* hand is always used; and the left hand is kept out of the way. In this case, water for washing hands is usually provided before and after the meal. In China and Japan, chopsticks are convenient and not too hard to master. Elsewhere you'll either use bread or similar scoops or cutlery.

Hindu religion rules that food is sullied if touched by those of a different caste or religion. In this case, when sharing a meal your lips should not touch the food of others, and if drinking out of a shared mug or bottle, pour the liquid directly into your mouth without touching the rim with your lips.

Your host will ply you with food. Tucking in is fine but remember that an empty plate is the signal to provide a refill. Leaving a little on your plate is a pleasing sign for your host that you've been fed enough.

If you are offered food and you aren't hungry, or you think it might be past its prime, then you have several options to decline gracefully. You can acknowledge the offer as a kind thought and state that you've just eaten. Often, though, this will be taken as politeness, and you may be urged to eat. In China, for example, it is customary to decline several times before accepting the offer of food.

You can also plead indisposition: doctor's advice against alcohol (for a weak liver) or against food (for an upset stomach). Or you can simply take a bite of what is offered and please your host by proclaiming it good. It is not expected that you will polish off the entire dish, but you should never offend the offerer with a gruff rebuttal. Always show your appreciation at the end of the meal; propose a toast, and praise the host and family for hospitality of such unexpected lavishness.

I have lost count of memorable hosted meals. In Sapporo, Hokkaido, I was mystified as to why a Korean restaurant owner was so keen to invite me to a lavish hotpot dinner until he moved in for the kill in the alcoholic haze at the end of the meal and requested the recipe for Yorkshire Pudding, an English specialty (duly posted to him later).

In Inner Mongolia, I landed up in a remote lakeside community recommended by a Chinese acquaintance. The bus conductor corralled the local official to organize a stupendous fish banquet, course after course of fish dishes from the local fish farm. As empty bottles lined up in marching order down the table, toasts and songs became more and more bizarre: wonderful, throaty Mongolian lyrics from the host, a rendition of *Twinkle Twinkle Little Star* from the local teacher, and my contribution of the first verse of *God Save the Queen*.

Staying Over

In many parts of Asia and the Far East, street shoes are not worn inside the house, but slipped off at the doorstep. Inside you either pad around in your socks or use house slippers. When seated, take care that your feet do not point at or touch others.

Bathing can also be different, for example in Japan you soap yourself outside the tub; only when you are scrubbed squeaky clean can you climb into *ofuro* (the bath). In Malaysia and Indonesia, dip water out of the *mandi* (a large water tank) with a ladle and splash it over yourself—immersing inside the *mandi* is a major cultural faux pas.

THE KINDNESS OF STRANGERS

"Walking along a remote and desolate track in north-west Iceland, I passed a fish farm. Uri, the owner of the farm, hadn't set eyes on a tourist for nearly a year, and he came hurtling after me in his car to invite me back to his house where I was given a bath in a clean fish tank filled with geothermal water! Uri and his wife then gave me a delicious Icelandic meal, put me up for the 'night' in a hut, and the next day took me along the rest of the road, to the start of the trek. A restoration of faith in humanity!"

—*Graeme Cornwallis*

VISITING RELIGIOUS SITES

Religion is a keystone for many cultures, and thoughtless dress, behavior, or photography is insulting. When visiting religious sites, you should treat their precincts, custodians, and worshipers with respect.

If admission for non-Hindus is allowed in a Hindu temple, remove your

Pilgrims, Okuno-in Temple, Japan

shoes (and other leather items, if required), and observe any regulations restricting access to the inner sanctum. In Buddhist temples, remove your shoes and follow pilgrim circuits in a clockwise direction. In the Himalayan region, white scarves (known as *kata* and obtainable at or near Buddhist temples) are presented as a sign of respect when meeting the local abbot.

If entry into a mosque is granted, shoes should be removed and dress should be conservative. Women should cover their head, arms, and legs, and men should wear full-length trousers (no shorts) and long-sleeved shirts.

◆ RECEIVING AND GIVING ◆

When you are offered something, respond with courtesy and tact. Turning down food or assistance outright can be considered a personal slight or inferred as an assessment of inferior quality.

Formal acceptance of a special gift may be best expressed by receiving with both hands and a nod of acknowledgment. For minor presents, such as a pen or receiving change at a shop, use your right hand (this applies especially in those countries where the left hand is considered unclean).

Although spoken thanks are commonly used in the West, elsewhere they may be implied in formal acceptance and reserved for less casual occasions where a favor has been extended rather than for a straightforward commercial transaction.

Reciprocating kindness with a gift requires tact and understanding. In some cases you will be offered hospitality or accommodation with no thought for remuneration. In this case, offering cash could damage your host's pride and possibly undermine the original intent. If you do offer a cash gift, in many cultures (especially Asian ones) it is appropriate to present it in an envelope. Perhaps your heartfelt thanks and a follow-up letter are more appropriate, or you can provide your host family with a few language lessons or buy them a selection of fruit from the market to be presented before you leave.

In many parts of the world, but especially in Asia, it is customary to play down the value of any gift you present as a mere trifle, and, conversely, it is usual to politely refuse a proffered present several times before acceptance.

BEGGING

In many countries the dominant view of Westerners is that they possess enormous wealth derived from a superculture. Sharing or giving away goods on a grand scale can produce the impression that the visitor's culture has such an abundance that it can fulfill virtually any request. This can in turn encourage locals to beg from light-skinned travelers who are clearly identifiable as a potential source of gain. Over the years the actions of visitors set the mold for begging. As a visitor yourself, you should be aware that you will be part of the continuing cycle.

Travel in rural areas in the developing countries can provide quite a jolt when you are confronted with apparently primitive living conditions. However, in many cases the inhabitants lead their lives on a subsistence basis with sufficient food, clothing, and shelter. Because they live outside a cash economy they may not possess the material goods of Westerners, such as videos, washing machines, and cars, but they also lack the concomitant problems of a Western lifestyle such as street crime and pollution.

One knee-jerk response to these subsistence conditions is the desire to assuage guilt feelings by showering the inhabitants with gifts of money, cigarettes, pens, and other presents. Although well meant, this action can quickly subvert their pride and lead to dependency on handouts or begging.

Giving pens, sweets, and other presents to children does nothing in the long term except encourage them to persistently badger for handouts. Rather than pens, what may be lacking is the schooling; and as for sweets, they generate the problem of dental decay with little hope of treatment. Rather than give the kids handouts, see if you can teach or exchange games and songs. If you want to provide pens, give them to the schoolteacher.

In some countries beset by endemic poverty, those who are destitute, homeless, or sick have no means for survival other than begging. The situation is complicated by the existence of career beggars who are not genuine.

Given the scale of the problem, you won't be able to address more than a fraction of those involved, but you may wish to give whatever you feel you can afford as a daily or weekly sum to those beggars you consider genuinely destitute. Rather than donate money, you may want to supply food instead, especially for child beggars who are often coerced into working for a group overseer who takes most of their daily earnings. Alternatively, you could decide to help at the community level either in person or by donating to charities and educational, agricultural, and conservation projects. Contact details for a selection of such organizations are listed in appendix A.

BRIBES

As an extension of the concept of giving on an official level, you may come across bribes, known in different parts of the world by various names, such as *la mordida* ("bite") in Mexico or *baksheesh* in the Middle East and most of the Indian subcontinent. Whatever the slang term used, bribes are demanded by officials as a little "extra" so that your visa, your border crossing, your currency exchange papers, your (alleged) traffic offense, or similar requirements and events are processed. The request might be aimed at cash or at goods, such as cigarettes or alcohol.

Whatever you do, don't attempt to explicitly bribe an official before you know if that really *is* what's at stake. If you misread the situation and attempt to bribe an upright official, that could in itself be a serious offense.

Bribes are rarely referred to as such, so your best approach is to circle around them using other terms. You can innocently inquire how the problem (delay, irregularity with papers, and so forth) is normally solved or perhaps ask if there is a processing "fee."

It will be up to you to decide if the bribe request is half-hearted or serious. At one very remote, rural police station in South America I was asked to contribute to the station's pencil fund and, in the same breath, was assured that my stay would be troublefree.

It's best not to encourage the bribery habit. Some officials merely try it on as a personal scam and back down if you don't comply or show signs of taking the matter to their superior. As a service to those that follow you, put up at least some good-humored token resistance.

Always keep cool and play for time. The easiest bribe mark is a traveler in a hurry, rather than one ready to sit in the corner of the office reading a novel for a few hours. Claiming that you are low on money or never carry foreign cash because it's too risky may be enough to convince the official that you are a lost cause.

If this doesn't work, then you'll need to quantify the sum involved, edging the conversation into ballpark figures. Make it show that you are depressed at the thought of such a high sum. Don't stimulate the official's appetite by acceding to the first demand, which may be ten or more times the amount you can finally agree upon. Once you reach an agreement, try and extract the right amount from your pocket without revealing a large wad of bills.

◆ BARGAINING ◆

One major bone of contention frequently discussed among foreign travelers is the "right" price. In many parts of the world, foreign visitors are charged different rates. Different usually means higher, although a pleasing exception is a scheme used by some Japanese Youth Hostels to give foreigners a substantial discount because their hosts recognize that Japan's cost of living is high compared to that of the home countries of some foreign hostelers (for example, indigent Brits or impoverished Americans).

Sometimes the higher rates are encouraged at a government level; in other cases, the locals set rates either as they think fit or in line with the estimated equivalent rates visitors would have to pay in their home country.

Prices set by locals for foreign visitors may follow local standards and regulate themselves according to competition. Contact with travelers can also induce a succession of price hikes, reflecting an increasing awareness of the visitor's relative wealth. Taken to extremes, this can lead to price distortion, where, for example, the price for local lodging might be equated with the price for a deluxe hotel in the visitor's home country.

The best rule of thumb is to consider if you are receiving value for money in relation to local standards. Overcharging means you are not getting what you pay for. The reason could be that what you want simply is not obtainable (or only obtainable as a hugely expensive import), you are faced with a greedy individual trying to take you for a ride, or you are expected to find a compromise price between what you wish to pay and what the seller wishes to charge—also known as bargaining.

Westerners used to the fixed-price concept usually require some mental sharpening to get to grips with the concept of bargaining, which is an essential ritual in everyday life in many parts of the world. It is worth emphasizing that this ritual involves a mutually agreed exchange: there is no point expecting to receive something for nothing.

Before entering into discussion, find out about the going rate for the goods (such as food and souvenirs) or service (such as transport and lodging) you need. One option is to chat to fellow travelers; another source would be to spend time sampling prices—for example, a quick pass through the market or a brief question to a taxi driver. This will also give you the chance to find out if the price is inclusive or exclusive of extras. If you use any form of intermediary (for example, a taxi driver taking you to a hotel or to a souvenir shop of their choice), you can automatically assume they are seeking commission from the shop and expect to pay a hefty percentage on top of the price quoted.

Traders set the "mark-up" on their goods or services at different percentages depending on location—there is clearly less overhead when running a bicycle-barrow on the street and more when renting a shop.

If you know what you want, it helps to set aside your specific interest and circle around casually looking at a few items, before returning to the item of interest. Always act as if you are happy to walk away—if you shout with glee it's obvious that your heart is set on your choice at just about any price.

When you are given a price, you can counter with a comment about the expense and offer to pay less—if you've already researched the price range, you'll know the rough target; if not, you can try the percentage that seems right to you (try between 25 and 50 percent of the asking price) and assess the response.

Throughout the discussion keep cool and focused and retain your humor. The trader may use various tactics: intimidation or indignation, cajoling with eulogies of praise for quality, switching (for example, offering an inferior product or room at the price previously discussed for a superior one), or a combination of these skills. For your part, you may want to show that your buying interest is ebbing: inspect the goods, point out any flaws, and voice doubts about its suitability for your requirements.

If you cannot agree on the price at this stage, you may decide you cannot afford it and start to walk away. This may prompt the seller to beckon or call you back for a special price either matching or close to your last price. Once you reach agreement on the price, keep your eye on the ball to make sure the deal is worked out in full.

◆ LOCAL PURCHASES ◆

During your travels, you'll probably be tempted by local arts and crafts, such as woven textiles, soapstone carvings, carpets, and much more. By checking whether or not the goods are locally produced, you will be able to encourage traditional arts and crafts rather than cheap imports from abroad. Note that some goods, such as carpets from the Indian subcontinent, may be produced by children and women working in conditions of near bondage in sweatshops.

As defined by the Convention of International Trade in Endangered Species of Wild Flora & Fauna (CITES), trading in wildlife products made from endangered species is illegal. Products of this kind include ivory (from elephant, narwhal, whale, and walrus), rhino horn, sea turtle goods (whole shells, stuffed specimens, leather items, soup, cream, tortoiseshell jewelry, combs, spectacle frames, and boxes), various kinds of furs (commonly blacklisted species include seal, polar bear, sea otter, tiger, jaguar, leopard, snow leopard, ocelot, margay, and tiger cat), butterflies, various bird products (feathers, skins, and mounted specimens), orchids, and cacti. Apart from the risk of prosecution if you return home with this sort of merchandise, you will also be trading in extinction.

◆ PHOTOGRAPHY ◆

The choice of photographic subject matter and its acceptability for the local culture also demands sensitivity to possible impact.

The political norms at your destination may be quite different from those in your home country. Various governments around the globe prohibit photography in "sensitive" areas. Depending on the country, you'll be risking trouble (at least a fine or a spell in jail) if you click away at military bases, bridges, airfields, industrial centers, and refineries. In this age of spy satellite technology, it's debatable whether or not travelers pose much of an espionage threat, and in some cases one suspects that antiquated regulations are kept on the books to provide local security with job justification. Photographing subjects that show the country to be technically less developed can also merit your detention. In the former Soviet Union, my snapping of impressive Siberian steam locomotives was firmly rebuked for this reason.

Enthusiastic subjects: Samoan kids, Aunu'u Island, American Samoa (**Deanna Swaney photo**)

On a social and personal level, photography requires tact and understanding. For religious, cultural, or personal reasons, some locals may not wish to be photographed—respect their viewpoint and their dignity.

Photographers fall into two broad categories: those who feel ill at ease when taking close-up portraits and either forego them or tote a zoom lens, and those who approach the subject for permission to take a photo. My own feelings sway between these two categories: sometimes I'm happy to forget the picture because it is such an obvious intrusion; at other times, permission materializes of its own accord when the acquaintance suggests a photo.

The best method is to establish a rapport with the subject and ask if you can take a picture. Most people react amicably to genuine interest as opposed to the impression that they might be set up for ridicule or curiosity value. If you promise to send a picture to your subject later, make good on your promise.

Telephoto lenses offer the opportunity to take unobtrusive pictures from a distance, but if you are observed in the act your behavior may be regarded with understandable animosity or suspicion.

On the subject of appropriate action, ponder the following possibly "super-photographic" tale:

"Hoping to bag some good cultural photos for a book project in Bolivia, I successfully snapped a few pictures of the mercado de hechicería, *the witches' market in La Paz. One of the vendors, an older woman, saw me and angrily warned that I'd regret the indiscretion—they aren't particularly happy with flighty foreigners taking snapshots of their rather bizarre wares. A month later, while I was traveling by boat on the Brazilian Amazon, all my exposed film of Bolivia—about 30 rolls—was stolen and tossed into the river. Of course this could have been a simple coincidence, but you never know. . . ."*

—Deanna Swaney

Some locals, for example in the remoter parts of Asia and Africa, have found they can supplement their income by posing for portrait photos. If you are happy with this arrangement, then avoid squabbles by agreeing on the price *before* the photo is taken. I have divided feelings on this type of fee because photos of this kind can form a passive dependency on tourism and reduce interaction to monetary transaction.

Instant photography with a Polaroid camera is a mixed blessing. It's quick, inexpensive, and easy and requires no postage; and as long as you carry a plentiful supply of film and are willing to dish out pictures, it can make instant friends or open doors. On the other hand, unless it is used very sparingly, it awakens expectations for more of the same "instant photo service" from any passing travelers. Misunderstandings may arise when locals encourage travelers to take photos. If the locals are expecting to receive prints, travelers using 35mm film then face a tough time trying to explain why no instant image issues from the camera.

At religious sites, such as mosques, temples, and monasteries, respect photography rules. These can vary from a total ban (particularly in Islamic countries), to a "fee scheme," to no rules at all. Certain shrines or sacred images may be off limits for photos, and, even if not discouraged, bear in mind that the use of a flash at religious gatherings can be highly disruptive.

◆   LOCAL INTERACTION   ◆

Throughout the world, a wide variety of traditions, beliefs, and religions have molded the roles of men and women. This may create attitudes toward gender and sexual interaction that differ profoundly from those in your own country.

For example, male dominance in the society at your destination may extend a high degree of control over women that constrains their movements and behavior to defined norms. Equally, different cultures have different restrictions on male behavior, especially in regard to contact with unmarried or married women, and gays or bisexuals may be low profile in public but an accepted facet of private life.

Some travelers feel that it is their prerogative to do as they please regardless of their surrounding culture. In many cases, however, they fail to understand that local outrage is not aimed at what they do in private but represents objection to their blatant show of disrespect to their hosts in public. If you feel you cannot adapt your behavior, then the best solution is to choose a destination where both you and the locals can feel at ease.

Bear in mind that even if you do not agree with some aspects of social interaction, you will have a tough time if you cannot adjust. What you wear or don't wear, how you make contact, and how you respect the social and religious etiquette of your host culture will be of prime importance for the enjoyment of your travels.

For an idea of what to expect at your destination, take a look at the appropriate title in the excellent *Culture Shock* series published by Kuperard (see details of this series in appendix B). More resources and references for women travelers are included in appendices A and B.

COUPLES

For couples, it is wise to take your cue from local custom: observe how local couples interact in public. What you may consider as light, amorous play behavior between sexes, such as necking, kissing, or holding hands in public, may be an affront to religious precepts or socially accepted decorum in your host country. Although you may see, for example, members of the same sex holding hands in public in Mediterranean Europe, Asia, or the Middle East, this is common social contact and doesn't necessarily indicate sexual preferences.

In general, couples are well received, and mixed couples of similar age will usually be assumed to be married.

SOLO TRAVELERS

In societies where unattached males or females normally remain under the supervision of their families, the idea of solo foreign travel for leisure (as opposed to work or family visits) can be a matter of concern. If you are young, there may be surprise that you have been allowed to travel without supervision; if you are of a mature age, there may be suspicion that you are unwanted or a misfit at home.

You may face a barrage of questions as to why you travel and like to travel alone or why you aren't married (or accompanied by your spouse). In many societies, it's normal to ask personal questions and equally normal (if you don't have an answer at hand or wish to leave the matter alone) to smile and simply ignore or switch the topic.

Solo Female Traveler

If you are a woman traveling solo, you'll probably be questioned about your reasons for traveling alone. It helps to explain the purpose of your trip—that you are traveling to meet friends and relatives, completing academic or medical research, or traveling for professional reasons.

In some societies it is a traditional assumption that unmarried women stay under the protection of their family until they marry, thereby authorizing the protective role to be transferred to their husband. As a visitor, you may feel indignant that women in some countries and cultures draw the short straw for equal status with men, but mounting a crusade to tell the locals how to change their traditions can provoke hostile reaction. In many parts of the world your appearance on the scene as a solo traveler can in itself be the subject of concern because it puts into question your expected womanly links with family, marriage, and children, and may even imply that you are an outcast for social or moral reasons.

Persistent sexual innuendo and pestering, almost always occurring as unwanted male attention directed at solo female travelers, can be a problem. It can be useful to create the impression that you have plenty of male backup available. Carry photos of your "husband" and your "brothers." Make sure that the photos have a neutral backdrop, nothing too opulent or flashy that might infer that you are made of money. Consider wearing a wedding ring; nothing of great value, but large enough to be recognized.

Passenger boat on the Brazilian Amazon (Deanna Swaney photo)

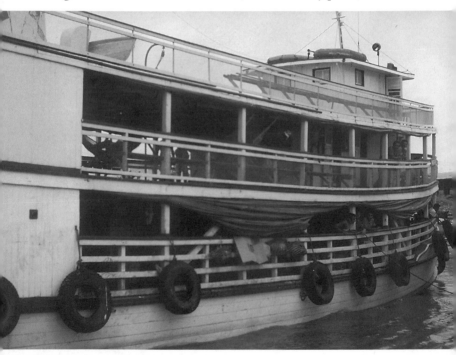

You may find it handy to know a word or two to deflect unwanted attention. Learn the equivalent of "no," "go away," and "don't touch," and for good measure add a stock of clear phrases that indicate, for example, you are "not interested," and "want to be left in peace/alone."

Apart from teaming up with another traveler, you can steer yourself into socializing on your own terms. Choose accommodation where you can mix on a personal basis—hostels, local bed and breakfasts, or home stays. Tourist offices and universities (especially the language department) can usually arrange for a good-will guide or student "buddy," keen to show a foreigner around and improve language skills. If you have a preference, you usually can request either a male or female guide.

Solo Male Traveler
As a solo male traveler, you may be considered an oddity, especially if you are of marriageable age yet neither travel with a partner nor assign priority to marriage. As indicated in "Solo Female Traveler," earlier in this section, it helps to provide some sort of reason and background to your presence—a special interest in the country and a prospective partner at home. In some societies, a single male traveler is viewed with suspicion and considered a threat. In other cultures, you will be seen as in need of life direction, which some people in your host country may be willing to supply.

The concern to help you run your life is often genuine. During a trip to the Middle East, I applied for a permit extension from a delightfully hospitable police chief at a mountain village in northern Syria who supplied the requisite stamp, refreshments, and an offer to act as a marriage broker.

DRESS AND PHYSICAL CONTACT
Observe and adapt to the dress code in your destination country, not just in the cities but also in rural areas, which can be more conservative.

The Female Perspective
For religious or cultural reasons, the uncovering of a woman's head, shoulders, arms, or legs can cause consternation or provoke harassment. This applies particularly in Islamic countries.

If you are in doubt, cover up. Avoid thin material or low-cut clothing; in some countries this is considered almost the equivalent of appearing naked in public. Skintight sportswear can also be considered provocative. A scarf or neat square of cloth draped over the head is standard dress code in some countries and may be deemed compulsory headgear when entering religious sites. Arms and shoulders, thighs, knees, and ankles should also be covered.

Looking into the eyes of a male in some countries can be considered an invitation to dalliance. Dark glasses lessen contact. Handshaking can also pose problems if the male considers that a shake can perhaps lead to a more substantial grip. In some countries, placing your right hand on your heart or making a folded-hands greeting will sidestep the issue.

Your physical appearance can also be a source of questioning amazement:

"The fact that I was a woman walking alone in Tibet was immaterial. When I occasionally came across nomads, the reaction was generally: 'Poo, poomo?' Are you a boy or girl? No matter that I had a waist-length plait; most nomad men had one or two plaits at least. No, it was the fact that my plait was ginger that threw them off kilter. I was treated with great kindness and courtesy nonetheless, and sometimes I wondered if I had not become androgynous; my periods stopped for six months and I didn't look in a mirror for three."

—Wendy Teasdill

The Male Perspective

For men the same sensitivity to local cues is advisable as for women. Stripping down to shorts and T-shirt or no shirt may be fine in the privacy of your room but considered unacceptable and disrespectful (to yourself and those around you) in public, especially when visiting religious sites or meeting officials. In public, long trousers and a long-sleeved shirt are usually more suitable. Take your cue from the locals.

Western travelers should be aware that some cultures closely guard their women against unauthorized contact with males. Authorized contact takes place when a male relative or friend is present. If you approach a woman in public, it may be considered an extreme insult and can trigger a threatening situation. Although younger women may have little influence in some cultures, the oldest woman often wields considerable matriarchal power within the household and family, and the traveler will earn approval for the measure of respect shown to her.

SEX

The wonders of global communications have put video, TV, and film within the reach of many societies that can view a lifestyle far removed from their own values. Curiosity about the Western world is fed by a lucrative trade in media products, mostly derived from Hollywood and porn movies. This can result in a grossly unbalanced portrayal of Western men surviving on violence and Western women living on a diet of sex, sex, and more sex. The total mismatch between screen characters and everyday life in the Western world provides powerful distortions.

This image of Western women may attract local males. Whereas local culture may consider a Western woman sleeping with a local man as an acceptable facet of the lust myth, the opposite scenario (Western man sleeping with local woman) can have dire consequences if it occurs outside wedlock. For example, where sexes are kept segregated and marriages are arranged, family honor is impugned if an unmarried daughter loses her virginity. Relatives may feel bound to exact blood revenge to restore family honor. Under Islamic law, adultery is an insult against Allah and punishable by flogging or even stoning to death.

Consequences may not be so drastic in every case, but remember that a foreign fling or sexual encounter with someone from a different cultural background may be dealing at rapid pace with different sets of values and feelings on both sides. Be sure to use high-quality condoms to protect against AIDS and venereal disease.

THE GAY ANGLE

In various parts of the world, open discussion of gay relationships or physical displays of affection between gays are treated as commonplace or may barely raise an eyebrow; in others it is not countenanced in public.

If you are traveling overseas and want advice on the gay scene, resources are provided in appendix A.

◆ RETURNING HOME ◆

By the time you are on your way home, you may find your life has turned full circle and the experience of homecoming is in itself another form of culture shock.

Give jet lag its due, and take it easy: allow a week to physically accept that you've returned and a month or so to corral your emotions. If you suffer health problems even several months after returning, be sure to visit your doctor and, most importantly, remind him or her that you were overseas.

If you are lucky, friends and family will be interested to listen to your tales and discuss your experiences. At the same time, they will want to fill you in on events at their end while you were away. Perhaps because we all assign different priorities to events in our lives, these two approaches don't always overlap equally. You may have trouble giving your attention to domestic matters while your mind still wanders abroad. Your listeners, especially those who have not traveled abroad, may have a very short attention span, possibly limited to those parts of your discussion that mirror media portrayal of the country you've just visited.

Take stock of what you have learned and achieved since you set out. What feels good about being back home? What do you miss from your travels? Have you become interested in learning a language or keeping up with political or environmental issues abroad (see appendix B for useful resources)? Do you feel differently about material possessions? Give yourself time to address questions such as these, which may give you personal answers to the attractions and rewards of travel and trekking abroad.

EMERGENCIES
Prepared and Alert

TO MAXIMIZE YOUR CHANCES OF A SAFE TREK, take time to plan and prepare, matching equipment and experience to the chosen route. Always have a contingency plan in case things go wrong, and take out appropriate insurance that provides solid coverage for both trekking and general travel (see chapter 2, "First Steps: Travel Arrangements").

◆ TREKKING EMERGENCIES ◆

Where possible, leave details of your group, your destination, and your estimated trek length in trailhead or mountain hut log books, or lodge an intentions form with a responsible authority or person, such as the ranger office at a park headquarters. This provides a healthy chance that you will be missed and searched for if you experience mishap and fail to turn up. Just as importantly, don't forget to sign off or report that you've completed the trek; otherwise, you may needlessly take up the time of the rescue teams and possibly endanger their lives.

Unless you are very experienced and know the area and the vagaries of its weather well, never trek solo.

EMERGENCY GEAR AND SUPPLIES
Always carry the Ten Essentials recommended by The Mountaineers: extra clothing, extra food, sunglasses, pocket knife, fire starter or candle, flashlight (with extra bulb and batteries), first-aid kit, waterproof matches, a map, and a compass. My preference is to supplement these essentials with an emergency repair

---

Symbolic spirit: **Unkatahe, Goddess Against Disease;** North American Indian

kit, a whistle, and a survival bag. All emergency gear and supplies should be carried in one bag and reserved strictly for emergency only.

Learn basic skills or brush up old ones before you go, and be sure you know how to use your equipment. The farther you go into the back of beyond, the more you will need to rely on your own resources if you get in trouble.

Food and Drink. Carry high-energy food such as trail mix (dried fruit and nuts), chocolate bars, glucose sweets, and a couple of dehydrated meals and soups. Keep it packed away separately for use only in an emergency. Don't be tempted at other times during your trek to nibble on this supply, as it may prove to be lifesaving food. Half a dozen fishhooks and a good length of fishing line packed into an empty film canister weigh next to nothing and could supplement the day's emergency food rations.

Always carry enough to drink, particularly at high altitudes or in hot or humid climates, so that you don't suffer from dehydration. Treat suspect water supplies by boiling or by using a water filter, purification tablets, or tincture.

Waterproof matches are useful for lighting a stove or fire in wet and windy weather, and half a candle will provide light and save batteries.

Warm Clothing. Your day's trekking may start in the warm sun, but a quick change in weather conditions or a delay reaching camp could leave you feeling chilled or worse. If you've been caught in a cloudburst, you'll appreciate dry clothing (such as a pullover, woolly hat, and pair of socks) to ward off hypothermia.

Survival Bag. A survival bag, made from brightly colored (for easy visibility), thick polyethylene, is large enough to completely cover the body. It is also waterproof and prevents heat loss. Lightweight "space blankets" are less durable.

Navigation and Signaling Equipment. For basic navigation you'll need a map and compass or, should no map be available for the area, at least a compass. Some compasses are manufactured with a sighting mirror that, apart from its navigational application, can also be used for signaling. A whistle is also useful for raising an alarm, especially in poor visibility. A flashlight is essential, not only for signaling but also for lighting up the path if you are caught on the trail after nightfall and for nighttime map-reading.

In remote areas, especially in dense or featureless terrain, you might pack a couple of smoke bombs or flares to draw the attention of an air search.

First-Aid Kit. Be sure to always carry a complete medicine kit (see "Medical Checklist" in chapter 4, "In Good Shape: Staying Healthy"). Attend a first-aid course and refer to appropriate manuals (see appendix B).

Emergency Repair Kit. To repair fabric tears, faulty zippers, and similar items, carry a supply of safety pins, a needle and strong thread, adhesive-backed tape, and rubber bands.

GETTING LOST

If you get lost, the cardinal rule is not to panic. As soon as you suspect you're off track, stop and think. Trace your last known point on the map and estimate the time elapsed and direction taken since you left it. Examine your surroundings and try to relate features to the map. Once you have clearly identified a feature, you can use your compass to fix your position. If visibility is very bad or progress impossible, seek shelter and wait for help. For a discussion on timing and navigation, see chapter 5, "Setting the Pace: Trek Preparation, Technique, and Navigation."

If a person disappears from your group, stop immediately and attempt to make contact by shouting or using a whistle. If there is no response, you should organize a search, but make sure that the search party keeps within sight and sound and agrees on specific signals to indicate respectively their whereabouts to each other, any decision to call off the search, the successful location of the missing companion, and the occurrence of a secondary emergency within the search party. Leave one person behind at the original stopping point, just in case the straggler turns up on the route.

EMERGENCY ACTION

The scope of this book does not cover the specifics of first-aid. Enroll in a first-aid course. Supplement the first-aid skills acquired in such a course by reading authoritative manuals, some of which are listed in appendix B. If a member of your party is injured and immobile, your only option may be to seek medical help. If there are only two in the group, then it may be necessary for the uninjured companion to leave and seek help while the victim stays behind.

In this case, the victim should be placed in a sheltered location, given a survival bag (preferably including some brightly colored piece of gear for easy identification from a distance), food and drink, and a whistle and headlight for signaling.

To move the victim for a short distance on your own, use the cradle method: place one arm under the thighs and the other under the armpit. If you are in a group, a stretcher can be rigged using poles or hiking staffs slid through jackets or a poncho. If a neck or spine injury is suspected, the victim should not be moved unless in danger—if you have to do this on your own, do not bend or twist the head and trunk, which must be kept aligned.

Take careful note of the victim's location, using distinctive landmarks and a compass bearing for future reference. Although the situation will be stressful, don't be panicked into causing another accident as you hasten (rather than race) for help.

Depending on the trekking region, help may be available at villages, park headquarters, or mountain huts where it may be possible to radio for assistance.

Helicopter rescue is extremely expensive. In some countries, payment must be assured before the rescue can proceed: yet another cogent argument for adequate travel insurance.

Exercise great care when you are at a rescue helicopter landing site. The violent rotor down-draught can easily displace objects and cause injury. At the landing site, remove any loose vegetation such as leaves or branches, and secure your equipment. Kneel down while the landing is in progress and stay away from the tail rotor. If landing is not possible and you are to be lifted off by the helicopter, let the winchline make contact with the ground first to discharge its accumulated static—otherwise you'll receive a strong electric shock.

Report. Your report on an emergency must be precise. Let the rescuers know the following:

❑ Your name
❑ The name of the injured person
❑ When the accident occurred
❑ The exact location
❑ The type and extent of injuries
❑ Treatment applied, if any
❑ The prevailing weather and any problems with access to the location

If the information is being relayed over the phone or radio, ask the person at the other end to repeat the details so that you are sure they have been understood. Before ending the connection, ask first if more details or discussion are required, and ask again for agreement before you end the connection. This double-check is very important to counteract possible communication confusion through poor reception, foreign languages, or local dialects.

If a porter or guide, who is more familiar with the terrain (hence, quicker), acts as a messenger, provide a written report with the preceding details.

SIGNALS

The internationally recognized mountain distress signal is six long whistle blasts, flashlight flashes, waves, or shouts in quick succession and then repeated after a 1-minute interval. Keep signaling as long as is necessary to bring rescuers within sight of you. The international response signal to acknowledge that the distress signal has been heard or seen is three whistles, waves, or flashlight flashes in quick succession and then repeated at 1-minute intervals.

If you anticipate helicopter rescue or an air search, raise your arms in a V shape to identify yourself to the approaching helicopter, or mark a V shape on the ground.

SURVIVAL

The following comments draw together some of the emergency aspects of health problems discussed in chapter 4, "In Good Shape: Staying Healthy." These general guidelines are based on regions. For survival techniques, refer to specialist manuals (see appendix B).

Mountains. In the mountains, you should watch for the effects of altitude and extreme weather conditions. Protect the skin and eyes from the effects of over-exposure to ultraviolet radiation, and respond promptly to the first sign of problems with altitude sickness (see chapter 4, "In Good Shape: Staying Healthy").

The best option for survival in driving rain, snow, and blizzards is to seek shelter. Insulate yourself from the ground by sitting on your pack or sleeping mat, and keep dry and warm inside your survival bag. If necessary, put on all your spare clothing and get into your sleeping bag. Top up your energy level at regular intervals by dipping into your emergency food supply. If weather conditions permit you to pitch a tent, its shelter value increases if you create a rock or snow wall as a windbreak.

On peaks, passes, and exposed ridges, there is a real possibility of lightning strikes during storms. Watch for darkening clouds, a buzzing in the air, hair standing on end, and a highly charged atmosphere, indicating an imminent strike. Act fast: Drop your pack to the ground to act as insulation against ground currents and curl up on it, keeping your profile as low as possible. Do not stand directly under tall trees or retreat into the mouth of a cave, and stay away from lakeshores and streams.

Desert. In desert climates, remember that you need to protect yourself especially from dehydration and direct sun, which can lead to heat exhaustion,

Fish River Canyon, Namibia (Deanna Swaney photo)

heat stroke, sunburn, and headaches. Your medical kit for the desert should include salt or electrolyte replacement powders to replenish losses through perspiration. Carry plenty of water and note any natural water sources marked on your map or indicated by lines of vegetation. As approximate figures for hot, dry conditions experienced with moderate exertion, you'll require 2 U.S. gallons (8 liters) of water per day. If you are low on water, seek shade and avoid walking during the heat of the day. Remember to keep up your salt intake. Make your way toward safety during the cool of the evening and early morning, when your body will sweat less, require less energy, and consume less water. Note that digestion requires more water, so it is advisable to eat frugally if water is short.

Tropical Rainforest. In tropical climates, you'll experience high temperatures and high humidity levels. Rainfall and damp conditions can quickly cause skin problems. Wearing loose-fitting clothing, preferably cotton, reduces irritation. Clean and treat any sores or gashes regularly to prevent rapid infection. Replace fluid lost through profuse sweating caused by high humidity. A plastic tarp tied off to trees provides shelter against frequent rainfall; if available, sling a hammock beneath the tarp.

◆ GENERAL TRAVEL EMERGENCIES ◆

If your woes are not specific to your trek, but more general in nature, you have various options to put things right. You'll be off to a flying start with adequate insurance, which should cover a wide spread of emergency situations, such as medical problems or loss of money or personal baggage.

GETTING ROBBED

With any luck, if you've followed the suggestions in chapter 6, "Look Sharp: Security Basics," to minimize the impact of loss, you'll survive getting robbed with nerves intact.

If you are robbed, you'll need to file a police report, detailing the place, time, manner, and quantity of items stolen. Request a copy of the report; send one to accompany the insurance claim, and make another for your own reference.

Traveler's checks should be replaced upon application to the issuer or their local agent within a couple of days or earlier—the commission paid on purchase is effectively your insurance against loss.

Credit cards should be canceled with a phone call to the appropriate number (most are toll-free or accept reverse charges) as quickly as possible.

Airline tickets will either be refunded (with a bit of paperwork) by the airline or covered by your insurance.

Your passport should be replaced by the local embassy or consulate. The process may be speeded up if you have kept separate copies (elsewhere in your remaining belongings or with a contactable friend or relative at home) of your birth certificate and the identification pages (and visa stamps) of the lost passport.

GETTING ARRESTED

If you are arrested, keep control of your temper, and try to establish who is in charge and why you are being held. At the same time, ask to speak to your consulate.

Registering with your consulate upon arrival at a destination, especially in known hotspots, is a good way to leave word of your approximate itinerary and contact details for next of kin in an emergency (either yours or theirs). If you are missing, the consulate will note your disappearance and make attempts to locate you.

OBTAINING EMERGENCY MONEY FROM HOME

One method of obtaining emergency money from home is to transfer funds from a bank in your home country to a correspondent bank at your overseas base. In countries with a Byzantine banking system, you may have to spend days trekking around various departments in search of your money. If you implement a bank-to-bank transfer, find out exactly which departments are involved, and ask the transmitting party to send you separate confirmation as soon as the money is sent.

A wire transfer may take a couple of days and the payout may be restricted to local foreign currency. In really dire emergency, such as accident, detention, or medical crisis, U.S. citizens can contact the Citizens Emergency Center, Bureau of Consular Affairs, U.S. Department of State, Washington, DC 20570 at (202) 647-5225. Arrangements can usually be made for rapid transfer of funds (a small fee is charged) to a local embassy or consular office.

• 10 •

THE WORLD AT YOUR FEET
Trekking Worldwide

 IT'S TIME TO UNLEASH YOUR IMAGINATION. DO
your interests lie in the Himalaya, amongst the highest peaks
in the world, perhaps in a three-week circuit of the Annapurna
region of Nepal? Are you intrigued by the idea of bushwalking
in the Blue Mountains of Australia, or tramping on one of
New Zealand's Great Walks? Would you like to experience the
alpine delights of hut-to-hut walking in Austria, or the birdlife and beaches of
the Pembrokeshire Coastal Path in Wales? Perhaps you are tempted by the landscapes of Africa, such as the volcanic beauty of Mount Kilimanjaro in Tanzania
or the mist-enshrouded Mountains of the Moon in Uganda? Are you attracted
to the contrasts of the Americas, perhaps the grizzlies and wilderness tundra of
Denali National Park in Alaska or the llamas and Inca ruins on trails in Bolivia?

This chapter offers an overview of trekking opportunities available around the
world. The selection is an eclectic mix of those treks that are popular or offer un-
usual variation. The descriptions are presented in broad strokes as a taster to prompt
you into active mode, so that you use the planning and research pointers offered
in this book to seek your own adventures rather than those prescribed by others.

The range of trekking options extends from the charted to the uncharted,
from trails and routes passing through remote communities, to pristine wilderness where you set your own path far from human contact. Your choice of destination depends only on your skills, experience, imagination, and interest. The
key to your enjoyment of any trek is to make a realistic assessment of your abilities and to prepare sensibly. Match your choice to your experience and skill, both
of which can be enhanced by the right partners, guides, or group.

Alchemic symbol: **Gravel**; origin unknown

• AFRICA •

The vivid landscapes, spectacular wildlife, and cultural interest of Africa ensure there is always adventure afoot. African landscapes are the stuff of dreams: snowcaps in the Atlas Mountains in the north; dense, mist-shrouded forests in Uganda; rolling savanna grasslands in East Africa; amazing dunescapes in the Namib Desert in the southwest; and wild coastline in South Africa.

The wildlife is equally diverse and impressive, ranging from gorillas in the forests, to the giant herds of roving wildebeest on the plains, to the big game species such as elephant, lion, buffalo, leopard, and the threatened rhino. Your visit may also provide a firsthand perspective on conservation issues.

Given the size and topography of the continent, it's scarcely surprising that there are major variations in the weather, ranging from the Mediterranean climate at the Western Cape to the alternating wet and dry seasons of the tropical rainforest climate close to the equator. There are trekking options to suit most tastes in national parks, game reserves, and bushwalking regions. For trekkers seeking experience or an introduction to Africa, both South Africa and Malawi have well-developed infrastructures of trail networks and mountain huts.

In some parks (for example, in Kenya, Malawi, and Namibia), where big game roams, for your own security it is compulsory to be accompanied by an armed ranger. Even if there is no compulsory hiring requirement, the skills and thorough knowledge of many of these guides can provide a very rewarding experience for a relatively modest fee, especially if you form a small group.

When assessing trekking costs, you'll need to budget for fees for park entry, ranger or guide fees, and camping. In many cases, the best means of access to remote parks and trailheads is by private or hired car, because public service may be nonexistent or infrequent.

ETHIOPIA

In northern Ethiopia, treks can be organized among the ravines, pinnacles, and rugged mountain scenery of Simien National Park, which hosts some rare local species, such as the lammergeyer, ibex, and extremely rare Simien fox. The park has an efficient infrastructure of trails, huts, and guides; and you can structure a trek for a week or longer, with or without pack animals.

INDIAN OCEAN ISLANDS

The tropical islands of the Indian Ocean are best known for their beaches, but for those ready to seek they also offer some good hikes and treks.

On Madagascar, the prime trekking destination is Isalo National Park, which has bizarrely eroded canyons, grasslands, woodlands, and an idyllic swimming hole. Park admission permits are required; and hiring a guide is advisable. Another

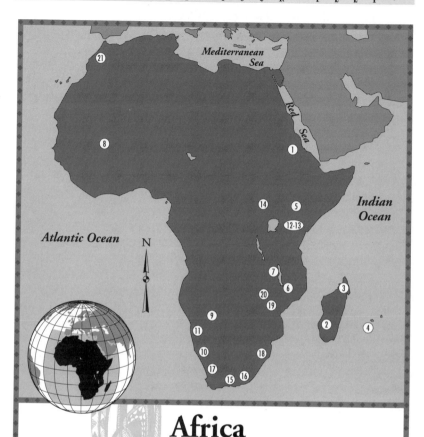

Africa

1 Simien National Park, Ethiopia
2 Isalo National Park, Madagascar
3 Masoala Peninsula, Madagascar
4 Cirque de Mafate Region, Réunion
5 Point Lenana (Mount Kenya National Park), Kenya
6 Mount Mulanje, Malawi
7 Nyika National Park, Malawi
8 Dogon Region, Mali
9 Waterberg Plateau Park, Namibia
10 Fish River Canyon Trek, Namibia
11 Namib-Naukluft National Park, Namibia
12 Mount Kilimanjaro, Tanzania
13 Mount Meru (Arusha National Park), Tanzania
14 Mount Speke (Ruwenzori National Park), Uganda
15 Tsitsikamma National Park, South Africa
16 Shipwreck Trail, South Africa
17 Cedarberg Wilderness Area, South Africa
18 Natal Drakensberg (Giant's Cup Trail), South Africa
19 Chimanimani National Park, Zimbabwe
20 Mavuradonha Wilderness, Zimbabwe
21 Atlas Mountains, Morocco

Rivière des Galets, Cirque de Mafate, Réunion (Deanna Swaney photo)

trekking option is a demanding 5-day trek, sleeping in villages en route, across the Masoala Peninsula in the north.

The dramatic volcanic character of Réunion has long made it a favorite haunt of French trekkers. There are many spectacular itineraries (5 days or longer), for example through the Cirque de Mafate where trails, partly hewn out of precipices, negotiate wooded valleys. Several routes are designated as part of the GR system (described later under the section on France), and mountain huts or local cabins can be reserved in advance.

KENYA

Kenya's major drawcard is the wildlife safari effected in a vehicle, but proficient trekkers can ring the changes by heading for the peaks of Mount Kenya National Park in the central highlands. A 5-day trek to Point Lenana (16,350 feet/4,985 meters) in the Mount Kenya massif, camping or staying in mountain huts en route, can be done with or without porters and guides. Rainforest on the lower slopes gives way to bamboo groves, which thin into moorland and, at higher altitude, the extraordinary, giant species of groundsel and lobelia. Wildlife in the area includes rock hyraxes, monkeys, elephant, and buffalo. Appropriate high-altitude experience and sufficient warm and waterproof gear are essential. Daily fees for park entry and camping are payable in advance.

MALAWI

In southern Malawi, the peaks and forests of Mount Mulanje are a focus for trekking. Permits are required prior to entry and there is a large network of trails that can be trekked for a week or longer, overnighting in mountain huts on the plateau. Highlights of the region include the towering Mulanje Cedar in thick forests, diverse flowers, and many kinds of birdlife.

Another popular destination is Nyika National Park, a high plateau of grasslands interspersed with moors and forests fringed by dramatic escarpments. Treks follow a network of trails to view wildlife such as baboons, antelope, and warthog as well as the park's extraordinary abundance of bird species. You must apply in advance for a permit and are required to take a guide.

MALI

In West Africa, the country of Mali draws trekkers to Dogon, an arid, scrubland region of special cultural interest. Here the unique culture of the cliff-dwelling inhabitants is shaped by cosmology, the characteristic architecture of conical or flat-roofed houses, colorful social gatherings at weekly markets, and superb artistic skills, especially the carving of masks for ritual dances. You can hire an official guide at towns such as Bankas or Bandiagara, negotiate routes and costs (apart from guide fees, you'll pay admission fees to villages and overnight fees to stay in local houses), and spend a week or longer trekking between the villages ranged along the sandstone Bandiagara escarpment.

MOROCCO

North Africa's premier trekking territory lies in the Atlas Mountains in Morocco. The two-day trek to the country's highest peak, Mount Toubkal (13,660 feet/ 4,165 meters), is of moderate difficulty (some scrambling and talus slopes) and affords great views from the top. The route is usually commenced from the village of Imlil and involves an overnight at the mountain hut below the summit. More extensive treks can be arranged from the nearby community of Tacheddirt.

NAMIBIA

Namibia attracts trekkers to the contrasts and delights of its landscapes and wildlife. Permits for the sample treks mentioned here should be booked well in advance. The sandstone wilderness of Waterberg Plateau Park features a wide variety of wildlife, including white and black rhino introduced as part of a conservation scheme. Guided or unguided trail tours last 4 days.

The awesome splendor of the Fish River Canyon, 100 miles (160 kilometers) in length and up to 17 miles (27 kilometers) wide, is accessible on a challenging 5-day trek that winds 52 miles (85 kilometers) along the rivercourse. You need to be fit, able to deal with heat, and self-reliant for food on this trek.

The Namib-Naukluft Park lies in the desert mountain massif of the Naukluft mountains. Trekking options include loop trails, varying in duration from 1 to 8 days, which take in spectacular scenery and offer the chance to see mountain zebra.

SOUTH AFRICA

South Africa has a well-organized trekking infrastructure for the management of trails and accommodation. Permits are often required—book well in advance to avoid disappointment.

In Tsitsikamma National Park in Cape Province, the Otter Trail is a prime 5-day trek, staying at huts en route, which follows the coastline for 25 miles (41 kilometers) from Storms River Mouth to Nature's Valley. The short stages, interspersed with river crossings and steep ascents onto the coastal plateau, give ample opportunity to enjoy the contrasts in fauna and flora between tidal pools and thick forests. Compulsory permits should be reserved far in advance from the National Parks Board, which supplies maps and further details.

Another excellent coastal trail extends for 39 miles (64 kilometers), between Great Fish River and Chalumna River, along the dramatic coastline of the Wild Coast in Transkei. Known as the Shipwreck Trail, it can be trekked in 4 days or linked to other coastal trails to form long-distance itineraries for several weeks. Highlights en route include shipwrecks, wild beachscapes, and abundant marine birdlife. Permits are required but you have a wide choice of sites to pitch your tent; and driftwood campfires on isolated sand are permitted.

The Cedarberg Wilderness Area, noted for its funky rock formations and unique fauna and flora (spring flowering is spectacular), covers part of the Cedarberg range in Western Cape province. A permit is required for access to the region's well-maintained network of trails, which are suitable for treks lasting several days.

The Natal Drakensberg (Dragon Mountains) are home to several national parks and reserves with a network of trails to enjoy the magnificent peaks of the country's highest range. The Giant's Cup Trail, a 5-day trek between Sani Pass and Bushman's Nek, is suitable as an introduction to hiking in the area. Permits are required and huts are available en route. The trail features mountain vistas, grasslands, caves, and rock art and many species of birds, including eagles and vultures.

TANZANIA

The volcanic peak of Mount Kilimanjaro, Africa's highest mountain at 19,344 feet (5,896 meters) and one of the continent's most impressive sights, lies in northern Tanzania. There are several routes to the summit, but the easiest is the Marangu trek, which crosses forest, moorland, and afro-alpine zones. The trip takes 5 days, including extra time for altitude acclimatization. The cost of the trip runs to several hundred dollars, which includes fees for park admission, camping or mountain hut stays, plus further miscellaneous charges. In addition you'll need to budget for the compulsory hire of guides and payment of their respective park fees.

In the nearby Arusha National Park, there's a 4-day trek (with compulsory guide) to the peak of Mount Meru (14,943 feet/4,556 meters), a tad smaller and less trekked than its famous neighbor but still with knockout views. Here, too, you'll have to budget several hundred dollars for the various park and ranger fees.

UGANDA

Trekking is popular in Ruwenzori National Park in the Ruwenzori Mountains, also known as the Mountains of the Moon, on the western border of Uganda. The only peak in the range accessible as a trek and climb, rather than a full climb, is Mount Speke (16,039 feet/4,890 meters). The scenery on the route ranges from dense rainforests, bogs, and heathland to lakes, waterfalls, and glaciers. Be equipped with warm clothing and raingear and prepared for strenuous gradients, high altitude, and slogging in heavy rainfall. Treks lasting a week or longer, staying in mountain huts or in tents, can be matched to the competence of the trekkers, either reaching the summit or choosing an itinerary at lower altitudes. Ruwenzori Mountaineering Services in Kasese currently organizes the entire trip, including compulsory guides and porters, for less than a couple hundred dollars per person.

ZIMBABWE

The most popular hiking venue in Zimbabwe is Chimanimani National Park, which takes in a spectacular range of mountains along the Mozambique border. From the base camp at Mutekeswane, there are several trails leading to the park's grasslands, streams, and lakes.

Friendly elephant, Matusadona National Park, Zimbabwe (Deanna Swaney photo)

Numerous hiking trails have been laid out in the recently designated Mavuradonha Wilderness, which occupies a range of mountains on the Zambezi escarpment.

◆ ASIA ◆

Asia offers trekkers a kaleidoscope of cultures and landscapes. Your trails might lead to the assembled white summits of the Annapurna Sanctuary in Nepal, high passes and remote monasteries in Tibet, the wildlife delights of Malaysia's rainforests, the ethnic diversity and color of northern Thailand, or the volcanoes and hot springs of Japan.

Asia presents broad contrasts in climate: from the icy winters and scorching hot summers of the windswept Central Asian steppes to the hot, humid, and rainy summers and cooler, drier winters brought by the monsoons in the southern sector of the continent.

For some treks (in Tibet, for example), you'll need to be self-sufficient for food and shelter, whereas hostels or mountain huts in Japan can provide meals and shelter, and teahouses on some trekking routes in Nepal offer simple lodging and food. In most cases you can trek independently or, as is commonly done in some Himalayan countries, organize the assistance of guides, porters, or pack animals. Some countries, such as Bhutan and Sikkim, restrict the numbers of independent travelers and set prices; elsewhere, trekking is inexpensive.

BHUTAN, SIKKIM, AND INDIA

At the eastern margin of the Himalaya are the territories of Bhutan and Sikkim, both of which restrict access to trekking groups in return for higher prices. In Bhutan, the Chomolhari Trek crosses high passes and provides spectacular views of Mount Chomolhari and neighboring peaks on the Tibetan border. In Sikkim, trekking groups are permitted on the Dzongri Trail, a trek that passes through pine and rhododendron forests and villages of Tibetan yak herders, and ascends to alpine meadows beneath the ramparts of Kanchenjunga, the world's third highest mountain.

Apart from Sikkim, other more accessible parts of the Indian Himalaya favored by trekkers are Garwhal, Himachal Pradesh, Lahoul, Ladakh, and Zanskar.

The headwaters of the sacred River Ganges in the mountainous region of Garwhal, in the western corner of Uttar Pradesh state, attract religious fervor, both Hindu and Buddhist. Apart from cultural interest, trekkers will also appreciate Garwhal's spectacular snow-covered peaks, alpine plateau, and tumbling rivers. The 4-day Dodi Tal Trek climbs through forests to Dodi Tal Lake and then past treeline to vantage points with superb mountain vistas, before descending again into the forests.

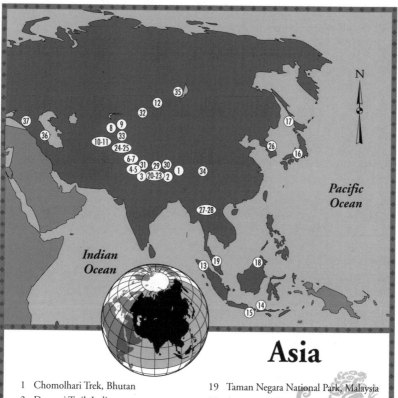

Asia

1   Chomolhari Trek, Bhutan
2   Dzongri Trail, India
3   Garwhal Region, India
4   Himachal Pradesh, India
5   Lahoul Region, India
6   Ladakh Plateau, India
7   Zanskar Valley, India
8   Bishkek, Kyrgyzstan
9   Almaty, Kazakhstan
10 Fansky Mountains, Uzbekistan
11 Samarkand, Uzbekistan
12 Gorno-Altaisk, Russia
13 Samosir Island, Indonesia
14 Gunung Rinjani, Indonesia
15 Bali Barat National Park, Indonesia
16 Japan Alps, Japan
17 Rishiri-Rebun National Park, Japan
18 Mount Kinabalu, Kinabalu National
    Park, Malaysia

19 Taman Negara National Park, Malaysia
20 Annapurna Circuit, Nepal
21 Jomsom Trek, Nepal
22 Everest Base Camp Trek, Nepal
23 Langtang Trek, Nepal
24 Fairy Meadows Trek, Pakistan
25 Concordia Trek, Pakistan
26 Sorak-San National Park, South Korea
27 Chiang Mai, Thailand
28 Mae Hong Son, Thailand
29 Mount Everest Base Camp Trek, Tibet
30 Samye Trek, Tibet
31 Mount Kailas, Tibet
32 Tianchi Lake Region, China
33 Mount Muztagh Ata, China
34 Hailuoguo Glacier, China
35 Lake Baikal Region, Russia
36 Dagestan, Russia
37 Mount Elbrus, Russia

The state of Himachal Pradesh draws trekkers to its hillstations and mountain ranges. From McLeodganj, a former hillstation and now residence-in-exile of the Dalai Lama and the Tibetan government, there are numerous trekking routes along forested valleys or across high passes with dramatic views of the Himalaya. The Kulu Valley is renowned for its orchards, meadows, and pleasant alpine scenery. From the hill resort of Manali, there are treks lasting 4 days or longer, to the glacial lake of Bea Kund, for example.

High-altitude acclimatization is required for treks farther north in Lahoul, Ladakh, and Zanskar, where there is the dramatic contrast of Tibetan-influenced culture; wild, desertland scenery; high passes; and occasional settlements with Buddhist monasteries.

RUSSIA

As a trekking destination in the making, Russia offers great scope across the continents of Europe and Asia for visitors prepared to live with a fair measure of impromptu facilities, minimal infrastructure, and flexible organization. Many trekkers from overseas currently sidestep direct involvement with logistics by taking organized or guided trips.

The spectacular alpine scenery of the Caucasus mountains affords fine hiking, for example, in the eastern region of Dagestan, and in the western ranges, which include Mount Elbrus (18,441 feet/5,621 meters), Europe's highest peak. An ascent of this mountain should be considered as a strenuous trek and climb, and prior acclimatization to altitude is essential. There's also a moderately difficult circuit of Mount Elbrus, which is rated scenically on a par with the circuit of Mont Blanc.

In eastern Siberia lies Lake Baikal, an extraordinarily beautiful lake holding the largest volume of freshwater on our planet. The region around the lake provides a wide variety of trekking options, some in remote wilderness without trails, others more readily accessible by road, rail, or ferry along its 400-mile (640-kilometer) length. Perhaps the most accessible option runs beside the Circumbaikal Railway (a former section of the Trans-Siberian Railway), which skirts the southern lakeshore for 53 miles (86 kilometers) between Port Baikal and Kultuk. Hikers camp out beside the line and follow its pleasant lakeside route fringed with taiga.

CENTRAL ASIA

The dismantling of the Soviet Union has redefined Central Asia as a travel destination and has brought the Tianshan, Pamir, and Altai ranges within reach of foreign trekkers, although the current lack of infrastructure for independent arrangements means that, in practice, most trips are organized by tour operators. Treks in the Tian Shan are more readily accessible from Bishkek (Kyrgyzstan) and Almaty (Kazakhstan), and in the Pamirs, a popular trekking destination, is the sparsely vegetated Fansky range, accessible from Samarkand (Uzbekistan). The Altai mountains stretch across the borders of Siberia, Mongolia, and China. The town of Gorno-Altaisk in Siberia provides access by road to trailheads for some excellent treks through the Altai's alpine scenery.

INDONESIA

The numerous islands of Indonesia provide trekking opportunities, including some at high altitude. Samosir Island, in the middle of Lake Toba (the largest lake in Southeast Asia), is a center for Batak culture. You can spend a couple of days trekking through the forest and scrub to cross the mountainous center from the eastern to the western shores and stay with Batak villagers en route.

On Lombok, trekkers head for the volcanic peak of Gunung Rinjani, which towers 12,221 feet (3,726 meters) above the island. Guides and equipment are available for hire locally, and basic provisions are sold at the main trailhead, Batu Koq. The return trip from this trailhead following the northern climb takes 3 days. The trail leads up through dense forest, gradually giving way to barren terrain as you approach the crater rim; from there it's a step descent to the soothing hot springs on the shore of the crater lake.

Seashore trail, Rebun Island, Hokkaido, Japan

On Bali, guided treks lasting several days allow you to explore Bali Barat National Park, a birder's delight (several hundred species, including the rare Bali mynah).

JAPAN

The cost of living in Japan is certainly steep, but one of the ways to stretch traveling money further is to head for the open spaces, especially the many national parks where hiking and trekking infrastructure (such as transport to trailheads and campsites, hostels, or huts within reach of the trail) is generally excellent.

On the main island of Honshu, the Japan Alps, also aptly termed the "Roof of Japan," provide excellent scope for hiking. From the resort of Kamikochi, a popular hiking center in the Japan Alps, trails (many with mountain huts offering lodging and food) lead along the forested river valley before making steep ascents of alpine ridges and peaks. Circuits can be tailored for three or more days, taking in major peaks, some of which are reached via fixed ropes, ladders, or chains.

Rishiri-Rebun-Sarobetsu National Park includes the islands of Rishiri and Rebun, both accessible within a couple of hours by ferry from the island of Hokkaido in the far north. You can spend several days trekking on the islands. Rishiri is dominated by its own volcanic peak, Rishiri-dake. An overnight at the mountain hut (unattended) below the peak gives you the chance to witness a superb sunrise or sunset (weather willing) and twinkling night views across to the Russian Far East.

MALAYSIA

An exciting mix of mountains and wildlife awaits the trekker in Malaysia. The country's prime trekking destination is Mount Kinabalu in Kinabalu National Park, Sabah. The 2-day trek to Southeast Asia's highest peak is best timed to coincide with sunrise, when the views across northern Borneo are superb. The climb demands dogged stamina; en route keep an eye out for orchids, insectivorous pitcher plants, and abundant birdlife—the park is a paradise for botanists and birders.

Another Malaysian highlight is Taman Negara National Park, peninsular Malaysia's largest park, where you can explore rainforest trails and observe wildlife from hides. Animals are less easily seen, but there is a profusion of hundreds of species of plants, birds, and insects. Apart from jungle walks, you can join up with guided treks to go deeper into the park for a week or longer.

NEPAL

The Kingdom of Nepal holds pride of place as the trekking center of the Himalaya. From the lowlands, where you'll find subtropical forest and rare rhinos in Chitwan National Park, to the terraced hillsides, glaciated valleys, and awesome peaks that top the world, the scenery is commensurate with the country's moniker, "Kingdom of the Gods."

Compulsory trekking permits (including park entry fees) for your chosen area are issued in Kathmandu for a fee within a day or so of application. Kathmandu is the place to stock up on maps, guidebooks, supplies, equipment; and enough Nepalese currency in notes of small denominations to pay for daily expenses. Trekking gear can be hired here (useful to save weight if trekking is only part of an overland trip). Many routes have an infrastructure of teahouses for accommodation and shops for provisions; this can reduce the amount of cooking gear and provisions you carry.

Routes and trails are rarely level; most deliver a constantly varying succession of climbs and descents. The prime trekking season is during the dry season, from October until May. Popular choices for trekking include the Annapurna region in central Nepal and the Mount Everest area to the east, whereas the Langtang valley, north of Kathmandu, receives fewer visitors.

Annapurna Region. The main gateway for this region is the town of Pokhara. From here you can embark on treks into the Annapurna mountain range lasting a couple of days, a couple of weeks, or a month or more. The Annapurna Conservation Area Project (ACAP), based in Pokhara, provides regional support for minimizing impact on the environment.

The Annapurna Circuit is a trekking tour de force, passing through landscapes varying from alpine forests to arid semidesert characteristic of Tibet, crossing over the Thorong La pass with dazzling views at 17,650 feet (5,295 meters), dropping into the Kali Gandaki gorge (the world's deepest), and leading through villages of different ethnic groups, such as Tamangs and Gurungs. The full circuit, usually accomplished in counterclockwise direction, takes around 18 days for seasoned trekkers putting in some 7 hours of hiking each day. Be prepared for the effects of high altitude and a possible wait to cross the pass if snowbound. The trail has plenty of teahouses and lodges en route.

The final 7-day segment of the circuit between Muktinath (famed for its Buddhist monastery), Jomsom, and Pokhara is known as the Jomsom Trek, which presents an alternative shorter trek (round trip of around two weeks), with stunning views and less altitude gain than the full circuit.

Another two-week trek in the area leads to the Annapurna Sanctuary, a natural amphitheater circled by several high mountains, including the distinctive fishtail peak of Machapuchare.

Mount Everest Area. The trek to Everest Base Camp takes around 21 days and leads into the homeland of the Sherpa people at the foot of the world's highest mountain—the base is at 17,515 feet (5,340 meters), but the classic view of Everest is gained after hiking a little higher up a nearby peak. The route requires stamina for frequent elevation loss and gain, and you should be prepared for the possible medical complications of high altitude. Although it is possible to fly in or out of Lukla, flights don't necessarily operate to schedule and if you fly in (rather than out) you should allow several days to acclimatize to the altitude.

Langtang Valley. The Langtang trek leads to the glaciers below the peak of Langtang Lirung (23,766 feet/7,246 meters), which lies north of Kathmandu.

Allow a couple of weeks for this trek, which features interesting wildlife, excellent views of peaks en route, and the option to stay in villages.

PAKISTAN

The northernmost region of Pakistan, where four ranges (Himalaya, Hindu Kush, Pamirs, and Karakorum) meet, boasts the largest number of high peaks in the world. Due to military or political friction, some border zones and parts of the Northwest Frontier Province are either off-limits to foreigners or access is regulated by permit and accompaniment by a government-authorized guide. Popular destinations in the north include Mount Nanga Parbat and Concordia, a glacier junction dominated by K2.

The 4-day Fairy Meadows trek to pine forests and alpine meadows (good camping) at the foot of Nanga Parbat, the eighth highest mountain in the world, starts at Raikot Bridge on the Karakorum Highway (blasted through the mountains to achieve the epic engineering feat of linking China and Pakistan by road).

The Concordia trek is rated as one of the world's best. Because it is currently included in a restricted zone, requiring permit and guide, most trips are organized through a tour operator. From the trailhead in Askole the trek takes a fortnight or longer (depending on routing and sidetrips) crossing awesome wilderness and glaciers into a natural amphitheater where colossal mountains (K2, Gasherbrum, Chogolisa, Broad Peak, and others) soar above you.

SOUTH KOREA

Sorak-san National Park in the northeast of the country is an area of outstanding beauty. The park contains historic temples and hermitages merged into a mass of rugged peaks, conifer and hardwood forests, and rivers and waterfalls. You'll need a map to plot your route along the many trails, staying overnight at campsites or basic mountain shelters. The deeper you hike into the interior, the quicker you leave behind the crowds.

THAILAND

In the north of Thailand, large numbers of foreign trekkers visit the hill tribes on treks organized, for example, out of Chiang Mai or Mae Hong Son. "Hilltribe trekking," as it is known, takes place in the drier season between November and February. Through their nomadic origin and relative isolation (until recent times), the hilltribes have evolved their own distinctive dress (ornate designs), beliefs (animist, Buddhist, and Christian), and customs. Treks, usually arranged with local companies and guides, last for a few days or a week and follow forested trails to tribal villages that provide overnight accommodation. Apart from travel on foot, these trips may also use boats, rafts, or elephants.

TIBET AND CHINA

On the northern margin of the Himalaya, trekking options in Tibet include the Mount Everest region and the valleys around Lhasa. The trek to Mount Everest Base Camp starts some 390 miles (690 kilometers) from Lhasa at a small side-track leading off the Tibet–Nepal Highway and takes 4 days. It should only be tackled if you are fit and acclimatized to high altitude (one pass exceeds 17,000 feet/5,000 meters) and prepared to be self-sufficient in food and shelter. The route follows trails across the barren plateau, passing the occasional settlement before reaching Rongbuk monastery at the head of the valley where the dramatic view of the north face of Everest (29,028 feet/8,848 meters), known to Tibetans as Chomolongma (Goddess Mother of the World), fills the sky. The base camp is a 2-hour trek beyond the monastery. A rugged, barely motorable track is also used by tour operators in Lhasa to bring visitors to Rongbuk.

View from Ganden Monastery, Tibet

Many routes throughout Tibet are ancient pilgrimage circuits actively used and revered by Tibetans. From Ganden monastery, just east of Lhasa, there's a 5-day pilgrim trek to Samye (the first monastery in Tibet). The route crosses high passes before descending into a gorge and continuing down valleys to Samye.

In the far west of Tibet lies Mount Kailas, one of the remotest and most sacred pilgrimage sites in the world, revered as the abode of the gods by Hindus, Jains, and Buddhists. The ritual circuit takes 3 days at extreme altitude. The region offers outstanding views across the plateau to the snowcapped Himalaya, but trekkers should be acclimatized, equipped to be self-sufficient, and sensitive to the sanctity of the site. Few independent trekkers reach Kailas; most arrange the trek through tour operators.

Further afield, popular destinations in China are the Tian Shan and Pamir ranges in the western province of Xinjiang, the mountains to the west of Sichuan province, and the rugged landscapes of Yunnan Province.

From Ürümqi, the capital of Xinjiang Province, you can take the 3-hour bus trip east to Tianchi Lake, which lies in a beautiful alpine area of the Tian Shan ranges. Local Kazakh herders camp here in their yurts and graze their livestock on the pastures. You can trek the hills and valleys with Kazakh guides who also have horses for hire.

In the far south of Xinjiang Province, close to the Sino-Pakistan border, the Pamir plateau, accessible via the Karakorum Highway, affords spectacular scenery, especially in the foothills of Mount Muztagh Ata, where Tajik herders graze yaks and camels.

Hailuoguo Glacier Park, in the mountainous western fringe of Sichuan Province and eastern Tibet, offers the opportunity to trek to the lowest glacier in Asia. The treks take between 4 and 5 days, and guides and ponies lead the way through subtropical forests to the glacier, which is below the snowline of Mount Gonga. At camps en route you can sleep in log cabins and enjoy natural hot springs.

◆   OCEANIA   ◆

Trekkers setting their sights on Oceania can sample attractions ranging from the rainforests, whitewater rivers, and diverse population (over 700 languages and cultures) of Papua New Guinea to the jagged coastlines, mountains, and glaciers of New Zealand and the wilderness areas, open spaces, and bushwalks of Australia.

AUSTRALIA

The oldest continent, Australia is also prime bushwalking (hiking/trekking) territory with a wide choice of landscapes, ranging from rainforest in the far north, alpine plateau in the Victorian Alps in the southeast, inland desert in the Flinders Ranges in the south, to coastal terrain in the west.

Bushwalking routes, many of which lie within the country's 500 national parks, vary in length from a day or so to a couple of weeks or more. Some heavily visited parks issue permits to regulate the numbers of hikers and reduce the environmental impact. In general, the country's size and the remote location of many trailheads make it more practical to get to them by car or shuttle bus, such as in Tasmania, although in some instances there is public transport.

Camping is commonly permitted in most of the national parks, and there are basic huts, for example, on Tasmania and in New South Wales. Bush fires are a major problem in several regions, where there may be a total ban on any type of fire, including fuel stoves, on high-risk days.

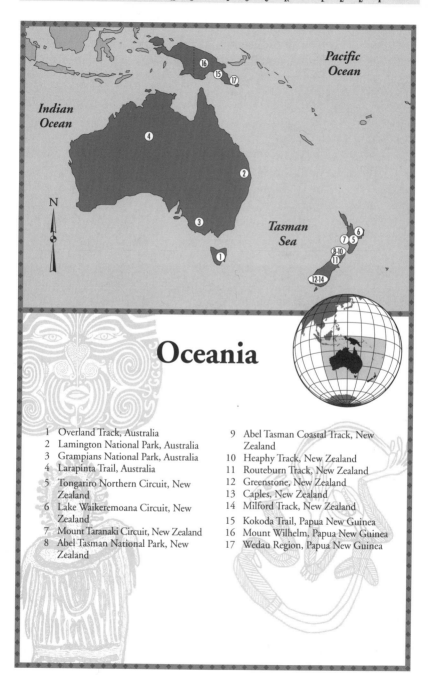

Pacific
Ocean

Indian
Ocean

Tasman
Sea

N

Oceania

1 Overland Track, Australia
2 Lamington National Park, Australia
3 Grampians National Park, Australia
4 Larapinta Trail, Australia
5 Tongariro Northern Circuit, New Zealand
6 Lake Waikeremoana Circuit, New Zealand
7 Mount Taranaki Circuit, New Zealand
8 Abel Tasman National Park, New Zealand

9 Abel Tasman Coastal Track, New Zealand
10 Heaphy Track, New Zealand
11 Routeburn Track, New Zealand
12 Greenstone, New Zealand
13 Caples, New Zealand
14 Milford Track, New Zealand
15 Kokoda Trail, Papua New Guinea
16 Mount Wilhelm, Papua New Guinea
17 Wedau Region, Papua New Guinea

The popular bushwalking period extends between September and February, spring and summer in the Southern Hemisphere, but as long as you can pick your region, the climate range allows for bushwalking anytime during the year. In the far north, the dry season, extending between May and September, is definitely more clement for bushwalking.

The delightful island state of Tasmania is a bushwalking magnet, as it offers a wide selection of wilderness routes through forests, lakelands, and grassy plains and along coastal bays. Weather can change with amazing speed, so be prepared with cold-weather and wet-weather gear.

In the center of the island, the popular Overland Track (50 miles/80 kilometers) in the Cradle Mountain–Lake St. Clair National Park can be covered in a week or less, but there's every reason to extend your time with side trips and enjoy even more of the moors, forests, and rockscapes. The trailheads at Cynthia Bay and Waldheim, at the southern and northern ends of the park, respectively, are served by a shuttle bus during the prime summer season. Permits are issued by park offices at both these points.

In Queensland state, Lamington National Park is renowned for its subtropical rainforests. Within the park, there are over 100 miles (160 kilometers) of well-maintained trails leading to ridges and valleys with scenic canyons, plunging waterfalls, and pools. Local wildlife, especially birdlife, is abundant and includes the bower bird (a close relative of the Bird of Paradise), which has a passion for interior decoration. Bus transport is available between Brisbane or Surfer's Paradise and Binna Burra and Green Mountains, the park's two major access points. Camping permits are issued on a limited basis. The dry season, between May and September, is popular with visitors, so give yourself plenty of time to reserve in advance.

Grampians National Park, a rugged region of cliffs and forests in the state of Victoria, offers a variety of bushwalking opportunities. The prime season to visit is between August and November, when the hundreds of species of flora produce a botanical extravaganza that is the park's major claim to fame. Permits and information are provided by the park's visitor center close to the town of Halls Gap, some 155 miles (250 kilometers) from Melbourne.

The arid Western McDonnell Ranges in the Northern Territory are characterized by sensational gorges and canyons and interspersed with pockets of vegetation, notably ghost gums or red gums, where moisture remains concealed. Ormiston Gorge, 62 miles (100 kilometers) west of Alice Springs, has long been popular as a trailhead (access by car) for excursions on foot into this region, including a 3-day trek up the gorge combined with a climb to the top of Mount Giles. Recently, the Ormiston Gorge has been linked as a section on the Larapinta Trail, a series of walks currently being combined to stretch 155 miles (220 kilometers) from Alice Springs to Mount Razorback. For completion details, advice on treks, and guided trek options, check with the tourist information center in Alice Springs.

Mount Cook, South Island, New Zealand (Deanna Swaney photo)

NEW ZEALAND

In New Zealand, tramping (the local term for hiking/trekking) has become a passion for the locals, who have developed a superb infrastructure to enjoy the outdoor attractions of the country's two main islands: the volcanic splendors, hot springs, peaks, and forests of the North Island and the rainforests, glaciers, fiords, lakes, and bays of the South Island.

The country has over a dozen national parks designated to protect their respective environments, such as forests, glaciers, or coastlines. In addition, large tracts of bush and wilderness are preserved in the forest parks system.

The prime tramping season runs roughly between November and late March. During the peak months of December and January, large numbers of international trampers can crowd major trails, especially those routes of notable scenic merit that have been nominated as "Great Walks," such as the Abel Tasman Coastal Track, Milford Track, and Routeburn Track. As a protective measure to prevent erosion and overcrowding, use of the Milford Track is regulated by permit (advance reservation strongly advised) issued for a fee. As an alternative to the dozen or so big name routes, which can attract considerable crowds, bear in mind the hundreds of lesser known trails, or try the Great Walks out of season.

The Department of Conservation (DOC) provides campsites, ranging from free areas with a place to pitch and a tap for cold water, to fee-paying sites with a variety of facilities.

The DOC also maintains several hundred backcountry huts. Hut facilities range from the minimum for a basic shelter to frills, such as tap water, gas or coal stove, and mattresses. Alpine huts are equipped with kerosene cookers and mountain radios.

To use the huts, purchase tickets in advance for a modest fee from DOC offices, park visitor centers, or outdoor shops. For the Great Walks you must purchase a "Hut and Campsite Pass." For some Great Walks, advance purchase of this pass is compulsory during the summer tramping season. All huts, except on the Milford and Routeburn tracks, operate on a first come, first served basis.

In the center of the North Island lies Tongariro National Park, which offers a variety of tramping options, the most popular being Tongariro Northern Circuit, a 4-day Great Walk of intermediate difficulty. The route skirts Mount Ngaruhuoe (7,514 feet/2,291 meters) and sends the tramper crunching through volcanic terrain in all its variations: craters, psychedelic-colored lakes, and hot springs for a welcome soak.

There are huts en route and Great Walks regulations apply. You must be prepared for flash changes in the weather; carry suitable gear to fend off cold and wet in the mountains. Public transport provides easy access, for example, to the major trailhead at Whakapapa Village, where the visitor center supplies Great Walk passes, information on weather, and track conditions.

Farther east, the circuit of Lake Waikeremoana, inside Te Urewera National Park, is an easier 4-day tramp over clifftops, affording great views across the lake, through beech forests, and along lake inlets with beaches. Great Walks regulations apply for the huts en route. Public transport and private shuttle services provide easy access to the main trailheads at Hopuruahine Landing and Onepoto—the visitor center at Aniwaniwa supplies information and advice.

On the southwestern margin of the North Island lies Egmont National Park, which is dominated by Mount Taranaki (8,259 feet/2,518 meters). The 4-day Mount Taranaki Circuit offers the variety of beech forest sections, high tussock slopes, and talus (scree) traverses, but it is essential that you are prepared and equipped for the vagaries of high altitude. Before you go, you are strongly advised to pop into the visitor center at North Egmont for information on weather and track conditions.

Abel Tasman National Park, on the topmost tip of the South Island, is the setting for an easy, 4-day tramp along the Abel Tasman Coastal Track, which runs between Marahau and Wainui Bay. One of the country's most popular tramps, the track's highlights include golden beaches, bays, tidal reaches, and tracts of native forest—more than enough for a picture postcard swoon, with the exception of the irritant sandflies, which you should be ready to repel.

At the southern end of the South Island lie Mount Aspiring National Park and Fiordland National Park, which are straddled by the Routeburn Track. This very popular 3-day tramp has great alpine scenery and passes through valleys covered by rainforest. A booking system for huts and campsites on the Routeburn has recently been introduced (less crowded tracks in the same area are the Greenstone and the Caples). Information is provided by the DOC in Queenstown, which provides a transport base to access the northern end of the trail, whereas Te Anau is convenient for the southern end.

Also inside Fiordland National Park is the Milford Track, an easy walk that runs between Milford Sound and Lake Te Anau and lays claim to being one of the world's finest. The scenic attraction of this 4-day Great Walk lies in its forests, cascading waterfalls, and mountain meadows.

The 5-day tramp on the Heaphy Track is an easy-to-intermediate–grade Great Walk in Kahurangi National Park at the northwestern tip of the South Island. The diverse delights of the route include subtropical forest along the coast, podocarp (native conifer species) forests, and tussock downs. Information is provided at DOC centers in Takaka and Karamea.

PAPUA NEW GUINEA

Papua New Guinea offers some wild cultural experiences and a wide choice of mountain or coastal treks. In the Highlands you may encounter the Huli wigmen, who adorn themselves with intricate wigs of flowers and tusks, topped off with Bird of Paradise plumes, or along the Sepik River you can change pace, taking to canoes and meeting villagers whose carving skills and magnificently crafted houses are legendary. The country's rainforests host hundreds of species of birds, such as the stunning Bird of Paradise; an enormous contingent of insects, including dinnerplate-sized butterflies; and thousands of plant species, notably the greatest diversity of orchids in any country in the world.

For those with stamina, the 7-day (58-mile/94-kilometer) Kokoda Trail is a challenging and popular option. Associated historically with the Japanese invasion of the country during World War II, the trail links the northern and southern coasts via the steep ridges of the Owen Stanley Ranges. Best trekked in a small group with a guide, the route involves river crossings, with forested sections where the vegetation is often slippery underfoot, and frequent elevation loss and gain with resultant shifts of climate from humid to cool.

The ascent of the country's highest peak, Mount Wilhelm (14,789 feet/ 4,509 meters), is best done as a 4-day trek. This should include acclimatization time at the hut several hours' walk below the summit where fine weather opens up sweeping views of the country's valleys, peaks, coastline, and islands laid out below.

For a less demanding alternative, there are coastal walks, one of which is along the palm-fringed coastline in the Wedau area.

♦   NORTH AMERICA   ♦

Those who are at home in North America may already appreciate its huge spread of trekking opportunities. Foreign visitors are rapidly catching on to the attractions of this trekking destination—the alpine delights of the Rockies, the deserts of the Southwest, the technicolor canyons of Utah, the spectacular wildlife of Alaska, and the coastal splendor of Atlantic Canada—with more than enough trails and wilderness to last a lifetime of exploration.

Given the continent's enormous climatic variations, you can visit during any season and seek out your preferred weather. In the Southeast, you'll encounter a generally humid, subtropical climate; in the Southwest, there's the drier heat of arid desert; in the northeastern and midwestern regions, you can prepare for humid summers and snowbound winters; the west coast experiences a mild, rainy climate from northern California to southeastern Alaska; and in the far north, there are long, harsh winters and short, warm summers with daylight almost round the clock.

In the United States, backpacking areas include national parks, state parks, national forests, national monuments, and lands administered by the Bureau of Land Management (BLM). In Canada, backpackers can visit national and provincial parks, reserves and recreation areas, and government-owned land (Crown Land). Camping reservations are a must at major national parks during the peak season in the United States and Canada. Book through MISTIX (toll-free 1-800-365-2267, or (619) 452-5956). For details of the outdoor opportunities on offer from the BLM, contact its Washington office at (202) 208-5717.

In terms of costs, backpacking in North America offers excellent value. Apart from remote wilderness where fees are seldom levied, expect to pay a couple of dollars for a basic designated spot to park a tent and some U.S.$15 or more for extensive facilities akin to a home away from home. Public campsites or commercial campgrounds are widely available.

In backcountry or wilderness areas, you may need a backcountry permit,

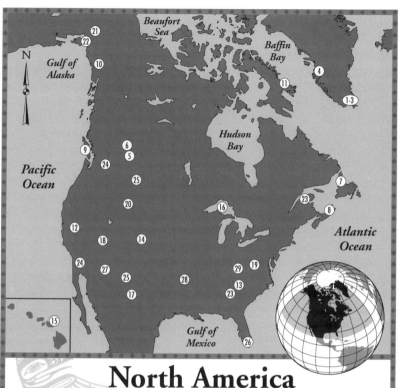

North America

Greenland
1 Narsaq Peninsula
2 Tasermiut Fiord
3 Qaqortoq–Igaliku Trek
4 Kangerlussuaq–Sisimiut Trek

Canada
5 Banff National Park, Alberta
6 Jasper National Park, Alberta
7 Gros Morne National Park, Newfoundland
8 Cape Breton National Park, Nova Scotia
9 West Coast Trail (Pacific Rim National Park), British Columbia
10 Kluane National Park, Yukon
11 Auyuittuq National Park, Northwest Territories

United States
12 Yosemite National Park, California
13 Great Smoky Mountains National Park, North Carolina–Tennesse

14 Rocky Mountains National Park, Colorado
15 Haleakala, Hawaii
16 Isle Royale National Park, Michigan
17 Guadelupe Mountains National Park, Texas
18 Zion National Park, Utah
19 Shenandoah National Park, Virginia
20 Yellowstone National Park, Wyoming
21 Denali National Park, Alaska
22 Chugach National Forest, Alaska
23 Appalachian Trail, Georgia–Maine
24 Pacific Crest Trail, California–Washington
25 Continental Divide Trail, New Mexico–Montana
26 Florida Trail, Florida
27 General Crook Trail, Arizona
28 Ozark Highlands Trail, Arkansas
29 Sheltowee Trace, Kentucky

obtainable for a couple of dollars from the park ranger's office, where you can also leave your trail plan and pick up advice on weather, fire regulations, and bear etiquette as appropriate.

GREENLAND

Greenland is dramatic wilderness on an incredible scale: vertical cliffs and deep fiords dotted with icebergs, glaciers, raging rivers, tundra, and mountains. It is also a challenging destination for trekkers ready to meet the requirements of experience and proper preparation for the demanding terrain, lack of trails (for navigation at these latitudes you'll need to adjust compass declination accordingly), and fickle weather.

The 5-day trek between Qassiarsuk and Narsaq, on the Narsaq Peninsula, passes through green pasturelands, skirts bright lakes, and ascends rocky uplands and ridges. Accommodation is available in shepherd huts.

The town of Nanortalik is a good staging point and source of information for challenging treks, lasting from a few days to a couple of weeks, to the valleys, glaciers, spires, and inlets of the Tasermiut Fiord.

The 5-day trek between Qaqortoq, the major town in southern Greenland, and Igaliku offers the scenic variety of bays, waterfalls, fells, and boulder fields; and the historic interest of church ruins dating back to medieval times. As an extended option, a two-week, long-distance (93-mile/150-kilometer) trek crosses plateaus and coastal mountains between Kangerlussuaq and Sisimiut.

CANADA

Canada is well stocked with trekking areas. Banff and Jasper national parks in Alberta possess splendid alpine scenery, snowy peaks, lakes, forests, and hot springs. The visitor information center in Banff supplies information on short hikes and backcountry treks.

On the east coast, Gros Morne National Park (Newfoundland) is a world heritage site, distinguished by its contrasts: fiords, tundra, lakes, and beaches. Excellent hiking is also to be found in the mountainous Cape Breton National Park (Nova Scotia).

In the Pacific Rim National Park on Vancouver Island (British Columbia) lies the West Coast Trail, a rugged trek of 44 miles (77 kilometers) between Bamfield and Port Renfrew. The trail takes around a week and is renowned for its spectacular coastal scenery.

If you prefer a wild hike off the marked trails, there's Kluane National Park (Yukon), which attracts large numbers of wildlife to its lakes, icefields, tundra, and alpine forests. A hiking trail booklet is available from the visitor reception centers at Haines Junction or Sheep Mountain, where you can obtain requisite backcountry permits. Even remoter trekking is available on the Pangnirtung Pass

Trail (60 miles/96 kilometers) in Auyuittuq National Park on Baffin Island (Northwest Territories), which lies on the Arctic Circle.

UNITED STATES

In the United States, you can take your pick from dozens of national parks, wilderness areas, and long-distance trails. A word of caution: In the most popular U.S. national parks, you will be falling over crowds unless you time your visit well. Think about an off-season trek, say, in March or October. Alternatively, select a lesser known venue. There are numerous spectacular but less utilized national forests, BLM units, state parks, and even unclassified wilderness areas.

Nearly all national parks have trail networks conducive to trekking; lodging or camping facilities abound. National parks that offer trekking options include climbing mecca Yosemite National Park (California); Great Smoky Mountains National Park (North Carolina/Tennessee), with its hundreds of miles of backcountry trails; Rocky Mountain National Park (Colorado), with stunning, high-elevation trekking; Haleakala (Hawaii), where you'll explore the world's largest dormant volcano; Isle Royal National Park (Michigan), the largest island in Lake Superior; Zion National Park (Utah), with its dazzling combination of red-rock canyons, sculpted cliffs, and deep-green waterfalls; thickly forested Shenandoah

Wonder Lake, Denali National Park, Alaska (**Deanna Swaney photo**)

National Park (Virginia); and Yellowstone National Park (Wyoming), with geysers, canyons, alpine meadows, coniferous forests, and abundant wildlife.

Alaska. Alaska is in a class of its own for numerous wilderness trekking opportunities throughout the southeast and in the extreme back of beyond. Alaska is a magnet for adventurous trekkers due to its enormous size (the state comprises a fifth of the United States). The sparse population of the state (only 500,000) contributes to its feeling of remoteness. The additional attraction is that three-quarters of the state's land is protected wilderness of extraordinary beauty.

Denali National Park is dominated by Denali (Mount McKinley), America's highest mountain at 20,320 feet (6,096 meters). In the park's millions of acres of tundra, spruce forest, and glacial terrain, there is thriving wildlife, such as moose, caribou, Dall sheep, and grizzlies.

Backcountry hiking is regulated through zoning and permit quotas, which ensure that there are only a set number of hikers in one place at the same time. Free permits are issued 1 day in advance by the Visitor Access Center (VAC)— get there really early in the day to front the queue. Once you have your permit and your loaned bear-resistant food container, you can pick up appropriate maps and hop on a shuttle bus that will drop you off at your assigned zone. The park has no marked trails; hikers find their way with topographical maps. Denali is accessible from Anchorage and Fairbanks by car, bus, and rail.

Also in Alaska, Chugach National Forest extends along the margins of Prince William Sound and offers amazing scenic contrasts between seashore, fjords, forest, and high mountains. Long-distance trails in the forest, noted for its abundant wildlife, include Crow Pass Trail and Resurrection Pass Trail. The forest is easily accessible from Anchorage.

Long-Distance Trails. If you fancy an odyssey of several months or just a few weeks on the trail, there are long-distance trails that are truly long. Contact details for conferences and societies providing information on these trails are provided in appendix A.

The *Appalachian Trail* extends 2,000 miles (3,220 kilometers) from the southern state of Georgia to the far northern state of Maine. The trail crosses fourteen states and seven national parks along a well-marked route, parts of which pass close to major cities (Atlanta, Boston, New York, Philadelphia, Pittsburgh, and Washington, D.C.). Those who trek its entire length take around six months.

The *Pacific Crest Trail (PCT),* running 2,600 miles (4,186 kilometers) from California to Washington state, is a remote wilderness option for trekkers. It is less clearly marked and much less trekked than the Appalachian Trail. If you don't have six months for the full route, then you can start with the John Muir Trail, a spectacular 180-mile (290-kilometer) section of the PCT, in the High Sierra of California.

The *Continental Divide Trail (CDT)* stretches 3,000 miles (4,860 kilometers) from New Mexico to Montana. Although plans are afoot to provide marking and route designation, wilderness navigation along unmarked trails is the norm for the CDT.

The semitropical *Florida Trail* runs 800 miles (1,288 kilometers) from Apalachichola National Forest past swamp forest, dry prairie, and wetlands to Lake Okeechobee—further extensions to the trail are in progress.

In Arizona, the *General Crook Trail* follows the Mogollon Rim for 138 miles (222 kilometers) through desert shrubland and coniferous forest. The *Ozark Highlands Trail* in Arkansas follows a scenic, 140-mile (225-kilometer) route through grasslands, steep ridges, and the dense woodland of the Ozark National Forest. In Kentucky, the Daniel Boone National Forest is crossed by the *Sheltowee Trace,* a 254-mile (408-kilometer) trail featuring coniferous forests, sandstone cliffs, and tumbling waterfalls.

◆ LATIN AMERICA ◆

Encompassing the southern and central parts of the American continent, Latin America hosts an extraordinary variety of interests. Although the Latin influences of the eclipsed colonial powers form part of the culture, they have overlaid ancient traditions of civilizations, such as the Inca, dating back many centuries.

The national parks, reserves, and wilderness areas of the region have plenty to offer the trekker. Choices for short or long treks might include the glaciers and lakelands of Patagonia; the deserts and volcanoes of Chile; the Bolivian coastline of Lake Titicaca, the world's highest lake; the mist-enshrouded forests and otherworldly summits of the *tepui* (tablelike mountains) in Venezuela; and the Inca Trail to the ruins of Machu Picchu, a "lost" ancient Inca city (only rediscovered this century), which perches on the peaks of the Peruvian Andes. En route in Patagonia or the Andean altiplano you may encounter unique species, such as the condor, guanaco, and the llama, whereas the forests of the Amazon Basin host an estimated half of all the world's species.

Climate ranges from the wet and dry seasons in the tropical rainforest of the Amazon Basin, to the arid deserts of northern Chile, to the alpine zones of the Andes. Because trekking infrastructure is not broadly available, it's best to be prepared for self-reliance. In much of the region, travel and trekking are inexpensive and generally represent good value.

ARGENTINA

Argentina attracts trekkers to the valleys of the Fitzroy range in the northern corner of Los Glaciares National Park, an awe-inspiring Patagonian wilderness dominated by glaciers. Treks provide stunning views of Cerro Torre and Cerro

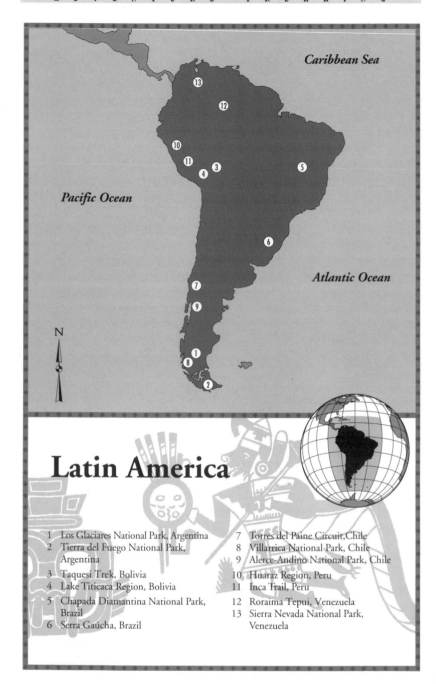

Caribbean Sea

Pacific Ocean

Atlantic Ocean

N

Latin America

1 Los Glaciares National Park, Argentina
2 Tierra del Fuego National Park, Argentina
3 Taquesi Trek, Bolivia
4 Lake Titicaca Region, Bolivia
5 Chapada Diamantina National Park, Brazil
6 Serra Gaúcha, Brazil

7 Torres del Paine Circuit, Chile
8 Villarrica National Park, Chile
9 Alerce-Andino National Park, Chile
10 Huaraz Region, Peru
11 Inca Trail, Peru
12 Roraima Tepui, Venezuela
13 Sierra Nevada National Park, Venezuela

Fitzroy—needle-shaped peaks that soar above 11,000 feet (3,353 meters). Farther south, at the tip of the continent, there is a network of trails through the peat bogs and beech forests of Tierra del Fuego National Park.

BOLIVIA

The Bolivian Andes, in particular the Cordillera Real and Cordillera Apolobamba ranges, provide plenty of scope for exploration on foot. The Taquesi Trek follows a route still partially paved as it was before even Inca times and features great mountain views, high lakes, and rushing rivers. Although the trek itself takes a couple of days, you should allow as many days again for transport to and from La Paz.

BRAZIL

Not just a country of beaches and Carnival, Brazil also provides scope for trekking. In the state of Bahia, there's a network of trails (but no

Armadillo, Pantanal, Brazil

infrastructure) accessible from the attractive old mining town of Lençois in Chapada Diamantina National Park. There's the option for self-reliant trekkers to take at least 5 days, preferably longer, on a circuit of the further attractions within the park, such as the splendid Glass Waterfall, at 1,377 feet (420 meters), Brazil's longest waterfall.

Farther south, the hiking is impressive in the forests and canyons of the Serra Gaúcha ranges in the state of Rio Grande do Sul.

CHILE

In southern Chile, a circuit of enormous granite pinnacles in Torres del Paine National Park tops the trekking bill. The Torres del Paine Circuit (53 miles/86 kilometers) is a one-week trek that takes in the full grandeur of the glaciers, turquoise lakes, beech forests, and pinnacles of this world biosphere reserve. The park also hosts silver fox, eagles, guanaco, and black-necked swans. En route you camp or stay in *refugios,* basic mountain shelters. The trek is of moderate diffi-culty, and vigorous meltwater streams may have to be forded.

Villarrica National Park lies in the Araucanía district, known for its charac-teristic *araucaría* (monkey-puzzle) trees. Villarrica volcano, still partially active, soars above the surrounding landscape and can be circuited on a 3-day trek.

Close to Puerto Montt in the Chilean Lake District is the Alerce-Andino National Park, where there is excellent scope for trekking for several days around the strings of lakes and forests of alerce, a conifer species of enormous size and age.

PERU

Trekking in the Peruvian Andes, especially in the Cordillera Huayhuash and Cordillera Blanca ranges, rates among the best in the world. The best base in the area is the town of Huaraz where transport, guides, porters, and pack ani-mals can be arranged for a wide range of treks and expeditions to the surround-ing scenic valleys and traditional villages.

The Inca Trail, a once-secret trail between Cuzco and Machu Picchu, the legendary lost city of the Incas, was rediscovered in 1911, wedged on high in a breathtaking position among forested peaks. The 3-day trek features high passes, forests, and ancient ruins. It is strenuous in parts and often crowded, as it is eas-ily the most well-known trekking destination in South America. For improved security, travel in a group and keep an eye on your tent and possessions. You should be self-reliant for food, shelter, and warm gear.

VENEZUELA

In the southeast of Venezuela is La Gran Sabana, a region renowned for its many tepui or tablelike mountains of sandstone that soar above the grasslands. The Roraima tepui rises 9,216 feet (2,810 meters) and is accessible via the village of San Francisco de Yuruaní. The trek to the top takes around 5 days or preferably longer if you spend more time in the otherworldly environment at the top. The trail commences in flat savanna, rising through rainforest, passing waterfalls, rivu-lets, and streams, before the final steep ascent to the stepped plateau. The swirl-ing mists, eroded rock forms, and trees draped with bromeliads and orchids provide an extraordinary experience. The trek is strenuous in parts and you'll need warm gear for the cold nights, raingear, and insect repellent. Given the confus-ing terrain and weather at the top, hiring of local guides is advisable. Overnighting en route consists of sleeping under rock overhangs or in caves; carry a tent and sufficient food.

The town of Mérida makes a pleasant base for hiking the high valleys and moorlands in the Sierra Nevada National Park in the Venezuelan Andes.

◆ EUROPE ◆

In Europe there's a wide variation in scenery, ranging from the breathtaking panoramas of hut-to-hut treks in the Alps, to the jagged cliffs and wild seas of the Welsh coast, to the birch forests of Scandinavia. The major mountain ranges of the Alps and Pyrenees provide plenty of scope for demanding treks (sometimes given a helpful kickstart or finish by a convenient cablecar).

Although few areas could be deemed uncharted wilderness, the long history of travel on foot in Europe has coalesced tracks or ways into long-distance trails—for instance, the Haute Route Pyrénée (High Level Pyrenean Route) following the Pyrenees from the Atlantic to the Mediterranean.

The European Rambling Association (for contact details, see appendix A) is promoting the implementation and upkeep of almost a dozen European long-distance footpaths, which are designated with an "E" and a number. Thus, for example, the E1 currently stretches (extension is continuing) some 1,740 miles (2,800 kilometers) from the North Sea (Flensburg, Germany) to the Mediterranean (Nice, France).

AUSTRIA

Alpine trekking in Austria matches the scenic splendors of its alpine neighbors and is complemented by a large trail network with conveniently placed huts, often with provision of meals. In the Tyrol region, hut-to-hut walks in the Stubai mountains are a good introduction to alpine walking, and the regional capital of Innsbruck makes a good base, while farther west, the Vorarlberg region also offers a wide choice of hikes of varying difficulty. For a drop in altitude, try the country's Carinthia region, which is a center for lakeland walks.

BRITAIN

Britain offers trekkers a variety of options. Apart from their scenic attractions, many of the routes also have historical connections dating back to the Middle Ages or even Roman times. Modern-day hikers can ponder the fortunes of wool merchants or the fate of Roman legionaries as they follow in their footsteps. British understatement tends to merge the trekking concept both at home and abroad into that of an extended "walk." Even the four-month odyssey from Land's End to John O'Groats is often referred to as an "End-to-End Walk."

With the exception of the wilder parts of Scotland, at the end of a days' trekking, accommodation (hostel or farmhouse) or a maintained campsite can usually be found nearby. Don't underestimate the British weather: equip for rapid change from fair conditions to foul, and be prepared to use your compass.

Atlantic Ocean

N

North Sea

Baltic Sea

Black Sea

Mediterranean Sea

Europe

1 Stubai Mountains, Austria
2 Vorarlberg Region, Austria
3 Carinthia Region, Austria
4 Peak District, England
5 Yorkshire Dales National Park, England
6 Southwest Peninsula Coastal Path, England
7 Pennine Way, England
8 Hadrian's Wall Walk, England

9 Offa's Dyke Path, Wales
10 West Highland Way, Scotland
11 Wicklow Way, Ireland
12 Kerry Way, Ireland
13 French Alps, France
14 Dolomites, Italy
15 Trento, Italy
16 Bolzano, Italy
17 Engadine Valley, Switzerland
18 Berner Oberland Region, Switzerland

England. Over a dozen long-distance trails link many of the national parks or combine regional routes. The following examples are but a brief look at a lengthy topic.

The Pennine Way follows the country's backbone, the Pennine range, for 270 miles (435 kilometers) from Edale in the Peak District to Kirk Yetholm in Scotland. Among its highlights are sections in the Peak District and Yorkshire Dales and a short sector along the old Roman structure of Hadrian's Wall; lowlights include notoriously boggy escapades past Kinder Scout Plateau. Allow three weeks for the walk and make sure you have proper foul-weather gear and navigation skills.

The Southwest Peninsula Coastal Path extends over 500 miles (800 kilometers), weaving up and over cliffs, following the coastline between Minehead in Somerset and Poole in Dorset. The full walk takes between six weeks and two months. Attractions along the way include rugged shores, sandy beaches, shipwrecked boat hulls, historic remains, and plentiful birdlife.

For a hardcore venture, you could take four months to walk Britain from end to end, pacing over a thousand miles from Land's End in the far southwest of England to John O'Groats at the tip of Scotland. Large sections of the route can be spliced together from existing long-distance trails, such as the Southwest Peninsula Coastal Path, Offa's Dyke Path, Pennine Way, and West Highland Way.

Wales. In the eighth century, Offa, King of Mercia, constructed an enormous earthwork dyke to mark the frontier between Wales and England. Following the line of the construction in some sections, the long-distance Offa's Dyke Path stretches 168 miles (270 kilometers) from the Severn Bridge near Chepstow to Prestatyn on the north coast of Wales. Highlights include the scenic Wye Valley and Tintern Abbey, the Black Mountains, castles, and Iron Age forts.

19	Rila Massif, Bulgaria	31	The Bear's Path, Finland
20	Pirin Massif, Bulgaria	32	Mount Halti, Finland
21	Tatra National Park, Poland	33	Landmannalaugar/Thórsmörk Trek, Iceland
22	Bieszczady National Park, Poland		
23	Bucegi ranges, Romania	34	Reykanesfölkvangur National Reserve, Iceland
24	Fagaras ranges, Romania		
25	Tatra National Park, Slovakia	35	Hornstrandir Peninsula, Iceland
26	Lake Bohinj Region, Slovenia	36	Jotunheimen National Park, Norway
27	Triglav National Park, Slovenia	37	The Lofoten Islands, Norway
28	Vikos-Aoos National Park, Greece	38	Lyngen Peninsula, Norway
29	Aigues Tortes National Park, Spain	39	Spitsbergen (Svalbard), Norway
30	Camino de Santiago, Spain	40	Kungsleden (Royal Route) Trek, Sweden
		41	Sarek National Park, Sweden

Scotland. For more experienced hikers, Scotland can provide the challenge of near-Arctic weather (proper equipment and navigation skills essential) and the rewards of truly splendid scenery. Midge repellent is essential to keep the pesky insects in check.

The West Highland Way runs 95 miles (151 kilometers) from Milngavie on the outskirts of Glasgow, rising from the lowlands via the shores of Loch Lomond to the splendors of the highlands, lochs, and mountains farther north, until it finishes at Fort William. Allow 10 days or a couple of weeks to suit your own pace for this walk for which you should be well prepared, especially if you top off the trip with a sideclimb of Ben Nevis (4,406 feet/1,445 meters), the highest peak in Britain.

REPUBLIC OF IRELAND

Irish landscapes offer walkers the charms of dazzling green pastures and lakelands, the drama of rocky coastlines, and the stark beauty of heather-covered moorlands.

The Wicklow Way stretches 83 miles (132 kilometers) from Rathfarnham (south of Dublin) to Clonegal (County Carlow) at the foot of the Blackstairs Mountains. The full route, a scenic mixture ranging from forested valleys to bogs and gorse-covered mountain slopes, takes 10 days. The Kerry Way is a loop walk that starts near Killarney in the southwestern county of Kerry. Circling 135 miles (215 kilometers) round the Iveragh Peninsula, the route's attractions include the Torc Waterfall and fine views of Macgillycuddy's Reeks, Ireland's highest mountain range.

FRANCE

Exploring France on foot is a passion for locals and foreign visitors. The country is crisscrossed by some 24,800 miles (40,000 kilometers) of major hiking routes maintained by the Fédération Française de la Randonée Pédestre (FFRP) (French Hiking Federation), which selects each route, designates it as a "grande randonnée" (GR), and assigns a specific number. Following special markings that differentiate between short walks, loop walks, and point-to-point routes, walkers can plan an excursion for a day, a week, or longer. Information, maps, and trail guides are available from tourist offices. Budget accommodation for walkers ranges from hostels and *gîtes d'étape* (locally provided hiker's accommodation) to mountain huts or refuges; some are open all year, others only operate during the summer season.

The French Alps, with their hallmark grandeur of snowcaps, glaciers, and pine forests, offer many hiking opportunities, especially in the national parks, but be prepared for crowds during both winter and summer. Major centers for hiking in the region include Grenoble, Chamonix, Annecy, and Chambéry, which offer access to GR long-distance trails. Excellent information, advice, and assistance with reservations are available locally from a tourist center or a specialist center for walkers, known as Maison de la Montagne or Maison de La Randonnée.

ITALY

Italy is a destination with an extensive trekking infrastructure, especially in the Italian Alps, and many national parks and hiking regions of interest. Italy's alpine gem is the Dolomite range in the north. The region is covered by a huge network of trails offering a wide choice of long-distance itineraries. Local tourist offices, such as those in the regional hubs of Trento and Bolzano, supply hiking maps and information and can provide advice on guided trips. Highly detailed trail maps are readily available. A number of long-distance high-level routes, including refuges en route, cross the mountains and can be trekked in their entirety for several weeks, or less if you opt for specific sections. Check the degree of skill required: some routes may require the use of fixed ropes or ladders, and there are many opportunities for scrambling or mountaineering. Alta Via 1 (High Level Route 1) is an easy- to moderate-grade, 10-day trek from Lago di Braes to Belluno.

SWITZERLAND

Alpine landscapes of soaring peaks, meadows, and lakes attract hikers and adventure sports enthusiasts to Switzerland. A well-organized and scrupulously maintained network of many thousands of miles of trails provides experienced and novice hikers with abundant choice. Tourist offices are well stocked with maps and have route information readily available.

For a kickstart on some hikes, you may be tempted to ease the pain of altitude gain by using one of the country's many cablecars. The Swiss Alpine Club (or SAC) maintains basic mountain huts on high level routes.

In the Graubünden region, the trails of the Engadine Valley are not overly difficult or steep and are accessible from, for example, the chic milieu of St. Moritz.

The town of Grindelwald, which lies below the Eiger peak (13,000 feet/3,970 meters), is a good base for trekking in the Berner Oberland, especially the Jungfrau region, which is packed with opportunities to trek trails at higher altitudes in superb alpine scenery: a visual feast of snowcaps, glaciers, and green valleys.

BULGARIA

Bulgaria's most popular hiking region lies in the Rila Massif, just south of the national capital, Sofia. The Rila Monastery, itself an architectural wonder, is a useful base. Options include wooded trails in the valleys and treks higher into the mountains where there are hostels providing basic bunk accommodation.

Farther south, the Pirin Massif attracts hikers to its mountain trails, glacial lakes, traditional villages, and mineral spas.

Tatra National Park, Poland (Deanna Swaney photo)

POLAND

In Poland, the mountain resort of Zakopane in the south of the country is a staging point for hikes into the stunning Tatra mountain ranges. The Polish portion of the Tatras is designated as the Tatra National Park and features alpine valleys and forests in the west and glacial lakes and exposed mountaintops in the east. Highly detailed mapping is available to make your choice of longer routes from a dense network of trails inside the park. Camping is not permitted within the park, and hikers use mountain huts, which may provide food and either a bunk or floorspace.

Farther east, the forests and meadows of the Bieszczady Mountains attract trekkers. The village of Ustrzyki Górne is a convenient staging point to explore the trail network within the Bieszczady National Park, which includes some of the most spectacular parts of the range. Mountain huts provide accommodation.

ROMANIA

Some of Europe's most isolated hiking terrain lies along hundreds of routes in the ranges of the Carpathian mountains in Romania. In Transylvania, prime trails crisscross the wooded valleys and alpine meadows in the Bucegi and Fagaras ranges. Sinaia is a convenient staging point for hikes in the Bucegi Mountains, whereas Sibiu serves the Fagaras. Accommodation in the mountains is provided by basic cabins, known locally as cabana.

SLOVAKIA

One of Europe's youngest countries, Slovakia has superb hiking in several national parks. In the east of the country, most of the Slovakian slice of the High Tatra Mountains has been included in the Tatra National Park. From the mountain resort of Stary´ Smokovec, several hundred miles of hiking trails provide access to jagged peaks, glacial lakes, and all-round stunning alpine scenery. Camping is not allowed within the park, but accommodation is provided at mountain chalets.

SLOVENIA

Formerly part of northern Yugoslavia, Slovenia is another recent addition to the fold of European countries. There's excellent hiking in the Julian Alps on Slovenia's northwestern boundary. Destinations for hikers include Lake Bohinj and Triglav National Park, an alpine extravaganza that has various hut-to-hut routes, including the ascent of Mount Triglav (9,393 feet/2,864 meters), the country's highest peak.

GREECE

As a change from the beach scene, more foreigners are exploring trekking options in Greece. Trail infrastructure is minimal, so you need to be self-reliant for equipment and shelter. Maps and trail guides are best bought in advance.

There is excellent alpine trekking among the forested peaks of the northern Píndhos mountains in the northwestern corner of the country. In the Zagoria region, north of Ioannina, lies the Vikos-Aoos National Park. Highlights of the area include picturesque villages, thick forests of oak and fir thinning at higher altitude to alpine pastures, and limestone peaks.

SPAIN

The mountains and rural regions of Spain attract both local and foreign climbers and trekkers. The country's trekking infrastructure is well supported by information centers, maps, and trail guides.

The mountains of the Pyrenees, shared between France and Spain, afford excellent scope for short or long treks. The scenery ranges from beech forests to alpine meadows and dramatic canyons, rock walls, and peaks. Mountain refuges provide shelter and often food. The Aigues Tortes National Park in the Catalan Pyrenees offers treks of varying lengths and difficulty through wild, glaciated landscapes studded with lakes.

The long-distance route, Camino de Santiago, forming part of the Way of St. James, stretches across Spain from the Pyrenees to Santiago de Compostela. Formerly used as an ancient pilgrimage trail, the route continues across France as the Chemin de Saint Jacques (GR65).

Puffins, Latrabjarg, Northwest Iceland (Deanna Swaney photo)

FINLAND

Finland offers many trekking opportunities in more than two dozen national parks, on designated trails, and in wilderness areas. Wilderness huts, basic shelters, and campsites are provided by the National Board of Forestry.

In North Karelia, the Bear's Path (48 miles/80 kilometers) leads the trekker close to the Arctic Circle and the 4-day route features mixed forests, lakes and waterfalls, raging rivers, and deep canyons.

The country's highest peak, Mount Halti (4,355 feet/1,328 meters), can be reached via a one-week return trek using wilderness huts en route.

ICELAND

Hiking in Iceland comes with a few surprises: hot springs, glaciers, active volcanoes, peaks, and waterfalls—the often quoted epithet "land of fire and ice" is apt. High-quality mapping is published by the Iceland Geodetic Survey, and mountain huts are available on the major trails. Due to the expense of importing goods from overseas, travel costs are very high, but setting off to explore on foot can reduce the budget to more manageable levels.

The 4-day trek between Landmannalaugar and Thórsmörk in the center of the island is rated a worldbeater, and you may be able to sidestep its growing popularity by starting in September. Trail highlights include hot springs, volcanic deserts and geological formations, churning torrents, boggy moors and grassy slopes, and spectacular views from the elevated trail sections. There are huts en route, which should be reserved in advance with the wardens, who can also advise on trail conditions. The route can be extended an additional 2 days by trekking south from Thórsmörk to Skógar.

Close to Reykavík lies Reykanesf lkvangur National Reserve, with a trail system that provides hiking access to spectacular lava formations and the bubbling vents and mudpots of geothermal fields.

For self-sufficient trekkers, the wilderness of Hornstranðir Peninsula with its vertical cliffs, rolling grasslands, deep valleys, and tidal flats, offers rewarding treks.

NORWAY

The highest mountain ranges in Scandinavia, arctic tundra in the far north, and deep-cut fiords zigzagging along its coast make Norway a fascinating outdoors destination. The Norwegian Mountain Touring Association (DNT) maintains mountain huts across the land and is an excellent source of information, advice, and mapping.

In central Norway, Jotunheimen National Park features dozens of glaciers and impressive peaks, including the country's highest mountain, Mount Galdhøpiggen (8,098 feet/2,469 meters). Throughout the Trollheimen and Jotunheimen ranges, trekkers can explore the peak trails, boulder fields, lakes, and deeply cut valleys, while camping or staying in mountain huts.

In the north of the country, trekking on the bristly peaks and ridges of the Lofoten Islands offers spectacular views as well as the chance to stay in a traditional fisherman's shanty and experience picturesque island life. Moving higher up the coastline to the province of Troms, there are many glaciers, valleys, and lakes on the rugged Lyngen peninsula, with a great variety of walks and climbs to suit all tastes.

For truly remote arctic splendors, you can visit the island of Spitsbergen (Svalbard), halfway between the northern coast of Norway and the North Pole. Guided treks lead through glacier landscapes and offer excellent opportunities for observing abundant birdlife and mammals, such as Arctic fox, whales, walrus, and, at a respectful distance, polar bear.

SWEDEN

Trekking in Sweden benefits from marked trails, detailed maps, and an efficiently maintained system of mountain huts.

The vast northern region of Sweden, known as Norrland—a landscape of birch and pine woods, whitewater torrents, moorland, rocky outcrops, and lakes—draws hikers in search of challenging wilderness. Experienced and hardened trekkers can try the routes in Sarek National Park, or take the long-distance Kungsleden (Royal Route) Trail, leading some 250 miles (400 kilometers) from Hemavan across the wilds to Abisko.

> *"I am now standing at North Cape . . . on the very edge of the world. Here the world ends, as does my curiosity, and I shall now return homewards, God willing. . . ."*
>
> **—Francesco Negri, on visiting Nordkapp (Norway) in 1664**

◆ Appendix A ◆

INFORMATION AND ADVICE
Useful Organizations and Addresses

The appendices have been compiled for largely English-speaking countries with mostly English-speaking trekkers in mind, so that they facilitate contacts at home and direct links abroad. At the same time I have included some contacts and data which fall outside this framework, because this information is less readily accessible elsewhere. I'd be happy to hear from readers with updates or expansions for these appendices, particularly where the trekking angle can be enhanced.

◆ BACKPACKING AND TREKKING ◆ CLUBS AND ASSOCIATIONS

Remember as a common courtesy to send any requests for information accompanied by a stamped, self-addressed envelope for local replies or an international reply coupon for international postage.

UNITED STATES

The American Alpine Club, 710 10th Street, Suite 100, Golden, CO 80401; phone (303) 384-0110.

American Hiking Society, P.O. Box 20160, Washington, DC 20041; phone (301) 565-6704, fax (301) 565-6714.

Sierra Club, 730 Polk Street, San Francisco, CA 94109; phone (415) 981-8634.

UNITED KINGDOM

The Backpackers Club, P.O. Box 381, Reading RG3 4LR; phone 01491-680684. Organizes local groups for meetings and publishes *Backpack,* a quarterly journal.

British Mountaineering Council, 177-179 Burton Road, West Didsbury, Manchester M20 2BB; phone 0161-4454747.

Long Distance Walkers Association, 10 Temple Park Close, Leeds, West Yorks LS15 0JJ; phone 0113-2642205. Publishes *Strider,* a quarterly newsletter.

Ramblers' Association, 1-5 Wandsworth Road, London SW8 2XX; phone 0171-5826878.

GERMANY

Europäische Wandervereinigung eV (European Rambling Association), Reichstraße 4, D-6000, Saarbrücken, Germany; phone 0681-390070. Encourages hiking and climbing and is active in the implementation of long-distance paths and trails across Europe.

SOUTH AFRICA

Hiking Federation of South Africa, P.O. Box 1420, Randburg 2125; phone 011-8866524, fax 011-8866013.

The Mountain Club of South Africa, 97 Hatfield Street, Cape Town 8001; phone 021-453412.

AUSTRALIA

New South Wales—NSW Federation of Bushwalking Clubs, GPO Box 2090, Sydney NSW 2001.

Northern Territory—Darwin Bushwalking Club, P.O. Box 1938, Darwin NT 5794.

Queensland—Queensland Federation of Bushwalking Clubs, GPO Box 1573, Brisbane QLD 4001.

South Australia—Adelaide Bushwalkers, 34 Strapsey Avenue, Hazelwood Park, SA 5066.

Tasmania—Launceston Walking Club, P.O. Box 273C, Launceston TAS 7250.

Western Australia—Western Walking Club, 57 Alderbury Street, Floreat Park WA 6014.

NEW ZEALAND

The Department of Conservation (DOC), Head Office, P.O. Box 10-420 Wellington; phone 04-4710726. Publishes and sells numerous publications of interest to the trekker.

Federated Mountain Clubs (FMC), P.O. Box 1604, Wellington; phone 04-3842448. Publishes a complete listing of affiliated regional clubs.

◆ GENERAL TRAVEL-RESOURCES ◆

UNITED STATES

Europe Through the Back Door, 120 Fourth Avenue North, P.O. Box 2009, Edmonds, WA 98020; phone (206) 771-8303, fax (206) 771-0833. Travel seminars, guidebooks, travel accessories, tours, quarterly newsletter, and catalogue.

Travel Info Exchange; BBS phone (508) 287-0660. Bulletin board service operated by travel guide author Tom Brosnahan. Offers interim updates for his guides, plus travel conferences hosted by other travel authors.

EUROPE

Expedition Advisory Service, Royal Geographical Society, 1 Kensington Gore, London SW7 2AR; phone 0171-5895466.

The Globetrotters Club, BCM/Roving, London WC1N 3XX. An association with no commercial affiliations that offers travellers a bimonthly newsletter, contacts, advice, and talks in regional centers.

SOUTH AMERICA

The South American Explorers Club, Casilla 3714, Lima 100 Peru. U.S. branch: 126 Indian Creek Road, Ithaca, NY 14850; phone (607) 277-0488. Serving scientists, travellers, trekkers, mountaineers, and explorers, offers members advice and information on the region, publications for sale by mail order, and the club's official journal, *The South American Explorer*.

◆ HOSTELLING ◆

UNITED STATES

Hostelling International—American Youth Hostels, 733 15th Street NW, Suite 840, Washington, DC 20005; phone (202) 783-6161.

CANADA

Hostelling International—Canada, 1600 James Naismith Drive, Suite 608, Gloucester, ON K1B 5N4; phone (613) 748-5638.

ENGLAND AND WALES

Youth Hostel Association of England & Wales (YHA), Trevelyan House, 8 St. Stephens Hill, St. Albans, Herts. AL1 2DY; phone 01727-55215.

NORTHERN IRELAND

Youth Hostel Association of Northern Ireland, 56 Bradbury Place, Belfast BT7 1RU; phone 01232-324733.

REPUBLIC OF IRELAND

An Óige, Irish Youth Hostel Association, 61 Mountjoy Street, Dublin 7; phone 01-304555.

SCOTLAND

Scottish Youth Hostels Association, 7 Glebe Crescent, Stirling FK8 2JA; phone 01786-451181.

AUSTRALIA

Australian Youth Hostels Association (AYHA), Level 3, 10 Mallett Street, Camperdown NSW 2050; phone 02-5651699.

NEW ZEALAND

Youth Hostels Association of New Zealand (YHANZ), P.O. Box 436, Christchurch 1; phone 03-3799970.

SOUTH AFRICA

South African Youth Hostels Association, 101 Boston House, Strand Street, Cape Town 8001; phone 021-4191853.

◆ FLIGHTS ◆

General Electronic Reference

PCTravel. Airline reservation and ticketing service for free public use. Telnet://pctravel.com

UNITED STATES
Consolidated Flights

Air Brokers International, 323 Geary Street, Suite 411, San Francisco, CA 94102; phone toll-free 1-800-883-3273.

Interworld Travel, 800 Douglas Road, Miami, FL 33134; phone (305) 443-4929.

TFI Tours International, 34 West 32nd Street, New York, NY 10001; phone toll-free 1-800-745-8000.

Travac, 989 Sixth Avenue, New York, NY 10018; phone toll-free 1-800-872-8800.

Unitravel, 1177 North Warson Road, St. Louis, MO 63132; phone toll-free 1-800-325-2222.

Discount Flights

Council Travel, 205 East 42nd Street, New York, NY 10017; phone toll-free1-800-743-1823. Over 50 branches in the United States, including Boston (phone (617) 266-1926), Chicago (phone (312) 951-0585), and Los Angeles (phone (310) 208-3551).

STA Travel, 48 East 11th Street, New York, NY 10003; phone toll-free 1-800-777-0112. Over ten branches in the United States, including Boston (phone (617) 266-6014) and Los Angeles (phone (213) 934-8722).

Standby Flights

AirHitch, 2790 Broadway, Suite 100, New York, NY 10025; phone (212) 864-2000.

AirHitch, 1341 Ocean Avenue, Suite 62, Santa Monica, CA 90401; phone (213) 458-1006.

Last-Minute Travel Club, 132 Brookline Avenue, Boston, MA 02215; phone (617) 267-9800.

Courier Flights

Air Courier Association, 191 University Boulevard, Suite 300, Denver, CO 80206; phone (303) 278-8810.

Discount Travel International (DTI), 169 West 81st Street, New York, NY 10024; phone (212) 362-3636.

International Association of Air Travel Couriers (IAATC), International Features, P.O. Box 1349, Lake Worth, FL 33460; phone (407) 582-8320. For a fee of $45 (US) or $50 (foreign), members receive the bimonthly *Air Courier Bulletin,* detailing courier routes currently open, and the bimonthly *Shoestring Traveler,* a newsletter containing bargain travel tips and air courier information. For last-minute flights and information, IAATC also operates a fax-on-demand service and an on-line 24-hour Bulletin Board Service (BBS) that is updated twice daily.

Now Voyager, 74 Varick Street, Suite 307, New York, NY 10013; phone (212) 431-1616.

Travel Unlimited, P.O. Box 1058, Allston, MA 02134. An inexpensive newsletter detailing airfares and courier flight options for routings around the world.

CANADA
Discount Flights

Travel CUTS (Canadian Universities Travel Services), 17 College Street, Toronto, ON M5T 1P7; phone (416) 979-2406. Branches in most major cities.

UNITED KINGDOM
Discount Flights

Bridge the World, 1-3 Ferdinand Street, Camden Town, London NW1 8ES; phone 0171-9110900.

Campus Travel, 52 Grosvenor Gardens, London SW1W OAG; phone 0171-7302101. Branches in Bristol, Cambridge, Oxford, and Edinburgh.

Council Travel, 28a Poland Street, London W1; phone 0171-4377767.

STA Travel, 86 Old Brompton Road, London SW7; phone 0171-9379971, North America; 0171-9379962, rest of world. Branches in Bristol, Cambridge, Edinburgh, Leeds, Manchester, and Oxford.

Trailfinders, 42-48 Earls Court Road, London W8 6FT; phone 0171-9383366. Branches in Birmingham, Bristol, Glasgow, and Manchester.

Travel Bug, 597 Cheetham Hill Road, Manchester M8 5EJ; phone 0161-7214000. Branch in London phone 0171-8352000.

Travel CUTS, 295 Regent Street, London W1; phone 0171-6373161.

Courier Flights

Bridges Worldwide, Unit 61/62 G, Building 521, Heathrow Airport, Middlesex TW3 3UJ; phone 0181-7595040.

British Airways (BA), Courier Enquiries; phone 0181-7541234. For flight details and prices, send a SASE to BA Travel Shop, World Cargo Centre, Export Cargo Terminal F126, Heathrow Airport, Hounslow, Middlesex TW6 2JS.

Linehaul Express, Building 252, Section D, Ely Road, Heathrow Airport, Hounslow, Middlesex TW6 2PR; phone 0181-7595969.

AUSTRALIA
Discount Flights

Flight Centre, 19 Bourke Street, Melbourne, VIC 3000; phone 03-96502899.

Flight Centre, Circular Quay, Sydney, NSW 2000; phone 02-2412422.

STA Travel, 256 Flinders Street, Melbourne, VIC 3000; phone 03-96547266.

STA Travel, 9 Oxford Street, Paddington, Sydney, NSW 2021; phone 02-3601822.

Courier Flights

Jupiter Air, P.O. Box 1219, Bondi Junction, NSW 2022; phone 02-3692704.

NEW ZEALAND
Discount Flights

Flight Centre, 205-225 Queen Street, Auckland; phone 09-3096171.

Flight Centre, 50-52 Willis Street, Wellington; phone 04-4728101.

STA Travel, 10 High Street, Auckland; phone 09-3099723.
STA Travel, 233 Cuba Street, Wellington; phone 04-3850561.

Courier Flights

TNT Express Worldwide, 6 Doncaster Street, Mangere, Auckland; phone 09-2750549.

◆ TRAVELER'S CHECKS ◆

American Express: in the United States and Canada, phone toll-free 1-800-221-7282; in the United Kingdom, phone toll-free 0800-521313; in Australia, New Zealand, and the South Pacific, phone 02-886-0689; in other locations, call US collect for referral, (801) 964-6665.

Thomas Cook: in the United States, phone toll-free 1-800-223-7373 or call collect (609) 987-7300; in the United Kingdom, phone toll-free 0800-622101 or call collect 01733-502995. Thomas Cook is affiliated with MasterCard, and charges no commission on traveler's checks purchased at Thomas Cook offices.

Visa: in the United States, phone toll-free 1-800-227-6811 or call collect (212) 858-8500; in the United Kingdom, phone toll-free 0800-895078 or call collect 0171-9378091. Visa traveler's checks are widely available around the world.

◆ INSURANCE ◆

UNITED STATES

Globalcare Travel Insurance, 220 Broadway, Lynnfield, MA 01940; phone toll-free 1-800-821-2488.

Travel Assistance International, 1133 15th Street NW, Washington, DC 20005; phone (202) 821-2828.

Travel Guard, 1145 Clark Street, Stevens Point, WI 54481; phone toll-free 1-800-7825151 or (715) 345-0505.

UNITED KINGDOM

Association of British Insurers, 51-55 Gresham Street, London EC2V 7HQ; phone 0171-6003333. Provides general advice on insurance and can put you in touch with mainstream or specialist insurers.

British Mountaineering Council, 177-179 Burton West, Didsbury, Manchester, M20 2BB; phone 0161-4454747. Provides insurance for trekking and mountaineering.

Club Direct, The Clock House, 39 North Street, Midhurst, West Sussex GU29 9DR; phone 01730-817533, fax 01730-815366.

Frizzell Financial Services Ltd., Frizzell House, County Gates, Bournemouth, BH1 2NF; phone 01202-292333.

Marcus Hearn & Co., 65-66 Shoreditch High Street, London E1 6JL; phone 0171-7393444, fax 0171-7397888.

◆ MAIL-ORDER TREKKING, CAMPING, ◆ AND BACKPACKING EQUIPMENT

The following is just a small selection of companies. You'll find many more advertised in the pages of travel, trekking, and backpacking magazines, some of which are listed in appendix B.

UNITED STATES

Campmor, P.O. Box 700-B4, Saddle River, NJ 07458; phone toll-free 1-800-230-2151 or (201) 445-5000.

Eastern Mountain Sports, One Vose Farm Road, Peterborough, NH 03548; phone (603) 924-7231.

Eddie Bauer, Fifth and Union, P.O. Box 3700, Seattle, WA 98130; phone toll-free 1-800-426-8020 or (206) 885-3330.

L. L. Bean, Casco Street, Freeport, ME 04033; phone toll-free 1-800-458-4438.

REI (Recreational Equipment Inc.), P.O. Box 1938, Sumner, WA 98390; phone toll-free 1-800-426-4840.

MontBell, 940 41st Avenue, Santa Cruz, CA 95062; phone toll-free 1-800-683-2002. Offers solar chargers—polycrystalline cell.

CANADA

Blacks Camping Equipment, 225 Strathcona and Bank, P.O. Box 4501, Ottawa, ON K1S 5H1.

Eddie Bauer, 50 Bloor Street West, Toronto, ON M4W 1A1.

Mountain Equipment Co-op, 1655 West Third Avenue, Vancouver, BC V6J 1K1.

UNITED KINGDOM

Blacks Camping & Leisure, Unit 3, Stevenson Industrial Estate, Washington, Tyne & Wear NE37 2SF; phone 0191-4170414.

Cotswold Camping, Broadway Lane, South Cerney, Cirencester, Glos GL7 5UQ; phone 01285-860612.

Field & Trek Ltd., 3 Wates Way, Brentwood, Essex CM15 9TB; phone 01277-233122.

Gulliver's Travels, The Wolfpack Trading Post, 52 Commercial Road, Poole, Dorset BH14 OJT; phone 01202-747096.

Taunton Leisure, 40 East Reach, Taunton TA1 3ES; phone 01823-331875.

YHA Adventure Shops, 19 High Street, Staines, Middlesex TW18 4QX; phone 01784-458625.

◆ COMPANIES SPECIALIZING IN REPAIR WORK AND RESOLING ◆

UNITED STATES

Dave Page, Cobbler, 3509 Evanston Avenue North, Seattle, WA 98103; phone toll-free 1-800-252-1229 or (206) 632-8686, fax (206) 632-2613.

Kenco Repair Service Center, 8141 West I-70, Frontage Road, Arvada, CO 80002; phone (303) 425-1201, fax (303) 425-9563.

UNITED KINGDOM

Shoecare Ltd., Unit 5, Yarrow Road, Chorley, Lancashire PR6 OLP; phone 01257-232333, fax 01257-232442.

◆ HEALTH ◆

General Electronic References

World Health Organization. International travel and health advice. http://www.who.ch/welcome.html

MCW International Travelers Clinic. Travel health information. http://www.intmed.mcw.edu/itc/health.html

UNITED STATES AND CANADA

Citizens Emergency Center, U.S. Department of State; phone (202) 647-5225. Provides general advice, including medical assistance, to U.S. citizens.

International Association for Medical Assistance to Travelers (IAMAT), 417 Center Street, Lewiston, NY 14092, USA; phone (716) 754-4883. Provides members with a worldwide directory of qualified English-speaking physicians.

IAMAT, 40 Regal Road, Guelph, ON N1K 1B5, Canada; phone (515) 836-0102. Provides members with a worldwide directory of qualified English-speaking physicians.

Dr. Leonard C. Marcus, Travelers' Health & Immunization Services, 148 Highland Avenue, Newton, MA 02165, USA. For a free list of travel health, tropical medicine, and parasitology specialists in the United States, send an 8½-by-11-inch, self-addressed envelope with 98 cents postage.

U.S. Center for Disease Control (CDC), Atlanta, GA, USA: international travelers' hotline, phone (404) 332 4559; malaria hotline, phone (404) 332-4555. Offers a quick check on the latest health risks. For fax service, call CDC International Travel Fax Service, (404) 332-4565, which will fax you information on health risks and prevention for specific countries or regions.

Medical products for travelers are available from various specialist outlets including the following:

Adventure Medical Kits, Bellevue, WA, USA; phone (206) 746-1896.

Chinook Medical Gear Inc., P.O. Box 3300, 725 Chambers Avenue, #12, Eagle, CO 81631, USA; phone (970) 328-2100 or phone toll-free 1-800-766-1365; fax (970) 328-4404.

Long Road, 111 Avenida Drive, Berkeley, CA 94708, USA; phone toll-free 1-800-359-6040.

Travel Medicine Inc., 351 Pleasant Street, Suite 312, Northampton, MA 01060, USA; phone toll-free 1-800-872-8633; fax (413) 584-6656.

UNITED KINGDOM

British Airways; phone 0171-8315333. Runs special travel clinics; call for the location of the one nearest you.

Dental Save, 144 High Street, Nailsea, Avon BS19 1AP; phone 01275-810291, fax 01275-858112. Provides emergency dental kits.

Health Literature Line, Department of Health, phone 0800-555777; TV viewers can consult page 50063 on Prestel. Publishes *Health Advice for Travelers* (also covers EC and non-EC reciprocal medical care agreements) and various other leaflets of interest to travellers.

The Hospital for Tropical Diseases, 4 St. Pancras Way, London NW1 OPE; phone 0171-3874411, fax 0171-3830041. Operates a travel clinic and shop, as well as a health line with recorded advice at 0898-337733.

Medical Advisory Service for Travellers Abroad (MASTA), phone 0171-6314408. Provides health advice, travel profiles, and medical supplies for specific countries. Operates the Travellers Health Line at 0891-224100 (calls charged at 49p per minute peak rate and 39p at other times) and will send callers a printout of the advice given. For a personalized health brief in greater depth, phone 01705-553933.

The National AIDS Helpline; phone 0800-567123 (free phone, national calls only). Provides information on AIDS.

NOMAD Travellers' Store and Medical Centre, 3-4 Wellington Terrace, Turnpike Lane, London N8 0PX; phone 0181-889-7014, fax 0181-889-9529. Opposite Turnpike Lane tube station (Piccadilly Line), offers advice in its travel shop and pharmacy. Also available at this center are travel health computer printouts, interviews with a pharmacist for specific requirements (phone in advance for an appointment), and customized medical kits.

Oasis Nets, Stoke Ferry, King's Lynn, Norfolk PE33 9SP; phone 01366-500466, fax 01366-501122. Specializes in protection and equipment advice on malaria.

SafariQuip, The Stones, Castleton, Sheffield S30 2WX; phone 01433-620320, fax 01433-620061. Stocks a wide range of medical products for travelers.

The Terrence Higgins Trust Helpline; phone 0171-2421010. Provides information on AIDS.

The UIAA Mountain Medicine Centre, St. Bartholomew's Hospital, London EC1A 7BE. Sells mountain medicine information sheets for climbers and trekkers; write for an order form.

AUSTRALIA

The Travellers' Medical & Vaccination Centre, Level 2, 393 Little Bourke Street, Melbourne, VIC 3000; phone 03-96025788.

The Travellers' Medical & Vaccination Centre, Level 7, 428 George Street, Dymock's Building, Level 7, Sydney, NSW 2000; for appointments phone 02-2217133, for recorded information service phone 02-2214799.

♦ SECURITY ♦

UNITED STATES

Citizens Emergency Center, U.S. Department of State, Bureau of Consular Affairs, Room 4811, NS, Washington, DC 20520; phone (202) 647-1488 during office hours, (202) 647-5225 24 hours, fax (202) 647-3000; use a computer and modem to access their Consular Affairs Bulletin Board (CABB) by phoning (202) 647-9225. Provides travel advisories. If you send a request by post, include a stamped, self-addressed envelope for the reply.

Consular Information Sheets and Travel Warnings. Available on-line; send a message to subscribe to travel-advisories-request@stolaf.edu

Using a program such as File Transfer Protocol (FTP), you can search archives: connect to ftp.stolaf.edu/pub/travel-advisories/archive. For travel information on a specific country, connect to ftp.stolaf.edu/pub/travel-advisories/country

Check in your phone book, library, or local sports center for self-defense courses, or contact Model Mugging, a company that offers instruction with offices nationwide; phone (415) 592-7300.

UNITED KINGDOM

Foreign Office Consular Section Travel Advice Unit, Clive House, Petty France, London SW1H 9HD; phone their advice line at 0171-2704129 or 0171-2704179, or check the BBC Ceefax service. Local call rate numbers have been introduced for the most requested countries, including India (0374-500935), Kenya (0374-500947), Russia (0374-500968), South Africa (0374-500974), and the United States (0374-500990). WWW electronic access for Foreign Office travel advice notices is on http://www.fco.gov.uk/

CATCH 22, 110 Chorley Road, Standish, Lancs WN1 2SX; phone 01257-473118. Specializes in travel security products, including personal alarms and pressure pads for tents, and lightweight, keyless door locks.

Check in your phone book, library, or local sports center for self-defense courses. Alternatively, contact Positive Response, St. Edmund's House, Taverham, Norwich, NR8 6PA (phone/fax 01603-2618690), a company that runs 2-day courses (or longer) in practical self-defense. Send a self-addressed, stamped envelope for a prospectus. Also available from the same address for £4.95 (check or postal order) is *Hands Off*, an excellent miniguide to self-defense, written by Fred Adams.

◆   CULTURAL AND ENVIRONMENTAL IMPACT   ◆

Remember as a common courtesy to send any requests for information accompanied by a stamped, self-addressed envelope for local replies or an international reply coupon for international queries.

General Electronic Reference

Greenpeace International: http://www.greenpeace.org/
Friends of the Earth. Environmental news and campaigns: http://www.foe.co.uk/

UNITED STATES

Conservation International, 1015 18th Street NW, Suite 1000, Washington, DC 20036; phone (202) 429-5660.

Cultural Survival, 53a Church Street, Cambridge, MA 02138; phone (617) 495-2562, fax (617) 495-1396.

The Ecotourism Society, 801 Devon Place, Alexandria, VA 22314.

Friends of the Earth, 218 D Street SE, Washington, DC 20003; phone (202) 544-2600.

Greenpeace, 1436 U Street NW, Washington, DC 20009; phone (202) 544-2600.

The Nature Conservancy, 1815 North Lynn Street, Arlington, VA 22209; phone (703) 841-5300.

North American Center for Responsible Tourism, 2 Kensington Road, San Anselmo, CA 94960; phone (415) 258-6594, fax (415) 454-2493. Publishes a newsletter and provides information in return for a stamped, self-addressed envelope.

Rainforest Alliance, 270 Lafayette Street, Suite 512, New York, NY 10012; phone (212) 941-1900.

Survival International USA, 2121 Decatur Place NW, Washington, DC 20006.

Transitional Network for Appropriate Technologies, P.O. Box 567, Rangeley, ME 04970.

Worldwide Fund for Nature, 1250 24th Street NW, Washingon, DC 20037; phone (202) 293-4800.

UNITED KINGDOM

Campaign for Environmentally Responsible Tourism (CERT), P.O. Box 4246, London SE23 2QB; phone 0181-291-0692. Encourages responsible tourism with both the travel industry and the traveling public.

Centre for the Advancement of Responsive Tourism (CART), 70 Dry Hill Park Road, Tonbridge, Kent TN10 3BX; phone 01732-352757.

Friends of the Earth, 26-28 Underwood Street, London N17JU; phone 0171-4901555.

Greenpeace, 30-31 Islington Green, London N1 8XE; phone 0171-3545100.

Kathmandu Environmental Education Project (KEEP), 72 Newhaven Road, Edinburgh EH6 5QG; phone 0131-554-9977. Provides members with environmental, cultural, trekking, and safety information via local offices, overseas associates, and its quarterly newsletter.

Survival International, 310 Edgware Road, London, W2 1DY; phone 0171-7235535.

Tourism Concern, Southlands College, Roehampton Institute, Wimbledon Parkside, London SW19 5NN; phone 0181-944-0464. Researches the impact of tourism and provides guidelines and reports.

GERMANY

Tourismus mit Einsicht, Arbeitsgemeinschaft Tourismus mit Einsicht, Herbert Hamele, Hadorferstr 9, D-8130 Starnberg.

SPAIN

World Tourism Organisation, Capitan Haya 42, 28020 Madrid; phone 01-5710628.

THAILAND

Ecumenical Coalition on Third World Tourism, P.O. Box 24, Chorakhebua, Bangkok 10230.

NEPAL

Kathmandu Environmental Education Project (KEEP), P.O. Box 9178,

Kathmandu; phone 977-1-410303, fax 977-1-411533. Provides members with environmental, cultural, trekking, and safety information via local offices, overseas associates, and its quarterly newsletter.

AUSTRALIA

Greenpeace, 1st Floor, 1 Lygon Street, Carlton, Melbourne, VIC 3053; phone 03-96629899.

Friends of the Earth, 312 Smith Street, Collingwood, Melbourne, VIC 3066; phone 03-94198700.

Wilderness Society, 130 Davey Street, Hobart, TAS 7000; phone 002-349366.

◆ TREKKING COMPANIONS ◆

In North America, *Escape* magazine runs advertisements for traveling companions in its Traveler's Exchange column; see also the back pages of *Backpacker* or *Outside* magazines. See appendix B for contact details on these magazines.

For the long-distance trails in the United States, try the following sources:

Pacific Crest Trail Conference, The Communicator, 365 West 29th Avenue, Eugene, OR 97405.

The Continental Divide Trail Society, P.O. Box 30002, Bethesda, MD 20814.

Appalachian Trail Conference, *Appalachian Trailway News Magazine,* P.O. Box 807, Harper's Ferry, WV 25425.

The Florida Trail Association, P.O. Box 13708, Gainesville, FL 32604.

In the UK, agencies such as Travel Companions (phone 0181-202-8478) or Odyssey International (phone 01223-861079) will match your needs with those of another traveler for a fee. The Globetrotters Club (contact details listed earlier in this appendix) publishes a members' newsletter with a "mutual-aid" column for travel companions. *Wanderlust* magazine (contact details in appendix B) has a "connections" column for prospective travel companions. *Triangle,* the quarterly magazine provided for members of the Youth Hostels Association (for contact address refer to the hostel association listing in this appendix), has a "companions" section in its classified pages. *Trail Walker* magazine (for contact details see appendix B) has a "trailmates" section. *Traveller* magazine runs a members' classified column for members of WEXAS (for contact details, see appendix B).

◆ WOMEN TRAVELERS ◆

UNITED STATES

Wander Women, 136 North Grand Avenue #237, West Covina, CA 91790; phone (818) 966-8857. Publishes a quarterly newsletter, *Journal 'n Footnotes*, with networked travel tips for women travelers in the 40-plus age range.

UNITED KINGDOM

Women's Travel Advisory Bureau (WTAB), Lansdowne, High Street, Blockley, Glos GL56 9HF; phone 01386-701082. Travel information service providing information packs for specific countries and seminars.

Women Welcome Women (WWW), Granta, 8a Chestnut Avenue, Bucks HP11 1DJ; phone 01494-439481. Offers the opportunity to find travel companions or stay in members' homes around the world.

◆ SPECIAL NEEDS ◆

UNITED STATES

The Itinerary, P.O. Box 2012, Bayonne, NJ 07002; phone (201) 858-3400. Travel magazine for the disabled.

Mobility International USA, P.O. Box 3551, Eugene, OR 97403; phone (503) 343-1284.

Society for the Advancement of Travel for the Handicapped, 345 Fifth Avenue #610, New York, NY 10016; phone (212) 447-7284.

UNITED KINGDOM

The Royal Association for Disability & Rehabilitation (RADAR), 25 Mortimer Street, London W1N 8AB; phone 0171-6375400, fax 0171-6371827, minicom 0171-6375315.

CANADA

Canadian Rehabilitation Council for the Disabled, 45 Sheppard Avenue East, Toronto, ON M2N 5W9; phone (416) 250-7490.

NEW ZEALAND

The Disabled Persons Assembly, P.O. Box 10-138, The Terrace, Wellington; phone 04-4722626.

AUSTRALIA

The Australian Council for the Rehabilitation of the Disabled (ACROD), P.O. Box 60, Curtin, Canberra, ACT 2605; phone 06-2824333. Please send self-addressed, franked envelope for any information requested.

◆ GAY TRAVELERS ◆

International Gay Travel Association (IGTA), P.O. Box 4974, Key West, FL 33041, USA; phone toll-free 1-800-448-8550. Provides lists of international members of the association.

International Lesbian and Gay Association (ILGA), 81 Rue Marche au Charbon, 1000 Brussels 1, Belgium; phone 032-25022471. Provides international information and advice.

◆ NAVIGATION ◆

GLOBAL POSITIONING SYSTEM (GPS)

United States

Magellan Systems, 960 Overland Court, San Dimas, CA 91773; phone toll-free 1-800-669-4477 or (909) 394-5000.

Panasonic, One Panasonic Way, Department 3G-9, Secaucus, NJ 07094; phone (201) 348-7000.

Silva, 333 Faulkenburg Road, Eastshore Center, Building D401, Tampa, FL 33619; phone (813) 654-1799.

Trimble Navigation, 9020-II Capital of Texas Highway North, Suite 400, Austin, TX 78759; phone toll-free 1-800-959-9567 or (512) 343-8970.

United Kingdom

Mobile Positioning Systems; phone 01908-604008.
Panasonic; phone 01344-853176.
Silva; phone 01784-471721.
Trimble; phone 01256-760150.

New Zealand

Trimble; phone 03-3713400.

Appendix B

BACKGROUND READING RESOURCES

CLIMATE AND WEATHER

Pearce, E. A. *The World Weather Guide.* Hutchinson, 1990. Provides information on the weather worldwide; temperatures, humidity, rainfall, and general climate are detailed for some 500 locations around the world.

U.S. National Weather Service, U.S. Government Printing Office, Washington, DC 20420. Publishes advisories and information documents on many topics related to weather and climate.

On-line weather information: http://web.nexor.co.uk/users/jpo/weather/weather.html

USEFUL BOOKSHOPS AND MAP SOURCES

Electronic Bookstores

Online Bookstore (OBS), WWW access on: http://marketplace.com/obs/obshome.html

Internet Book Shop (IBS), WWW access on: http://www.bookshop.co.uk/

UNITED KINGDOM
Maps and Travel Bookshops

Daunt Books, 83 Marylebone High Street, London W1M 4Al; phone 0171-2242295.

The Map Shop, 15 High Street, Upton Upon Severn, Worcs WR8 OHJ; phone 01684-593146.

Stanfords, 12-14 Long Acre, London WC2E 9LP; phone 0171-8361321.

The Travel Bookshop, 13 Blenheim Crescent, London W11 2EE; phone 0171-2295260.

The Travellers' Bookshop, 25 Cecil Court, London WC2N 4EZ; phone 0171-8369132.

UNITED STATES
Specialist Store for Overseas Mapping
Maplink, 25 East Mason Street, Department G, Santa Barbara, CA 93101; phone (805) 965-4402.

Specialist Travel Bookstores
Adventurous Traveler Bookstore, P.O. Box 577, Hinesburg, VT 05461; phone toll-free 1-800-ATB-3963, or (802) 482-3330. Specializes in mail order.

Backcountry Bookstore, P.O. Box 6235, Lynnwood, WA 98036; phone (206) 290-7652.

Book Passage, 51 Tamal Vista Boulevard, Corte Madera, CA 94925; phone (415) 927-0960 or phone toll-free 1-800-999-7909.

The Complete Traveler, 199 Madison Avenue, New York, NY 10016; phone (212) 685-9007.

The Complete Traveler, 3207 Filmore Street, San Francisco, CA 92123; phone (415) 923-1511.

Elliot Bay Book Company, 101 South Main Street, Seattle, WA 98104; phone (206) 624-6600.

Rand McNally, 150 East 52nd Street, New York, NY 10022; phone (212) 758-7488.

Rand McNally, 595 Market Street, San Francisco, CA 94105; phone (415) 777-3131.

The Savvy Traveler, 50 East Washington Street, Chicago, IL 60602; phone (312) 263-2100.

Traveler's Bookstore, 22 West 52nd Street, New York, NY 10019; phone (212) 664-0995.

CANADA
Open Air Books & Maps, 25 Toronto Street, Toronto, ON M5R 2C1; phone (416) 363-0719

The Travel Bug, 2667 West Broadway, Vancouver, BC V6K 2G2; phone (604) 737-1122.

Ulysses Travel Bookshop, 4176 St-Denis, Montréal, QUE; phone (514) 289-0993.

World Wide Books and Maps, 1247 Granville Street, Vancouver, BC V62 1G3; phone (416) 363-0719.

AUSTRALIA

Bowyangs, 372 Little Bourke Street, Melbourne, VIC 3000; phone 03-96704383.

Hema Maps, 239 George Street, Brisbane, QLD 4000; phone 07-2214330.

The Map Shop, 16a Peel Street, Adelaide, SA 5000; phone 08-2312033.

The Melbourne Map Centre, 740 Waverley Road, Chadstone, Melbourne, VIC 3148; phone 03-95695472.

Perth Map Centre, 899 Hay Street, Perth, WA 6000; phone 09-3225733.

The Travel Bookshop, 20 Bridge Street, Sydney, NSW 2000; phone 02-2413554.

JAPAN

Travelers Bookshop Tokyo, Wako 5 Building, 5th Floor, 1-19-8 Kakigaracho Nihonbashi, Chuoku, Tokyo 103; phone 03-36617458, fax 03-36679646. Close to Tokyo City Air Terminal (TCAT); also provides mail-order service.

HONG KONG

Wanderlust Books, 30 Hollywood Road, Central; phone 852-25232042, fax 852-25234001. Also provides mail-order service.

◆ SELECTION OF PUBLISHERS OF ◆ TREKKING AND WALKING GUIDES

For the many series of trekking guides for countries worldwide, keep up-to-date with catalogues from the publishers listed here. There are also many trekking guides that are individual labors rather than part of a series—for example, Torbjoern Ydegaard, *Trekking in Greenland* (Skarv Guides, 1990), and Paul Hunt, *Hiking in Japan* (Kodansha International, 1988). Consult reference works in your library or ask for advice at travel bookstores for the full picture on guides in print.

UNITED STATES

Falcon Press, P.O. Box 1718, Helena, MT 59624; phone toll-free 1-800-582-2665.

Lonely Planet Publications, Embarcadero West, 155 Filbert Street, Suite 251, Oakland, CA 94607; phone (510) 893-8555, fax (510) 893-8563.

The Mountaineers Books, 1001 SW Klickitat Way, Suite 201, Seattle, WA 98134; phone toll-free 1-800-553-4453, fax (206) 223-6306.

Sierra Club, 730 Polk Street, San Francisco, CA 94109; phone (415) 981-8634.

UNITED KINGDOM

Bradt Publications, 41 Nortoft Road, Chalfont St. Peter, Bucks SL9 OLA; phone/fax 01494-873478.

Cicerone Press, 2 Police Square, Milnthorpe, Cumbria LA7 7PY; phone 015395-62069.

Compass Star Publications, Kyre Park, Tenbury Wells, Worcestershire WR15 8RP; phone/fax 01885-410352, e-mail cpstar@delphi.com

Cordee Books & Maps, 3a de Montfort Street, Leicester LE1 7HD; phone 0116-543579.

Lonely Planet Publications, 10 Barley Mow Passage, Chiswick, London W4 4PH; phone 0181-7423161, fax 0181-7422772.

AUSTRALIA

Lonely Planet Publications, P.O. Box 617, Hawthorn, Victoria 3122; phone 03-98191877, fax 03-98196459, e-mail talk2us@lonelyplanet.com.au

WWW access on: http://www.lonelyplanet.co.au

◆ GENERAL TRAVEL REFERENCES ◆

Brandenburger, Caroline, ed. *The Traveller's Handbook.* London: Wexas, 1994. Offers a vast array of information, general articles, and lists—from tips on travel in a Buddhist country to traveling by Microlight or public holidays in Zaire. Editions are usually updated every three years.

Moore, Fred. *Fred's Guide to Travel in the Real World.* Chicago: Chicago Review Press, 1989.

◆ GENERAL TRAVEL–ELECTRONIC REFERENCES ◆

Air Traveller's Handbook. Advice around the globe for air travelers. http://www.cis.ohio-state.edu/hypertext/faq/usenet/travel/air/handbook/top.html

CIA World FactBook. Background information across the globe. http://www.odci.gov/94fact/fb94toc/fb94toc.html

City.net. Global resource for tourist information. http://www.city.net/

Endicott, M. L. *The Electronic Traveler.* Available for U.S.$50 from the author, P.O. Box 20837, Saint Simons Island, GA 31522, USA. Directory of travel information sources available on computer networks.

GNN Travel Resource Center. Assorted travel sites for travel publishers, travel companies, traveler's tales, and more. http://gnn.com/cgi-bin/imagemap/HOME?457,190

Grand Canyon National Park. Highly detailed resource for trails, trail maps, reservations and background reading. http://www.kbt.com/gc/

Koblas Currency Converter. WWW access on: http://www.ora.com/cgi-bin/ora/currency

Rec. Travel Library. Travel experiences, advice and resources collated from Usenet newsgroups. http://www.nectec.or.th/rec-travel/index.html

Travelmag. Electronic magazine includes travelogues, health tips, and flight deals. http://www.travelmag.co.uk/travelmag

◆ GENERAL TRAVEL–NEWSLETTERS ◆

UNITED STATES

Planet Talk, Lonely Planet (see addresses under "Selection of Publishers of Trekking and Walking Guides," earlier in this appendix). Travel newsletter.

Transitions Abroad, P.O. Box 3000, Denville, NJ 07834; phone (413) 256-0373, phone toll-free 1-800-293-0373. Resources for travel/work/study programs worldwide.

Travel Books Review, P.O. Box 191554, Atlanta, GA 31119. Bimonthly newsletter with reviews from travel journalists plus general advice.

Travel Matters, Moon Publications, P.O. Box 3040, Chico, CA 95927; phone toll-free 1-800-345-5473. Travel newsletter. For information about the on-line version of this newsletter, the e-mail address is info@moon.com

Travel Smart Newsletter, 40 Beechdale Road, Dobbs Ferry, NY 10522; phone toll-free 1-800-327-3633. General travel newsletter.

Travelin' Woman, Nancy Mills Communications, 855 Moraga Drive #14, Los Angeles, CA 90049; phone (310) 472-6318. Monthly newsletter for the woman traveler; available by subscription.

LATIN AMERICA

The Latin American Travel Advisor, Latin American Travel Consultants, P.O. Box 17-17-908, Quito, Ecuador; fax 02-562-566, e-mail rku@pi.pro.ec. WWW access on: http://www.amerispan.com/latc. Quarterly news bulletin—books, maps, and videos are also available by mail order.

UNITED KINGDOM

Globe, The Globetrotters' Club, BCM Roving, London WC1N 3XX. See club details in appendix A.

FRANCE AND BELGIUM

Aventure Au Bout du Monde, 116 Rue de Javel, 75015, Paris. A French-language magazine for travelers.

Farang, La Rue 8 á 4261, Braives, Belgium. A French-language newsletter for travelers.

GERMANY

Der Trotter, Deutsche Zentrale für Globetrotter e.V., Birkenweg 19, D-2359, Henstedt-Ulzburg; phone 04193-3914. A German-language newletter.

◆ BACKPACKING AND ◆
GENERAL TRAVEL MAGAZINES

UNITED STATES

Backpacker, Rodale Press, 33 East Minor Street, Emmaus, PA 18098; phone (610) 967-5171, fax (610) 967-8181. Electronic trailhead accessible for subscribers to America Online; phone toll-free 1-800-827-6364.

Ecotraveler, P.O. Box 469003, Escondido, CA 92046; phone toll-free 1-800-334-8152, e-mail ecotrav@aol.com

Escape, P.O. Box 5159, 2720 Neilson Way, Santa Monica, CA 90409; phone toll-free 1-800-738-5571 or (310) 392-5235. Travel magazine with emphasis on tales, tips, contacts, and advice for the adventurous traveler.

HIMAL, P.O. Box 470758, San Francisco, CA 94147; phone toll-free 1-800-203-8600. A bimonthly magazine on cultural, environmental, and development issues for readers interested in the Himalaya.

Outside, 1165 North Clark Street, Chicago, IL 60610; phone (312) 951-0990. WWW access on: http://www.starwave.com/outside

Walkabout, P.O. Box 5143-S, Portsmouth, NH 03802. Bimonthly newsletter with articles, anecdotes, and advice covering budget, adventure, and cultural angles on travel.

CANADA

Explore, Suite 410, 310-14 Street NW, Calgary, AB T2N 2A1; fax (403) 270-7922. Adventure travel magazine.

UNITED KINGDOM

Climber & Hillwalker, The Plaza Tower, East Kilbride, Glasgow G74 1LW; phone 013552-46444, fax: 013552-63013.

The Great Outdoors, The Plaza Tower, East Kilbride, Glasgow G74 1LW; phone 013552-46444, fax: 013552-63013.

Outdoors Illustrated, Discovery Publications, Studio Two, The Courtyard, 114-116 Walcot Street, Bath BA1 5BG; phone 01225-443194, fax 01225-443195.

Trail Walker, EMAP Pursuit Publishing, Bretton Court, Peterborough PE3 8DZ; phone 01733-264666.

Traveller, Wexas Ltd., 45-49 Brompton Road, London SW3 1DE; phone 0171-5890500.

Wanderlust, P.O. Box 1832, Windsor SL4 5YG; phone/fax 01753-620-426. Magazine aimed at travelers with independent and adventurous wanderlust.

SOUTH AFRICA
Getaway, P.O. Box 180, Howard Place 7450; phone 021-5311391. Magazine covering outdoor travel, game parks, and conservation.

AUSTRALIA
Wild, P.O. Box 415, Prahran, VIC 3181; phone 03-98268482. Magazine covering hiking and adventure sports.

NEW ZEALAND
Adventure, P.O. Box 4335, Christchurch; phone 03-379-6401. Magazine covering all types of outdoor adventures in New Zealand and abroad.

◆ FLIGHTS ◆

Consumer Guide to Air Travel, Superintendent of Documents, Consumer Information Center, Department 133B, Pueblo, CO 81009. Supplies information on overbooking, frequent flyer programs, and more.

International Association of Air Couriers (IAATC), International Features Inc., P.O. Box 1349, Lake Worth, FL 33460; phone (407) 582-8320, fax (407) 582-1581. Publishes *The Shoestring Traveler* newsletter, which contains tips and information for travelers; and the bi-monthly *Air Courier Bulletin,* which lists budget flights to and from major destinations around the world. Members also have access to the IAATC bulletin board, BBS phone (407) 582-0425, which details airfare news and updates for courier and non-courier tickets to overseas destinations; and the IAATC fax-back service (phone (407) 582-3829), updated daily.

◆ HEALTH ◆

Dawood, Richard. *Travellers' Health: How to Stay Healthy Abroad.* Oxford: Oxford University Press, 1992.

British Red Cross. *First Aid Manual.* London: Dorling Kindersley, 1995.

Hackett, Peter. *Mountain Sickness: Prevention, Recognition and Treatment.* New York: American Alpine Club, 1979.

Hatt, John. *The Tropical Traveller.* London: Penguin, 1990.

Isaac, Jeff, and Goth, Peter. *Outward Bound Wilderness First Aid Handbook.* New York: Lyons and Burford, 1991.

Lentz, Martha; Carline, Jan; and Macdonald, Steven. *Mountaineering First Aid.* Seattle: The Mountaineers, 1990.

Lessell, Colin. *The World Travellers' Manual of Homeopathy*. Saffron Walden: C. W. Daniel Co., 1993.

Schroeder, Dirk. *Staying Healthy in Asia, Africa & Latin America*. Chico: Moon Publications, 1993.

Wilkerson, James. *Medicine for Mountaineering & Other Wilderness Activities*, 4th ed. Seattle: The Mountaineers, 1992.

◆ ENVIRONMENTAL IMPACT ◆

Hampton, Bruce, and Cole, David. *Soft Paths: How to Enjoy the Wilderness Without Harming It.* Mechanicsburg: Stackpole Books, 1988.

Hart, John. *Walking Softly in the Wilderness.* San Francisco: Sierra Club Books, 1992.

Meyer, Kathleen. *How to Shit in the Woods: An Environmentally Sound Approach to a Lost Art.* Berkeley: Ten Speed Press, 1989.

◆ CULTURAL IMPACT ◆

Culture Shock! series. Published by Kuperard (London Ltd), No. 9 Hampstead West, 244 Iverson Road, London NW6 2HL, UK; phone 0171-3724722, fax 0171-3724599. An excellent and expanding series available for many countries detailing cultural differences and do's and dont's.

Norberg-Hodge, Helena. *Ancient Futures: Learning from Ladakh*. London: Century, 1992.

Scott, Graham. *Handle with Care: Responsible Travel in Developing Countries.* Chicago: Noble Press, 1990.

◆ HIKING, BACKPACKING, AND TREKKING ◆

Fletcher, Colin. *The Complete Walker*, 3d ed. New York: Alfred Knopf, 1984.

Graham, Scott. *Backpacking in the Developing World*. Chicago: Noble Press, 1989.

Ross, Cindy, and Gladfelter, Todd. *A Hiker's Companion: 12,000 Miles of Trail-Tested Wisdom.* Seattle: The Mountaineers, 1993.

Schad, Jerry, and Moser, David S., eds. *Wilderness Basics: The Complete Handbook for Hikers & Backpackers.* 2d ed. Seattle: The Mountaineers, 1993.

Silverman, Goldie. *Backpacking with Babies and Small Children*. Berkeley: Wilderness Press, 1986.

◆ NARRATIVES ◆

Abbey, Edward. *Desert Solitaire: A Season in the Wilderness*. New York: Ballantine Books, 1986.

Fletcher, Colin. *The Man Who Walked Through Time*. New York: Random House, 1989.

Fletcher, Colin. *The Thousand-Mile Summer*. New York: Random House, 1989.

Lopez, Barry. *Arctic Dreams*. Tucson: University of Arizona Press, 1988.

Muir, John. *The Eight Wilderness Discovery Books*. Seattle: The Mountaineers, 1988. A compendium of John Muir titles, including *A Thousand Mile Walk to the Gulf, My First Summer in the Sierra, Travels in Alaska*, and *Steep Trails*.

Newby, Eric. *A Short Walk in the Hindu Kush*. London: Picador, 1981.

Pilkington, John. *Into Thin Air: A Walk Across Nepal*. London: Century Hutchinson, 1989.

Townsend, Chris. *Walking the Yukon: A Solo Trek*. Camden: Ragged Mountain Press, 1993.

◆ NAVIGATION ◆

Cliff, Peter. *Mountain Navigation*. Published by Peter Cliff, Ardenbeg, Grant Road, Grantown-on-Spey PH26 3LD, UK; 1991.

Fleming, June. *Staying Found: The Complete Map & Compass Book*. Seattle: The Mountaineers, 1994.

Kellstrom, Bjorn. *Be Expert with Map and Compass*. New York: Macmillan, 1976.

Letham, Lawrence. *GPS Made Easy*. Seattle: The Mountaineers, 1996.

◆ EMERGENCY AND SURVIVAL ◆

Dodwell, Christina. *An Explorer's Handbook: Travel, Survival & Bush Cookery*. Sevenoaks: Hodder & Stoughton, 1984.

Herrero, Stephen. *Bear Attacks: Their Causes & Avoidance*. Edmonton: Hurtig Publishers, 1985.

McManners, Hugh. *The Commando Survival Manual*. London: Dorling Kindersley, 1994.

Wiseman, John. *SAS Survival Guide*. London: HarperCollins, 1986.

◆ WOMEN TRAVELERS ◆

Davies, Miranda, and Jansz, Natania. *More Women Travel*. London: Rough Guides, 1995. Personal accounts of women travelers, plus brief travel notes on individual countries.

Moss, Maggie, and Moss, Gemma. *Handbook for Women Travellers*. London: Piatkus Books, 1995.

Robinson, Jane. *Wayward Women: A Guide to Women Travellers*. Oxford: Oxford University Press, 1990. Inspiring and entertaining historical survey of 400 women travelers, their feats and antics.

◆ SPECIAL NEEDS◆

Smooth Ride Guides. Series of travel guides for disabled travelers. London: FT
Publishing, 1995.

Walsh, Alison. *Able to Travel/Nothing Ventured: Disabled People Travel the World.*
London: Rough Guides, 1991.

Weiss, Louise. *Access to the World: A Travel Guide for the Handicapped.* New York:
Facts on File Inc., 1983.

◆ GAY TRAVELERS ◆

Spartacus International Gay Guide. Provides worldwide coverage. Available in the
United States from: 100 East Biddle Street, Baltimore, MD 21202; phone
(410) 727-5677; and in Europe from: Bruno Gmünder Verlag, Luetzowstraße
10, P.O. Box 301345, D-1000 Berlin 30, Germany; phone 030-25498200.

USA & Worldwide Gay Accommodations. Part of a series of gay travel titles published by Ferrari Publications, P.O. Box 37887, Phoenix, AZ 85069, USA;
phone (602) 863-2408.

Gaia's Guide. Geared to lesbian travelers. Available in the United States from:
147 West 42nd Street, Suite 603, New York, NY 10036; and in UK from Gay's
The Word, 66 Marchmont Street, London WC1N 1AB; phone 0171-
2787654.

Women Going Places. Travel resource directory with lesbian angle and general
coverage of travel topics for women. Available from Inland Book Co., P.O.
Box 120261, East Haven, CT 06152, USA; phone (203) 4674257.

Giovanni's Room. 345 South 12th Street, Philadelphia, PA 19107, USA; phone
(215) 923-2960. Bookstore (also mail order) offering travel and general publications of gay interest.

◆ PHOTOGRAPHY AND WRITING ◆

A & C Black. *Writers' and Artists' Yearbook.* London: A & C Black, published
annually.

Australian Writers' Professional Services. *The Writers' and Photographers' Market
Guide for Australia and New Zealand.* Melbourne: Australian Writers' Professional Services, published annually.

Calder, Julian, and Garrett, John. *The Travelling Photographer's Handbook.* London: Pan, 1985.

Calder, Julian, and Garrett, John. *35mm Photographer's Handbook.* London:
Pan, 1990.

Writers' Digest Books. *Photographers' Market*. Cincinnati: Writers' Digest Books, published annually.

Writers' Digest Books. *Writers' Market*. Cincinnati: Writers' Digest Books, published annually.

◆ Index ◆

ABOUT THE AUTHOR

In the early 1970s, Robert Strauss took the overland route to Nepal and then studied, taught, and edited in England, Germany, Portugal, Hong Kong, and Australia. Robert is the author of travel guides to countries in Europe, Asia, South America, and the Indian Ocean and has trekked on six continents. He has also contributed articles and photos to other books, magazines, and newspapers in the United States, Europe, Australia, and Asia. Currently based in England, he is enjoying lakeside wildlife and writing and publishing more adventure titles.

Comments, suggestions, updates, and feedback for this book are welcome. Please mail them to the author c/o The Mountaineers Books, 1001 SW Klickitat Way, Seattle, WA 98134, USA, or to Compass Star Publications, Kyre Park, Tenbury Wells, Worcestershire WR15 8RP, UK. To contact the author on-line, send your message to cpstar@delphi.com—a World Wide Web site should be available by the time this book goes to press.

THE MOUNTAINEERS, founded in 1906, is a nonprofit outdoor activity and conservation club, whose mission is "to explore, study, preserve, and enjoy the natural beauty of the outdoors. . . ." Based in Seattle, Washington, the club is now the third-largest such organization in the United States, with 15,000 members and four branches throughout Washington State.

The Mountaineers sponsors both classes and year-round outdoor activities in the Pacific Northwest, which include hiking, mountain climbing, ski-touring, snowshoeing, bicycling, camping, kayaking and canoeing, nature study, sailing, and adventure travel. The club's conservation division supports environmental causes through educational activities, sponsoring legislation, and presenting informational programs. All club activities are led by skilled, experienced volunteers, who are dedicated to promoting safe and responsible enjoyment and preservation of the outdoors.

The Mountaineers Books, an active, nonprofit publishing program of the club, produces guidebooks, instructional texts, historical works, natural history guides, and works on environmental conservation. All books produced by The Mountaineers are aimed at fulfilling the club's mission.

If you would like to participate in these organized outdoor activities or the club's programs, consider a membership in The Mountaineers. For information and an application, write or call The Mountaineers, Club Headquarters, 300 Third Avenue West, Seattle, WA 98119, USA; (206) 284-6310.

Send or call for our catalog of more than 300 outdoor titles:

The Mountaineers Books
1001 SW Klickitat Way, Suite 201
Seattle, WA 98134, USA
1-800-553-4453